The Storms Below

The Storms Below

The Turbulent Life and Times of Hugh Garner

Paul Stuewe

James Lorimer & Company, Publishers
Toronto, 1988

Canadian Cataloguing in Publication
Stuewe, Paul, 1943-
The storms below

ISBN 1-55028-150-X (bound) ISBN 1-55028-148-8 (pbk.)
1. Garner, Hugh, 1913-1979 - Biography.
2. Authors, Canadian (English) - 20th century -
Biography.* I. Title.

PS8513.A7Z78 1988   C813'.54   C88-094502-8
                    68978

PR9199.3.G36Z78 1988

James Lorimer & Company, Publishers
Egerton Ryerson Memorial Building
35 Britain Street
Toronto, Ontario M5A 1R7

Printed and bound in Canada

6 5 4 3 2 1   88 89 90 91 92 93

For Christina and Sarah

Contents

ACKNOWLEDGEMENTS

I am grateful to all those whose friendship and aid were essential for the writing of *The Storms Below*.

I am particularly indebted to Barbara Wong, without whose enthusiastic co-operation this book could not have been written. Other members of Hugh Garner's family have also been very helpful. Alice Garner and Ronald Garner were important sources of information and insight, and the assistance of June Clow and Margery McFarlane was also appreciated.

Grants from the Canada Council and the Ontario Arts Council made it possible to complete this project while I took a prolonged respite from the perils of free-lance journalism. I would like to collectively thank Jack David, Doug Fetherling and Robert Weaver for recommending me to the Canada Council's attention and must also gratefully acknowledge their individual contributions. Robert Weaver has generously shared both his reminiscences and his literary contacts, Doug Fetherling has provided an extensive memoir as well as constant encouragement and Jack David was instrumental in first arousing my interest in Hugh Garner.

Anne MacDermaid, Shirley Spragge, Mario Creet, Helen Cobb and George Henderson at the Queen's University Archives were most tolerant of an obsessed researcher's requests, as were Barbara Clarke at the CBC Archives, Gail Gregory at the archives of the Toronto Board of Education, Eugene Martel at the Archives of Ontario, John Paveling at the National Archives of Canada and the extraordinarily efficient staff at the City of Toronto archives.

Many others offered their help in various ways. James Bacque, William French, Robert Fulford, Greg Gatenby, Betty Gerow, Ruth Hartman, M.T. Kelly, Dave MacDonald, Doug Marshall, Donald Nethery, Irene Parker, Ollie Plunkett, Frank Rasky, William Rowe, Helmut Schwar, Beverly Slopen, Jocko Thomas, Susan Traer, Ann Vanderhoof and Jean Wright all made valuable contributions to the completion of *The Storms Below*. Stephen Temple Books and Annex Books, both of Toronto, were of great help in obtaining out-of-print material that made it possible for me to read almost all of Garner's published work.

A special thank you goes to my wife, Deanna Groetzinger, who, while I burrowed in archives and mastered the intricacies of word processing, coped brilliantly with our three delightful but demanding children as well as her own career. She also made many helpful suggestions regarding improvements in the manuscript. Our friend and neighbour, Lois Cook, filled in ably when neither of us was able to answer the call of parental duty.

Editors are traditionally thanked last, which is why Heather Robertson's support and advice have not been mentioned previously. As the commissioning editor of *The Storms Below*, she was an active participant at every stage of the book's progress, and along with James Lorimer and Naomi Frankel made many constructive recommendations for revisions in the final text. The responsibility for its contents, however, is entirely mine.

Introduction

In the summer of 1931, as the Great Depression tightened its grip upon the world, a young Toronto man hopped a freight train and headed west in search of a job. During the next three years he travelled all over North America while working as a farm-hand, dishwasher and construction labourer; if there was no work to be had, he spent his nights in jail cells and hobo jungles. Maybe the worst time was on a flatcar crossing the prairies, when another kid on the bum caught his foot in a coupling and stared with agonized eyes at the blood welling up out of his boot ...

On a fine summer's morning in Spain in 1937, a Loyalist soldier took cover as a Fascist machine-gun held up his unit's advance on a small village. Fear tasted like a copper coin in his throat as he tried to burrow deep beneath the sparse camouflage of an untilled wheat field. In the church steeple overlooking the field the enemy machine-gunners could be seen pointing out likely targets, while from the village's other buildings a growing volume of small-arms fire beat against the dry ground and its frightened crop of decimated infantry ...

In the last days of December 1942, German submarines attacked a U.K.-bound convoy during the Battle of the North Atlantic. On board one of the outnumbered Canadian escort vessels, a veteran sailor saw a third of the convoy's ships torpedoed by the inexorable U-boats. After a night of sudden explosions that hurled men into ice-cold waters, the surviving escorts braced themselves for a last-ditch defence ...

If Hugh Garner had cared to go in for self-dramatization, he might have used these experiences to make a larger impression upon the consciousness of his time. Ernest Hemingway, after all, parlayed much less knowledge of combat into far greater notoriety as the chronicler of war's atrocities and ecstasies. But

Garner's reluctance to boast about his martial qualities, based on the firm conviction that he was no more of a hero than the next guy, kept this aspect of his life largely concealed from those who did not know him well. At the time of his death in 1979, his fellow Torontonians were for the most part content to view him as that curious phenomenon, a writer from "Cabbagetown", the city's traditional slum district with which Garner remained linked long after he had ceased to either reside or keep in touch with what was going on there. Garner's reputation as an abrasive critic of middle-class mores, intolerant of "phoney-balonies" and "sob-sisters" and never known to refuse a drink, often overshadowed his literary accomplishments. As I discovered when writing a short critical study of his work (*Hugh Garner*, ECW Press, 1986), although he had won the Governor General's Award for Fiction in 1963, by the mid-1970s his attempts to produce best-selling novels had led to his being dismissed as a serious writer by many readers and critics.

Garner himself, in characteristically maladroit fashion, had encouraged such a view with his 1973 autobiography, *One Damn Thing After Another!*. Just as Anthony Trollope in his 1883 *An Autobiography* had shocked Victorian readers by confessing that he enjoyed making money from his books, so Garner's trenchant remarks regarding the stupidity of university professors, the ineptitude of his fellow writers and his refusal to take his own work too seriously (any symbolism or allegory "were placed there quite unconsciously," he assured over- zealous academics) might have been deliberately calculated to offend just about everyone on the Canadian literary scene. Those literary critics who considered Garner beneath serious notice were given an ample supply of ammunition by *One Damn Thing After Another!*, which suffered from severe structural defects as well as some very sloppy writing: much of the book had been cobbled together from journalistic articles published piecemeal over the years, and its garrulous prose displayed little evidence of helpful editorial hands. In it, Garner was also extremely reticent about his family life, generally shied away from anything resembling psychological introspection and spent far too much time on the petty details of the writer's trade. Despite this, *One Damn Thing After Another!* revealed enough about Garner's life to suggest that a researcher willing to probe beneath its portrait of an obnoxious malcontent might reap a rewarding biographical harvest.

Here, then, are the results of one such attempt at sketching a more accurate picture of an author who deserves to be ranked as one of the major figures of modern Canadian literature. In his novels *Cabbagetown* and *Silence on the Shore*, in many of his short stories and in much of his non-fiction, Hugh Garner demonstrated that he could be a very fine writer indeed; and if he also produced a good deal of mediocre and even quite poor work, at his best he combined an intuitive comprehension of human nature with a craftsperson's attention to careful construction and telling detail. Here is his story.

Chapter One

Early Years in England and Toronto (1913-1929)

Hubert Garner was born on February 22, 1913 in Batley, England, a West Yorkshire town whose woollen mills and coal mines provided employment for its largely working-class population. Although his mother addressed him as "Hubert" until the day she died, others quickly learned that "Hugh" was the name of choice for a young lad who identified with G.A. Henty's combative heroes rather than the Tom Swifts and Frank Merriwells approved by society's do-gooders. Even at this early age, Garner was demonstrating that he preferred good scraps to good deeds: he always viewed the latter as some stuffed-shirt's idea of how to interfere in other people's lives, whereas the former put you right up against whomever or whatever deserved a good thrashing.

The house in which he was born, Number 7 Back Henrietta Street, was typical of the accommodations provided for the inhabitants of England's booming industrial centres:

> In West Yorkshire ... the normal house was a four- or five-room back-to-back terrace type, which was still being built in the 1900s. In almost all these northern towns more than a quarter of the houses had no drainage, so that excrement from the privies had to be shovelled out at intervals by sanitary gangs into barrows, and emptied from these into carts standing in the streets, a process creating overpowering stench. Although these undrained houses might otherwise be structurally sound, there would also normally be some older housing, perhaps a tenth of the town's total, built around narrow alleys and courts, with no damp courses, loose brick

floors laid direct on the earth, roofs and gutters letting in the wet, ceilings bulging and wallpaper peeling off the damp walls, broken window panes stuffed with paper or rags. The only water supply might be a common tap in the yard, shared with other tenants.

Garner was later to write that he recognized his birthplace in D.H. Lawrence's *Sons and Lovers*, where the Morel household is described in the following terms:

The houses themselves were substantial and very decent. One could walk all round, seeing little front gardens with auriculas and saxifrage in the shadow of the bottom block, sweet-williams and pinks in the sunny top block; seeing neat front windows, little porches, little privet hedges, and dormer windows for the attics. But that was outside; that was the view on to the uninhabited parlours of all the collier's wives. The dwelling-room, the kitchen, was at the back of the house, facing inward between the blocks, looking at a scrubby back garden, and then at the ash-pits. And between the rows, between the long lines of ash-pits, went the alley, where the children played and the women gossiped and the men smoked. So, the actual conditions of living ... were quite unsavoury because people must live in the kitchen, and the kitchens opened on to that nasty alley of ash-pits.

The human population of these communities was a sometimes volatile mix of stable working-class families and single young men and women drawn there by the many employment opportunities, and the union of Garner's parents was an example of the mismatches that sometimes occurred. His mother, Annie Fozard Stephenson, born on January 24, 1889, came from a long line of woollen workers: her grandparents had been sent to Germany in the mid-1800s to teach their craft to the employees of its new mills, and at the age of thirteen she herself had begun working in the "shoddy mill" of the local Taylor's Woollens factory, where old rags were reprocessed into an inferior grade of yarn. There she met her future husband, Matthew Garner, born on January 19, 1889, whose ancestors had been "labourers, soldiers and instrumentalists in town and army bands." Matthew was a handsome young lady-killer from the nearby town of Dewsbury, whose other favourite activities were playing the tenor horn and drinking, not necessarily in that order.

Young Hubert — or Hugh, as he will from this point be known — was born seven months after his parents' wedding, and since he was not a premature baby, it seems likely that he was the proximate cause of their marriage. For a few months the young couple lived with Annie's family at 7 Back Henrietta Street, but toward the end of 1913 Matthew emigrated to Canada, leaving behind only vague assurances that he would eventually send for his wife and child. Annie returned to her job at Taylor's and left Hugh in the care of his widowed grandmother, an intensely religious woman who dutifully enrolled her grandson in Batley's Parish Church School on his third birthday.

But instead of bringing his family to Canada, Matthew returned to England as a member of the 18th Battalion of the Canadian Expeditionary Corps, signing up at Galt (now Cambridge), Ontario in October 1914. He enlisted as a bandsman, specializing in the playing of his beloved tenor horn, and in September 1915 was posted to France. After less than two months' service he was admitted to hospital, diagnosed as suffering from sciatica and transferred back to England for further medical treatment. Discharged from hospital in February 1916, he took a clerical course at a British Army stenographic school in Bath and was then assigned to duties with the Canadian Army Pay Corps.

The Pays Corps was stationed in England, and by the beginning of 1917 Annie was following her husband from billet to billet, giving birth to another son, Ronald, later that same year. Matthew did well in the Pays Corps, rising from private to staff sergeant during his three years in this branch of the Canadian Expeditionary Force. Since he had enlisted in Canada, Matthew was returned there for his formal demobilization in May 1919, once again promising to send for his family when he got settled. This time, however, Annie decided that she would follow him and attempt to establish something resembling a stable family life.

Unfortunately, her decision seems to have caught Matthew by surprise: when she and her sons arrived in Toronto in July 1919, they found him living with another woman, and after many harsh words and mutual recriminations the marriage was effectively dissolved. Later that year Annie had Matthew brought before a Police Court magistrate on a charge of non-support, but the case was adjourned and Matthew left for parts unknown before it was resumed. Hugh, who was present at the hearing, would later tell family members and close friends that he had been overwhelmed by the emotions he felt at the sight of his father standing in the witness box.

At this point Annie found herself in an unfamiliar city with two small children, very little money and no network of friends and relations to fall back upon. Her family in England urged her to return but, in a manner that speaks volumes about the sheer obstinacy so often remarked upon by those who knew her, she decided that she would make the best of her new circumstances. She took rooms at 11 Ontario Street, just above King Street and abutted on the north side by a busy livery stable, and found a job at the nearby Blackford Shoe Manufacturers factory. In September Hugh began his Junior First year (equivalent to today's Grade One) at Duke Street School and discovered that he was by far the best reader among his fellow students: he had already developed a taste for the robust adventures featured in *A Boy's Own Annual* and would soon become a devotee of the English public school boy heroes of comic papers such as *Triumph* and *Magnet.*

The Cabbagetown neighbourhood in which Hugh spent most of his first three years in Toronto had received its name from the gardening habits of its largely English, Scotch and Irish residents, who grew vegetables in their front as well as their backyards. This distinctly proletarian practice — the respectable middle class grew only flowers in their front gardens — had largely died out by the time of the First World War, but the name had stuck as an indication of its inhabitants' fierce pride in their class origins. As Garner put it in his 1936 essay "Toronto's Cabbagetown:"

The people who live east of the [Don] river in the Riverdale district are working people too, but they wear good suits to work and then change into overalls. The workers in Cabbagetown can't be bothered changing their clothes like that. They are proud to be recognized as workmen.

Toronto at the beginning of the 1920s was experiencing one of its periodic housing shortages as returning veterans and their long-deferred young families put even more strain upon an already critical situation. Between 1913 and 1918 the city's health department had ordered the demolition of more than 1,600 substandard dwellings, and little had been done to replace them. In 1918 a Toronto Housing Commission was established, but it was dominated by business interests and ultimately produced a grand total of only 236 homes. As rents soared and real wages fell as a consequence of the post-war economic slowdown, families doubled up in ageing, overcrowded houses, and those on the bottom rungs of the social ladder found it difficult to afford even this sort of accommodation.

Under these conditions landlords were able to raise rents arbitrarily and get rid of any tenants who might have the gall to complain about their living conditions, and both factors undoubtedly contributed to the frequent moves made by the sharp-tongued Annie and her family. In addition, she was laid off from the shoe factory in the spring of 1920 and was forced to apply for public welfare, which was granted but was inadequate to cover the rapidly escalating cost of housing. Although there is no way of assessing the relative weight of these circumstances, it is clear that they resulted in a pattern of constant changes of address and schools attended that made the family's first three years in Toronto extremely hectic ones.

In April of 1920 they moved to 87 Pape Avenue in the Riverdale district, where Hugh attended Morse Street School until the end of June. Autumn found them back in Cabbagetown, initially at 234 Berkeley Street, then at 140 Sumach Street and finally at 13 Wascana Avenue, with Hugh going to Lord Dufferin School until the Christmas break. Just before the holidays, returning home with his mother and younger brother after a visit to both the Eaton's and Simpson's Santa Claus, he was hit by a car at the intersection of Queen and George Streets and only narrowly escaped serious injury: years later he remarked, "You had to really *search* for an automobile in Toronto in 1920, but I found one."

Garner spent most of the remainder of the academic year at Park School, residing at 327 Ontario Street and 360 Berkeley Street during the winter and spring of 1921. In mid-June he moved back to Riverdale, where he resided first at 63 Lewis Street and then at 267 Erie Terrace, and attended Roden School until the end of June 1922. Here, according to his school attendance card, someone must have asked him about his father's occupation: he listed it as "British government employee in Germany," which indicates that Annie must have contacted the authorities in Ottawa regarding her husband's whereabouts. The last address given for Matthew on his military records is "Inter-Allied Commission of Control, Armament Subcommission, Berlin, Germany," an organization responsible for ensuring that Germany did not rearm following its defeat in the First World War. At this point Matthew's subsequent movements are lost in the minutiae of history, although Hugh later made several efforts to find out what had happened to his father.

One of the highlights of these early years in Toronto, drab and impoverished though they generally were, was the arrival of the service club hampers and *Toronto Star* Santa Claus Fund boxes that marked the advent of Christmas. The hampers contained "foodstuffs we never saw any other time of the year" and usually included a chicken; on one memorable occasion they received two chickens, one of which was stored in their icebox — meaning outside on the windowsill — for a New Year's feast as well. The *Star* boxes offered a small toy, candy, socks and an object that became one of the banes of Garner's childhood:

> a knitted woollen sweater of a color I can only describe as puce.
> On the day after New Year's when we charity recipients went back to school it was possible to pick us out by our uniforms. The boys' sweaters had a high roll-neck, and they seemed to have been

knitted out of steel wool. We knowledgeable charity-hounds would cut a slit down the front of the itchy, unwearable collar, re-making the sweater into an open-neck creation.

In Garner's later years, he would sometimes receive letters from readers whose memories had been jogged by his accounts of an earlier Toronto. One of these, a 1969 letter from Robert Moore of Port Credit, Ontario, provides a glimpse of the Sumach Street neighbourhood Garner's family lived in during the autumn of 1920 and then again from the summer of 1924 to the fall of 1925:

> 140 Sumach St. — that must have been a few doors below the shoe repair shop at the corner of St. Davids and Sumach. Joe, an un-married, quiet Macedonian ran it. He was fond of kids, who liked him too. One day during the war he arranged all his business af-fairs, left a short note, drove his car to High Park and hanged him-self.
>
> The Hines family must have lived almost across from you. Mr. Hines rode a bicycle to work all his life. ... He liked to drink, which often made his bike riding interesting to watch. His wife was hard of hearing, his daughter Gertie was almost totally deaf, his daughter Norma half deaf, the other two girls, Margaret and Velma were both partially deaf.
>
> On a summer day or evening when the house doors and win-dows were open and the women were having a casual conversa-tion you could easily hear them from the corner ...
>
> Mr. Yankoff ran the little grocery store at the north-west corner of Sumach and St. Davids for years ... He made the greatest pickled brown onions as a little sideline. His other sideline was helping a male cousin run a handbook [an illegal betting operation] ...
>
> ... the kids used to take their wagons down to the Consumers Gas and steal a load of coke, picking up loose bits piece by piece.
>
> I remember kids getting ten cents on a Saturday to take a bath at the Public Baths at the corner of Sackville and St. Davids. In-stead they would hit for the Bluebell Theatre at Parliament and Dundas. After the movies they would dunk their heads in the drink-ing fountain, run home with wet hair, which proved they had bathed.

While Mr. Yankoff was running his handbook, a young newspaper reporter who would soon become one of Hugh's formative literary influences was taking a broader look at this phenomenon in the December 29, 1923 issue of the *Toronto Star Weekly*. In an article entitled "Betting in Toronto," Ernest Hemingway observed that much of the action was handled by "bookmakers who operate behind the cigar counters of certain restaurants, in certain cigar stores, ice cream parlors and poolrooms. These men are mostly accepting commissions for larger bookmakers."

Several factors link Garner with Hemingway, and there is a case to be made for Garner being considered as a kind of Canadian version of his American idol. Both began as, and to a degree always were, journalists; both would be linked, however misleadingly, with the cult of rampant masculinity; both achieved the highest standards as short-story writers and were markedly less successful as novelists. Moreover, Garner's literary indebtedness to Hemingway is evident as well as explicitly acknowledged. Although Hugh's reputation was severely damaged by the amount of sheer hackwork that, for reasons of economic necessity, he published during his career, at his best I think that he can be spoken of in the same terms as his much more famous literary hero.

To return to the biographical story, Garner's account of these years in *One Damn Thing After Another!* is the only other reliable evidence we have concerning this period of his life, and one does not have to read too far between the lines to conclude that his description of himself as "a contented loner" who lived in a milieu where "we kids had everything going for us except money for clothes, fruit juices, and a stomach full of food, and what we didn't have we didn't particularly miss" paints an excessively rosy picture. One particularly false note is struck by his assertion that his lack of knowledge about his father is a matter of "no interest" to him: in fact, according to his daughter Barbara, he made many attempts to find out what had happened to his father and was saddened by his inability to do so. Even more noticeable, however, is what can only be described as a high degree of ambivalence concerning his mother, which is strikingly evident in the way he concludes his account of her life:

> I suppose that the professional sociologists and psychologists could find a great many errors in my mother's life-style and in the way she brought her children up. Her conduct at times, out of sheer ignorance of the consequences and what it might do to the psyches of her children, especially to me who was the oldest, was lamentable and injurious. Nevertheless she was a good, clean, hardworking mother to us all, and a credit to the working class.

Garner never spells out what this "lamentable and injurious" behaviour might have been, even though these are strong words that necessarily whet the reader's curiosity. In the process of researching his family background, however, I think that I have discovered the circumstances which provoked such a double-edged tribute to his mother's influence.

One Damn Thing After Another! contains only one brief reference to the two different men who were the fathers of Garner's two half-sisters. Actually, the men themselves are not referred to at all, but one of the relationships — which resulted in the birth of the older of his half-sisters, Margery, in 1925 — is characterized as "a disastrous common-law union." The language is again rather strong, especially when one considers that Garner was a stickler for the precise use of words: if he had meant merely "regrettable" or "unfortunate," he would have said so. But his choice of "disastrous," like his earlier use of "lamentable and injurious," suggests a depth of feeling which is not articulated in his autobiography, although it turns out that it was forcefully expressed to some members of his immediate family.

At some time in 1922 or 1923 Annie Garner, now working as a waitress at the T. Eaton Company's employees' cafeteria on Hayter Street, began living with a man who used the then readily available drug paregoric as a stimulant. Paregoric is an opium tincture usually prescribed as a treatment for diarrhea, although during the period in question it was also routinely prescribed as a cough suppressant. Ron Garner, Hugh's younger brother, re-members being taken to local drugstores to serve as what he even

at the age of five or six felt was "window dressing:" the paregoric was supposedly being purchased as children's medicine,
but Ron was aware that the syringes and cotton swabs he found
lying around the house were being used by his mother's common-law husband. Hugh, four years older and already streetwise,
knew exactly what was going on: according to his daughter Barbara, he often referred to the man as a "drug addict" and was
ashamed of the fact that his mother had borne such a person a
child.

There were other men who either visited, or for short periods
of time resided in, the Garner household — one of whom became the father of Hugh's younger half-sister, June, born in 1929
— and the effects of this upon a young boy, keenly aware of his
real father's absence and perhaps aspiring to be the male head of
the family, can easily be imagined. According to his brother Ron,
none of these men served as fathers to the two young boys: "One
day they were there, the next day they weren't there, and nothing was ever said about it to us." Although we are now in the
realm of speculation rather than fact, it could also have been the
lack of communication, and not just the relationships themselves, that made Hugh describe his mother's behaviour as sometimes "lamentable and injurious." He could not help but be
jealous of these mysterious visitors who usurped his rightful
place, and his mother's failure to help him understand the situation is what almost certainly lies at the root of his ambivalent
feelings about her.

His bitterness was apt to surface at any time: in a 1965 *Star
Weekly* article entitled "The Women in My Life," which begins
as a pleasant reminiscence of past sexual indiscretions and con-
quests, Garner suddenly blurts out that "As a small boy I lived
in a broken home and was thrown on my own resources by a
mother who worked and left me alone all day." It was only
toward the very end of his life, according to his daughter, that he
began to appreciate just how difficult his mother's situation had
been.

But it would be misleading to imply that Hugh spent most of
his time brooding about his mother's inadequacies. Although life

at home might be pretty depressing — there was never enough money for even a small radio, and Hugh and Ron slept in the same bed until the former was sixteen and the latter twelve — there were all sorts of interesting things to do in the streets and parks of downtown Toronto. And there was almost unlimited opportunity to do them: since Annie often worked afternoons and evenings, the boys were pretty much on their own after school, if indeed they had bothered to attend school at all. Ron Garner recalls that one of the advantages of having no father and a working mother was that if the school authorities wanted to speak to your parents, this was literally impossible: "We would just say she couldn't come because she had to work, and that would be the end of that."

And then there were the frequent moves, which along with the absence of a telephone (Annie Garner would not appear in the phone book until 1948) would have made it difficult for anyone to get in touch and keep in touch with the family. From the fall of 1922 to the summer of 1924 they did at least reside on the same street: first at 267 Erie Terrace, then at number 221 and finally at 273 Craven Road after the street's name had been changed in 1924 (according to local legend, this change had been advocated in 1914 but had been postponed because of the cowardly connotations of "craven"). During this period Hugh attended Duke of Connaught School, where he experienced his first intimation of the joys of authorship when he "hand printed a class newspaper in pen and ink."

In the summer of 1924 the family moved back to a previous Cabbagetown address, 140 Sumach Street, and the boys spent the next academic year at Park School, where Hugh played "a pair of polished beef bones" in the rhythm section of the school band. In October 1925 it was back to Riverdale, first at 5 Napier Street, then in 1927 at an unknown address on Booth Avenue, and at 194 Logan Avenue by the beginning of 1928. Hugh went to Queen Alexandra Senior School for most of the 1925-26 school year, which left him with never-to-be-forgotten memories of his eighth grade class' cacophonous renditions of a sea shanty called "The Mermaid." Led by a "formidable lady in a

pince- nez," the class worked its way up to a thunderous cater-
wauling of the song's concluding lines, "and the landlubbers
lying down below, below, below — AND THE LANDLUB-
BERS LYING DOWN BELOW!" He would later be glad that
he remembered this phrase when he was searching for a title for
his first published novel, but in the autumn of 1926 he was
delighted to move on to the less musically inclined program
offered by Riverdale Technical School.

Ron Garner provides a glimpse of the kinds of lodgings the
family lived in during these years:

> We usually shared a house, living in the downstairs flat in a kitchen
> and two other rooms, renting it unfurnished. We had practically no
> furniture. There were some wooden chairs and a cheap rocker, and
> at one point we did have an old round dining-room table, although
> that went pretty quickly. We didn't have a radio until about 1931.
> We all slept in army cots. When we moved, sometimes somebody
> where my mother worked would give us a hand, but we really
> didn't have that much to move.

If her family's life was in many respects chaotic, Annie Garner
did insist on Sunday attendance at church services. During 1924
and 1925 Hugh was a "front-row boy soprano" at St. Bar-
tholomew's Anglican Church at Dundas and Parliament Streets,
and he also sang in the choir at St. Monica's Anglican Church
on Hiawatha Road when the family lived in Riverdale, first in
1923 and then again in 1926 and 1927. *One Damn Thing After
Another!* includes a photograph of the ten- year-old Hugh decked
out in his choirboy garments, looking as neat, angelic and
thoroughly respectable as any middle-class lad of the day; only
the rickety board fence in the background hints at the material
and emotional deprivation of which he was so conscious at this
time.

A book that offers a helpful perspective on the social context
of Garner's childhood, Robert Thomas Allen's *When Toronto
Was For Kids*, portrays the contemporary educational system this
way:

Not learning anything at school was a mark of manhood, like not being neat. The kid who stood thirty-first in my class ... wore a beam of triumph on his face that made you feel like a sissy.

... at best, school was just something that temporarily barred the way to the real world.

Allen, two years older than Garner, came from a solidly lower middle-class family that believed in the value of education, which increases one's sympathy for those teachers who had to deal with young Hugh's feeling that "I didn't give a damn about learning anything, so I didn't."

Garner's educational performance wasn't helped by the constant shifts from one school to another. Although these became somewhat less frequent as the decade went on — in the 1919-1922 period Hugh had attended five different schools, whereas in the years from 1922 to 1926 this was reduced to three — he was usually in the position of the "new kid" who had to suffer rites of initiation before being accepted by his peers. Writing about his school-days in a 1953 magazine article, he averred that he could still remember the names of three bullies who had made his recesses hell but could only recall the names of two of his teachers. And one of these was a "feared strap wielder," adept at applying the long rubber strap to the tender parts of the victim's palm in the days when this was a common form of punishment.

If Hugh wasn't learning a great deal in school classrooms, he was certainly picking up all kinds of other knowledge and experience. Writing of 1925 Toronto in a 1960 magazine article, he remembered:

On a warm evening in July I can close my eyes and transport myself back 35 years into the city streets of my boyhood. They were streets filled with the sounds of games of Ink-pink-pannigan or Bluebottle, Bluebottle from one sidewalk to the other ... the daytime bread wagons with the rear step to ride on ... the ice wagon with its cool, wet floorboards, and its fantail of children sucking slivers of ice as black as their hands ... the scooters made of a wooden box, a length of board, the wheels off a roller skate and ingenuity ... the automobile tires we pushed along the sidewalks, tirelessly, like hoops ... the collecting of old bottles and baskets under the cellar stairs in order to see Ruth Roland at the Saturday matinee. ...

The best times were the summers, when life could be lived outdoors and it was easy to forget that you would eventually be returning to a "crummy house or flat." Riverdale Park had not yet been invaded by major highways such as the Don Valley Expressway and the Bayview Avenue Extension, and it offered a large expanse of grass and trees as well as swimming in the as yet only moderately polluted Don River. Here Hugh and his friends spent the long summer days playing with a freedom denied to them in their crowded residential neighbourhoods: they "hiked, fought, climbed, built forts, swum, roasted stolen potatoes," and did it all without any sort of parental or official supervision.

Summer also held the threat of being sent away to one of the camps operated by charitable organizations such as the Salvation Army, whose Jackson's Point facility on Lake Simcoe provided him with one of his first — and by no means the last — brushes with evangelical religion. One year his mother signed him up for a second two-week session after he had grimly toughed out the first, which led to the following totally uncharacteristic behaviour:

> No convict lifer, finding that his parole had been withdrawn, felt worse than I did at that moment. I even sought refuge at the next evening's bible session by going forward to the mercy bench and confessing to an indifferent deity that from then on I would forego the pleasures of sin and become as dour and nutty as my keepers.

Many years later he would use memories of this experience in one of his most powerful short stories, and throughout his life he would have nothing but contempt for those who claimed to have had direct contact with God.

Toronto's summers also provided many other forms of free entertainment. As a lifelong lover of parades — his daughter describes him as a "parade fanatic" — Garner especially appreciated the pomp and circumstances of the "Derry Drums" march on the 12th of July, during which the fife-and-drum bands of the city's Orange Lodges strutted their stuff. Almost every weekend there were the annual Sunday School and service club picnics to sign up for, and later in life he remembered how "Most of us suddenly blossomed out as Anglicans, Methodists, Baptists, Sons of Scotland, junior Lions and Orange Young Britons," enjoying a free lake steamer ride to Port Dalhousie or Queenston Heights as well as all the food they could eat.

His personal record for number of Sunday School picnics attended was six, set at the age of twelve when he registered himself with St. Matthew's Anglican, First Avenue Baptist, Woodgreen United, Queen East Presbyterian, Pentecostal Tabernacle and the local Salvation Army branch; he thought about trying for the St. Anne's Roman Catholic Church picnic as well but decided that the chance of being identified as a "dirty Prot" made it not worth the risk. In a way that anticipated the sociological interests of much of his later work, he noticed that there was a direct relationship between the evangelical fervour of the church and the cheapness of its children's fêtes: the Anglicans really put on a spread, the Presbyterians did a pretty good job and the Baptists and Pentecostals were so niggardly that their picnics weren't anywhere near as much fun.

Locally, amusement parks at Sunnyside, Hanlon's Point and Scarborough Beach had some free attractions, notably the latter's "The Bumps:"

> a polished hardwood slope literally covered with gentle bumps over which you slid on the seat of your pants. At the bottom of the slope you found yourself on a speedily revolving polished saucer around which you too revolved until you were discarded by centrifugal force, unless you became an expert who could quickly crawl to its axis and there amaze the girls with your boyish expertise.

And then there was the Canadian National Exhibition, at this time more of a big country fair than the tawdry carnival it has since become, which on Children's Day let in the youth of Toronto for free. Hugh was always among the first in line, "clutching my half-a-buck and free admission ticket in my grubby little hand." After a judicious selection of midway rides he would stagger home with as many free samples as possible from the numerous commercial exhibits. Robert Thomas Allen offers an evocative sense of the holiday atmosphere:

> you could smell the sheep, horses, pigs, and cows from the time the streetcar groaned around the corner of King and Dufferin Streets, with the city kids hanging out the windows inhaling the air with looks of rapture. ... We wedged ourselves into the crowds of grown-ups like ping-pong balls, and shuffled through smells of hot butter, popcorn, mothballs, and floor wax collecting samples of Kellogg's Corn Flakes, Quaker Oats, Bon Ami, Mentholatum, Old Dutch Cleanser, booklets on stoves, industrial sites, the Royal Bank of Canada.

Hugh and his friend Chuck Sanderson were first in line for the 1928 CNE, sleeping overnight in front of the gates and getting their pictures in the daily papers.

The summers passed quickly in a feverish haze of perpetual activity, but with colder weather life returned to a much slower and duller pace. Since, in the words of his brother Ron, "There was nothing to hang around the house for," hanging around an interesting street corner became the usual thing. The corner of Broadview Avenue and Gerrard Street was one favourite spot, since a public library, a YMCA and the nickel java at Joe the Greek's coffee shop offered something for just about everyone. Unknown to most of his cronies, Hugh had become an active user of the public libraries, joining the Ashdale Avenue and Gerrard Street branch as soon as he had reached the minimum age of twelve. There he read widely and unselectively in everything from the classics to current popular fiction. At a local Owl Drugstore lending library, he paid three cents per day to rent titles the public libraries of the day refused to stock: Henry Miller's *The Tropic of Cancer*, Erskine Caldwell's *Tobacco Road* and — from the under-the-counter, five cents per day section — D.H. Lawrence's *Lady Chatterley's Lover*.

Given a more elastic educational system, Garner might well have qualified for some form of alternative schooling, which would have satisfied the intellectual hunger lurking beneath the tough-kid exterior. Instead, in the fall of 1926 he began a vocational course at Riverdale Technical School, at the Danforth and Greenwood Avenues location that would in the 1930s be renamed Danforth Technical School. Here he strenuously resisted Riverdale's half-hearted efforts to force him to learn a trade and secretly wished that he could become a member of the tight little cliques that ran the newspaper and the drama club. Since he had to work every day after school at a Danforth Avenue fruit store, he was unable to participate in extracurricular activities; but the urge to write something of his own was nonetheless growing within him, and he submitted several of his poems to the editorial judgement of the *Tech Tatler* and his class newspaper. All of these were rejected, and in *One Damn Thing After Another!* Garner piques the reader's curiosity by describing them as "short pieces of horrible verse" while failing to quote any examples. But in the process of reading his more than 400 newspaper and magazine articles, I did come across two of these early ventures into authorship, and they have their points of interest.

The first, characterized as "atrocious doggerel" by its creator, echoes both his early reading of G.A. Henty and the preoccupation with his relationship with his mother. It is entitled "The Burglars:"

> The night was dark the weather was cold
> The boy was frightened the man was bold
> Go to the window you he said
> Or I will cave in your ungaily head
> I wont I cant the boy he cried
> Ive been so sick since mother died
> Just then a shot a scream rang out
> The boys red blood began to spout
> And then as his brave life blood spent
> To his mother in heaven the boy he went

Besides displaying an indifference to the niceties of spelling, punctuation and contraction, which had been Garner's undoing in the grammar section of his high school entrance examination,

"The Burglars'" only other notable literary quality is its absence of literary quality: there is nothing here that would lead us to predict an author's career for the writer.

But the second piece Garner cites, a "proletarian free verse" effort called "Dawn," is much more interesting:

A field of grey lawns
Smoking chimneys
Twittering birds
Pure air
a few milkmen
And an array of garbage pails.

A selection of impressions intended to convey a general effect, "Dawn" reveals an intuitive apprehension of literary technique that, however uncertain its expression, is several light years beyond the crude rhymes of "The Burglars." It would be wrong to make too much out of a poem Garner considered nothing more than a kind of adolescent doodling, but it is interesting to note that "The Dawn" precedes his next dateable work — the 1936 essay "Toronto's Cabbagetown" — by seven or eight years and demonstrates that his reading was beginning to have an impact on his writing.

If Hugh couldn't get his poetry published in the *Tech Tatler*, he did appear in its pages in the somewhat unlikely role of an athlete. Sports generally played very little part in Garner's life, but during his third and final year at Riverdale he was a member of the school's cross-country team. On November 2, 1928 he participated in a race for which M.P.P. George Smith was the starter, and the *Tatler* reported that he was the "sweetheart" (sentimental favourite) of the event and "ran splendidly." Otherwise he does not appear in the *Tatler*'s chatty chronicles of corn roasts, masquerade balls, tennis tournaments and the joys of life at the summer cottage, which are complemented by pre-Depression humour such as the following:

Dear Editor,
I am in poor circumstances, have a family of ten children and I am

out of work. What would you advise me to do?
Alex Taylor

Dear Alex,
I'd advise you to have the family secure work.
Editor

For someone who later visualized himself during this period as "The dirty little kid sitting in the back row wearing a *Star* Santa Claus-box sweater," this was ample proof that he wasn't wanted by the well-dressed sophisticates who ran the *Tech Tatler*.

Hugh failed his first Grade Nine year at Riverdale, getting off to a bad start by standing eighteenth out of twenty-four in his class at the 1926 Christmas break and being described as "Late and absent too often." In *One Damn Thing After Another!* he attributes this to "psychological reasons beyond [the school's] comprehension" but does not elaborate; presumably this refers to how upset he was by the presence at home of his half-sister Margery, who had been born in 1925. His 1927-28 repeat of Grade Nine was an entirely different story, as he consistently stood first in his class despite failing Algebra and Woodworking, and was seldom absent, if occasionally late. He earned very high marks in Literature, Printing, Art and — of all things — Conduct, which he ascribed to his desire to show his teachers what he could do "when I wanted to."

In September of 1928 he began Tenth Grade knowing that he would be leaving the following February, and he slacked off a bit: he stood sixth out of twenty at the Christmas break, due mainly to his scoring nine out of one hundred on his Arithmatic exam, and had accumulated quite a few absences and latenesses. He was still doing well in Literature and had pulled up his Composition grades, in previous years usually in the fifties and sixties, to the same eighties level; his deficiencies in grammar were showing signs of yielding to his interest in literature. While Hugh was certainly no academic superstar, his marks were somewhat better than one would gather from a reading of his autobiography.

Any account of Garner's school-days, and indeed any account of his experiences with social institutions, must take note of the virulence with which he verbally abused the teachers, social workers and other authority figures who loomed large in his childhood. One thing which should be stressed is that Garner's ancestors were not the products of what would today be considered a "culture of poverty:" they had always been *workers*, at times unemployed or subject to the temptations of demon rum, to be sure, but never the regular recipients of any form of social welfare:

> To the unemployed workmen, most of whom were the descendants of the workhorses of the Industrial Revolution, being without a job was morally wrong, and applying for relief was tantamount to holding out your hat for a handout. As a consequence many Torontonians of my acquaintance used up their pitiful savings, gave up their houses, and cashed in their insurance policies before applying, out of desperation, for Home Relief.

After spending his early years in such a milieu, Garner at the age of six suddenly found himself a member of a new class: the poor, those unfortunates who in the neo-Victorian climate of 1920s Toronto could count on a minimum of charity and a maximum of patronizing attention from the public and private institutions responsible for their support. Having been brought up to believe that he was just as good as anyone else, young Hugh now had to learn that in a very real sense this was no longer so: the Garners were now at the bottom of the social scale, and subject to the whims and caprices of everyone from policemen to social workers to teachers to petty bureaucrats of all descriptions. A child with his innate intelligence and less stubborn pride in himself as a worthwhile human being would have learned the proper kinds of social humility demanded by the authority figures of the day, but Hugh instead chose to wage a ceaseless guerrilla battle against those who presumed to know what was good for him. His memories of his first encounters with the era's social institutions are very bitter:

> The two things I hated most during my childhood were bedbugs
> and social workers. ... The social workers, like the schoolteachers
> and librarians of the day largely untrained and uneducated, were
> not as numerous as the bugs but too numerous for *my* comfort at
> least.
>
> Middle-class liberal bleeding-hearts whose ego demands that
> they throw themselves into causes aimed at helping the slum kids
> are ... a complete pain in the ass ...
>
> Though I frequently received the highest marks in school for lit-
> erary composition, to my teachers it was a fluke. Their favourite
> pupils were the snotty little swotters who could repeat parrot-like
> most historical dates, the division of fractions and the genealogi-
> cal musical chairs of the English monarchy ...

With these kinds of attitudes firmly ingrained in his youthful
persona, Garner was well on his way to being labelled a social
deviant. By his teen-age years he and his family were in the files
of several social agencies, one of which attempted to provide a
male role model for this little hellion from a fatherless home. Unfortunately, the putative role model dandied Hugh on his knee,
kissed him on the cheek and left a lasting impression concerning the real motives of volunteers from charitable organizations.
Garner would later take this essentially innocuous event and use
it as the basis of a scene in *Cabbagetown*, where the homosexu-
ally inclined bachelor "Clarence Gurney" attempts to seduce the
novel's protagonist with photos of men and boys practicing "coi-
tus and other sexual aberrations." This is among the earliest examples of Garner's use of his own experiences as basic elements
of his fiction, although here he has exaggerated the original occurrence to a marked extent.

In any case, by his teen-age years Hugh was "completely anti-
social and on my way to becoming a chronic juvenile delinquent." Allowing for a certain amount of bravado — he was
holding down a job from 3:30 p.m. to 6:00 p.m. after school and
from 9 a.m. to midnight on Saturdays, and his friends were for
the most part high-spirited rather than potential criminals — his
frustrations with society were finding outlets that could lead to
serious trouble. Thus in the fall of 1928 he appeared before Juvenile Court Judge Mott, charged with "malicious damage to

property " and in some danger of being sent to an institution for delinquent boys.

The experience did have its comic side. The whole thing had started when his brother Ron, part of a younger but equally rambunctious gang, came home and told him of the great time he had had vandalizing a wintering lake boat down on the waterfront: they had even come across a plate of cold spaghetti and had impersonated biblical characters by draping it over their heads in wig-like fashion. Then, becoming bored with a game that must have reminded Ron of enforced attendance at Sunday School, they had smashed up the place and gone on their merry way. Hugh replied that if he thought that was something, "Just wait until *we* get through with the place."

So Hugh and his cronies set off to complete the trashing of the lake boat. Unfortunately, they had not given sufficient thought to the significance of the spaghetti: the vessel was in fact being lived in by a watchman, who preferred to spend his evenings in a tavern and had therefore been out when Ron's bunch came to call. But he had returned later that night, been appalled by what he discovered and arranged for increased surveillance by the local police. Hugh and his friends were seen leaving the boat after another orgy of destruction — during which they had a wonderful time "breaking all the dishes, and spattering the galley, and ourselves, with a nauseating mixture of flour, lard and fire-extinguisher fluid" — and a summons to appear in court arrived a few days later.

Dressed in their Sunday clothes, shoes shined and hair combed and faces scrubbed, the boys were ordered to approach the bench. Judge Mott lectured them sternly about the gravity of what they had done and asked them how it had happened. When Hugh admitted that it had been his idea, he was singled out for a special warning: the Judge advised him that it was within his power to have him sent to the Working Boys' Home for a few months, and left that possibility up in the air for several very uncomfortable minutes. Finally, however, he let the boys off with a fine of ten dollars each plus costs, threatening them with a term at the Home if they appeared before him again.

Although at the time Hugh refused to admit that he had been sobered by this experience, the fact remains that both he and his friends went back to hanging around the corner of Broadview Avenue and Gerrard Street and avoided any further serious trouble. But in retrospect, he viewed this as "the most dangerous period of my life" and recognized that he was very close to taking the path of overt conflict with authority and suffering the consequent legal penalties. In years to come he would again run afoul of legal and military authorities, but would always draw back from any final, irrevocable act of total defiance; it was almost as if he needed to establish the territory within which he could operate by periodically crossing its boundaries, after which he would carefully follow the straight and narrow path until once more compelled to test society's limits.

As his sixteenth year drew to a close, Hugh Garner was by conventional standards an unlikely candidate for either fame or fortune. He would be celebrating his birthday by leaving school, where with the occasional exception he had not distinguished himself in either academic or extracurricular activities and had resisted all efforts to teach him a marketable skill. At home, his mother's few free moments were devoted to the care of her two young daughters, and the grinding poverty of their existence was about to be further exacerbated by the imminent economic depression. On the streets, he could at least look forward to sympathetic companionship, although for a young man with a vivid imagination and no money there were also temptations to get rich quick by challenging the forces of the law. But for the moment, these considerations were overshadowed by the prospect of being delivered from school's restrictions: Hugh Garner was about to escape from one set of authorities, although others lay in wait for a youth who stubbornly refused to accept the world's assessment of his chances.

Chapter Two

On His Own, and Down and Out (1929-1936)

O n February 22, 1929, his sixteenth birthday, Hugh Garner shook hands with the principal of Riverdale Tech and said goodbye to formal education for the remainder of his life. After a similar ritual handshake the protagonist of *Cabbagetown,* " Ken Tilling," reflects on his past and future in these terms:

> He had believed somehow that the school would release him from his shabby district and even shabbier home and make him a belonging part of its cleanliness and comradeship and happier life. It had not done this. The failure was not so much that of the school, or of his fellow students, as it was his own. The contrasts between life inside and outside its association were too great to be bridged so easily.
>
> Almost immediately he had run head-on into social consciousness and snobbery. ... He had remained an outsider from the cliques revolving around athletics, the school magazine, the auditorium stage, the possession of a Model T Ford —
>
> But now all this was past. Tomorrow he would get a job, and the money he earned would give him equality with those among whom he had not been equal before.

Ordinarily, one would hesitate to equate fictional and real-life experience in such a direct manner, but in the case of Hugh Garner and Ken Tilling it is clear that we are talking about an almost complete identity between the author's persona and that of his protagonist. When he discussed this in *One Damn Thing After Another!*, Garner tried to downplay the question of such correspondences in order to protect his family and friends from being associated with *Cabbagetown*'s other characters, but the Garner-Tilling relationship still comes through:

> My protagonist, Ken Tilling, lived on a street I lived on as a small boy, Wascana Avenue. He shared some of the jobs I had held at his age, took some of the boxcar trips to Western Canada that I had taken, hung around with a gang in Riverdale Park, and finally went off to fight in Spain in 1937. I made him about my size, gave him my personality, but that was all. Other than that he is a fictional figure.

At this point, it is not immediately clear that there are any significant differences at all. But Garner's intentions are revealed in the sentences that follow: "His alcoholic mother is completely fictional (my own mother never took a drink in her whole life), his girl friend Myrla Patson is also completely fictional, as are all the other characters in the novel."

Whatever the truth of this last statement — and we have already seen that Garner used one social agency volunteer as "my model for Mr. Gurney in *Cabbagetown*" — the important point is that *Cabbagetown* should be viewed as an autobiographical novel. And since the years between Garner's leaving school and his involvement in radical politics are not well documented, the book offers a valuable account of what he was feeling and thinking during this period.

But the correspondences are not absolute, as the matter of Hugh's service in the Canadian militia demonstrates. On February 11, 1929, just before his sixteenth birthday, he enrolled in what was then known as the Non-Permanent Active Militia of Canada and remained a member until June 1931, when he resigned in good standing. Militia units normally met twice per week for low-level military training, and Garner's record of service indicates that he attended regularly. He was also described as both a "bugler" and a member of the "trumpet band," which is corroborated by his brother Ron's memories of Hugh bringing home a bugle to practice on.

But he never mentioned the militia in any of his autobiographical writings and certainly did not enlist Ken Tilling in its fictional counterpart. It is of course possible that Hugh deemed this an insignificant episode in an eventful life, but there are also grounds for suspecting that he deliberately suppressed this information. When he began writing his autobiography in the early 1970s, he presented his late teens and early twenties as a period of increasing radicalization and political awareness, and voluntary military service obviously wouldn't have fit well with this self-image. Although there may have been economic motives involved — members of the militia received a small stipend as well as their uniforms — this is most likely the earliest formal indication of that side of Garner which loved a parade and the romantic aspects of soldiering. He would later write of his "emotion when the regiments march down University Avenue ... the Queen's Own Rifles bugle band swinging down the street with the setting sun glinting on their silver bugles.... " Although there is no way of knowing for sure, it is quite possible that Hugh marched in just such a parade as a bugler in the militia.

Hugh's post-secondary career also began on a very different note from that of Ken Tilling. Where his fictional alter ego found work at a wholesale grocery warehouse, Garner was fortunate enough to get his foot on the bottom rung of a ladder that had been climbed by many a famous writer: on February 23, 1929 he became the youngest copy boy at the *Toronto Daily Star*, where one of his literary heroes, Ernest Hemingway, had in the early 1920s been a reporter and foreign correspondent.

He got off to an auspicious start. Although the basic responsibility of a copy boy was to pick up copy from reporters in the field and deliver it to the newspaper's editorial department, there were many opportunities to learn other aspects of the journalistic profession. Hugh was soon operating the switchboard, helping out in the "slot" — where final decisions about a story's layout and placement were made — and learning to type. Most importantly, he tried his hand at writing up some short items himself, and caught the approving attention of the managing editor, H.C. Hindmarsh. His wages were raised from $6 to $8 per week, and he began to think of himself as an unofficial member of the *Star*'s "flying squad," a crack team of reporters mobilized when a major news event required extensive coverage.

Then came his big chance. On his way to pick up some copy at City Hall, Hugh saw a policeman refuse to let a young man park his car in front of the building. The young man, enraged, hurled a test-tube onto the ground and told the policeman that he could deliver it himself. When Garner learned that the test-tube contained a diptheria culture being sent in for analysis, he wrote a story about what he had seen and had another copy boy rush off with it to the *Star*'s offices on King Street:

> I was called into the managing editor's office, congratulated by Mr. Hindmarsh, given another two dollar raise (which gave me $10 a week, equal to the head copy boy's salary) and personally conducted around the third, fourth, and fifth floors of the building and introduced to Mr. Joseph Atkinson the president ... Mr. Atkinson gave his secretary, Mr. Palmer, instructions to teach me shorthand to boot, every Thursday afternoon.

If Hugh Garner's life had been destined to follow the Horatio Alger pattern, this would have been the first step in a successful career as a writer. But having achieved, through a combination of good luck and innate ability, a position that would have been the envy of almost anyone else in his circumstances, Garner then threw it all away: in December of 1929 — after helping pack Santa Claus Fund boxes with the same itchy sweaters he had detested as a boy — he refused to sully his new-found prestige by acting as a tour guide for "a party of giggling teenagers," and was immediately fired. Although he doesn't say so, it's more than likely that these teenagers came from middle or upper-class backgrounds — the use of "giggling" implies a frivolity alien to the world of Hugh and his peers, who were in any case unlikely to be invited on specially arranged tours of newspaper offices. This would certainly have aroused his already well-developed class consciousness and suggests that his refusal to guide the group wasn't simply a case of his characteristic inability to accept direction from authority.

Jocko Thomas, who joined the *Star* in October 1929 and is now its senior police reporter, has vivid memories of Hugh's constant squabbling with his immediate superior:

> The head office boy was Robert Burnett, who was later nicknamed "Red" and became a well-known hockey writer. He and Garner used to feud, because Hugh was a fellow who didn't like to take orders. Burnett used to time how long it took the office boys to run their copy from City Hall or Osgoode Hall down to the *Star*. But Hugh liked to stop off and play a game of snooker in a billiard parlor at Bay and Queen, and so of course he'd be late, and would have words with Burnett. And when you got in Red's bad books you were ordered to sweep the floor, and Hugh really hated that. They finally had it out with their fists in back of the building, and it was Red who got his nose bloodied.

Burnett was thus more than willing to fire Garner when he refused to guide the tour group, which effectively nipped in the bud a promising journalistic career. Years later Hugh would attempt to rationalize his stubbornness as a wise decision that kept him from ending up "like so many newspapermen, wishing I had written the book I had once promised myself to write, but know I never will." But since he would in the future make much of his living from journalism and would write books under circumstances much more difficult than those of a working newspaper reporter, this rings rather false. In terms of his development as a writer, leaving the *Star* was almost certainly a regressive move: it would be another six or seven years before he made a serious attempt at authorship, and several more years after that before he finally mastered the rudiments of fictional story-telling. In the interim, of course, he was accumulating the experiences which would be transmuted into some of his best work. But the examples of several of his acknowledged literary influences, Hemingway, Theodore Dreiser and John O'Hara among them, suggest that newspaper reporting is an excellent place to begin for writers who take an essentially realistic approach to their craft.

Whatever the possibilities of what might have been, Hugh Garner found himself out of a job at a time when the stock market crash of October 1929 had signalled the onset of the economic slump that would soon become known as The Great Depression. His next job did make use of some of the skills he had learned as a copy boy, but these had nothing to do with writing: delivering telegrams for Canadian National Telegraphs required pedal rather than pen pushing, and the pay was much less than what he had earned at the *Star*.

Hugh worked as a bicycle messenger for most of 1930 and found that the job could be enlivened by "defying all the rules of safety and prudence as I dared the motorists to hit me." On a warm evening in May of that year, outdoors in the Don River Valley, he made love to a girl for the first time: her name was Lily, she was sixteen years old and wore flannel bloomers, and she made Hugh's sexual initiation a pleasant and untraumatic one. For the remainder of the decade his relationships with the opposite sex were conditioned by his determination to avoid serious involvements:

> As a youth and young man many of my affairs were with women rather than girls. I met them on the street, in restaurants, parks, at the beach. Some were neighbor's wives or women who lived in the same rooming houses and hotels I did. Some were married but others were single, widowed or grass-widowed. These casual affairs took the place of youthful courtships. I quickly gave up any girl who responded to me romantically, mentally seeing myself running the gauntlet every evening past their porch-sitting neighbors, meeting their families, being shown off to their friends, having them "do things for me," becoming one of the family, letting them tie me down to a life I was trying to escape.

One way of ensuring deliverance from the snares of matrimony was to spend his free time hanging out with "the gang," a group of young men in their late teens and early twenties who had met each other during their childhood explorations of Riverdale Park. Membership was highly elastic, since many of them spent much of their time on the road during the Depression, working on the

Western wheat harvest, bringing in the tobacco crop in south-western Ontario and hopping freights between relief camps. But when they were in Toronto, they could be certain of meeting each other in the park, where

> the wide green playing fields and steep grass- covered hills ... furnished us with a ready-made summer resort. In the evenings the pathways, hills and wooded ravines of Riverdale came alive with courting couples or members of both sexes on the make. Lovemaking — that cheapest and most satisfying of all human pursuits — took the place of such sham and expensive imitations of life as the movies....

Winter evenings presented more of a problem, especially if a shortage of funds put even the dime games at the bowling alley and the nickel hamburgers with the works at the White Tower out of reach. Many of the area's churches did offer free social evenings, and in the same way that young Hugh had become a joiner when summer picnics were put on by organizations of all varieties, his young adult years found him becoming a temporary Anglican, Presbyterian and Roman Catholic. This was somewhat ironic, since at the age of fifteen he had become a "non-practicing Anglican" when "both my voice and my illusions changed;" but the prospect of "a warm and friendly place in which to escape cold and snowy winter evenings," as *Cabbagetown*'s Ken Tilling describes his local church's socials, was sufficient to overcome whatever religious doubts Hugh might have developed.

Just about anything could serve for an evening's entertainment. When a new lonely-hearts club advertised its free opening night in the Toronto papers, Garner and several friends attended. Although they must have made an awkward contrast with what he describes as "older ladies of indeterminate age, looking for husbands," the young men did their duty by dancing the night away and doubtless adding an element of raucous fun to what otherwise must have been a pretty dreary occasion.

But if the members of the gang were in funds, several inexpensive dance-halls beckoned to those who, like Garner, had become adept at the intricate steps of the Big Apple, the Lindy Hop and the popular foxtrots and waltzes of the day. The Silver Slipper at Sunnyside, the Fallingbrook at Balmy Beach and Playter's Hall up on the Danforth were among the most popular spots for a young man to venture his twenty-five cents admission charge on a chance at romance. Hugh and his friend Alex McCartney, however, preferred the Columbus Hall on Linden Avenue. After sharing a cheap bottle of wine under a Don River bridge, they would spend the rest of the evening dancing to the dulcet strains of bands such as Jack Evans and his Manhattan Blues Blowers, who advertised that they played "the sweetest music this side of Yonge Street."

Underlying all these frenetic searches for a good time was the realization that bad times were never far away. The Depression hit the working class first and hardest, and it was not long before families such as Garner's were forced to rely on the municipal relief offices for the necessities of life. Even though Hugh gave almost all of his wages to his mother, they had a hard time paying the rent on the flat at 42 Lewis Street to which they had moved in 1930. When Canadian National Telegraphs reduced its staff at the beginning of the next year, Hugh could not find another steady job. He was able to get occasional part-time or temporary work — mostly unskilled factory or warehouse jobs, although he once worked as a solderer of cemetery flowerholders — but with his mother's meagre waitressing wages the only other source of income, the family had no choice but to go on relief.

The growing numbers of relief recipients were required to report each week to a central office, where

> There were two long queues of men and women winding through a high-fenced yard and into a building where several men at long tables filled paper bags and cartons with such staples as prunes, white beans, peanut butter, porridge oats, cocoa, tea dust, dried apples, and cans of treacle, tomatoes and canned vegetables ...
>
> The people in the slowly shuffling lines at the relief depot were no longer exclusively members of the *lumpen proletariat*, or chronic unemployables of the year before, but were quickly becoming a cross-section of the city's workers and members of the lower middle-class. To have to apply for relief was a shameful

thing for most of them, but the municipal authorities, who still had a Victorian attitude towards the poor, believed that poverty was a sin and that its penance was humiliation. An individual's weekly food requirements had been carefully ascertained by Health Department dieticians, and its portions weighed as scientifically as those given to laboratory rats. It made no allowance for personal preferences, and as a consequence most relief families found themselves the involuntary hoarders of bags upon bags of rolled oats and dried apples, while their kitchen cupboards groaned under the weight of tins of treacle. I used to hear my fellow sufferers say, "We burned our porridge oats in the stove, but they plugged up the stovepipes."

Streetcar tickets were not among the items provided by the municipal authorities, which meant that to save money Hugh walked the approximately three miles between his home and the relief office, carrying heavy bags of foodstuffs on the return trip.

In these circumstances, Hugh and his younger brother Ron were tempted to hit the open road in search of both work and adventure. The now fourteen-year-old Ron actually left first, hopping a freight for "down East" at the end of the school year in June 1931. Hugh headed in the other direction the following month, riding the rods west as far as Regina to work on the wheat harvest. On the way there, on a CPR freight train coming into Broadview, Saskatchewan, he watched in horror as a young man caught his foot in the couplings between two flatcars; the youth could not be freed until the train reached the top of a grade and the couplings momentarily went slack, and his foot was completely crushed.

Garner soon got a job harvesting wheat in southern Saskatchewan, where a good "stooker" — the person who stacks the bound sheaves of wheat into pyramids — earned a dollar a day and board. *Cabbagetown*'s Ken Tilling offers a graphic description of the stooker's lot:

the sun bakes you, and the sweat under your arms dries into salt patches that rub you raw. Clouds of grasshoppers fly into your face as you bend over to pick up the sheaves. The sheaves get heavier every hour during the morning, and every ten minutes during the afternoon. While all this is happening you're trying to keep up with the farmer on his binder ... He keeps going around and around the field, and every time he passes you he stares over to see how much you've done. You can't possibly keep up with him . ...

At the end of the harvest season Garner went on to Vancouver, where he rented a room in the east-central area of the city and hung out at the local employment office, "where I was September, 1931, euchre champion." He spent most of the winter at a relief camp near Kamloops, British Columbia, working on a section of the Trans-Canada Highway. Camps of this kind provided temporary accommodations for the thousands of men out of work, who in exchange for twenty cents a day, board and war-surplus army uniforms were expected to clear bush, build bridges and highways and stay out of trouble. The camps were run by the army, and discipline was harsh: any breach of the rules was liable to be cause for expulsion, and there were no appeal procedures for anyone who felt unjustly treated. One of the anonymous contributors to Barry Broadfoot's *Ten Lost Years* describes another British Columbia relief camp this way:

> the thing most wrong was they treated us like dirt. And we weren't. We were up against it, broke, tired, hungry, but ... we were shit. Dirt. Slaves. ... What else would you call a man who is given twenty cents a day and is expected to believe their bullshit that he is an important part of the country. They just wanted us out of sight, as far out of sight as they could manage.

It would be the British Columbia camps that, in May of 1935, boiled over into the open rebellion that culminated in the March on Ottawa and the Regina Riot.

Garner returned to Toronto in the spring of 1932 and for several months spent his days hanging around the headquarters of the Boy's Department of the National Employment Offices. Here he and other youths aged sixteen to nineteen talked, played cards and waited for any openings to be posted, although these were usually temporary jobs such as "delivering handbills, pulling wooden wagons filled with stationery, or helping load or unload trucks." For a few months he worked as a packer of soap flakes in a factory where those in his department "were forced to wear gauze masks over our mouths and nostrils to cut down the inhalation of soap dust, which seared our throats and sent us into sneezing fits." Garner hated this job so much that he had *Cabbagetown*'s Ken Tilling engage in some industrial sabotage after the latter has made up his mind to quit the soap factory:

> Ken stood well back from the tumbling, tearing mess on the packing table and watched in awe as the machine-fed boxes of Flako ground together in a spreading jam that would have to be freed later with iron bars and shipping hooks.
>
> When the machinery was finally halted half the packing room was hidden under grotesque piles of broken boxes and spilled soap flakes, and Ken was standing against the wall, his face-mask in his hand, gazing on it with a look of incredulous satisfaction.

Given the kinds of jobs available to him in Toronto, it's not surprising that Hugh elected to head west again in the summer of 1932. He again worked on the wheat harvest, this time at both stooking and, when he could, as a teamster, since the drivers of the gigantic hay wagons were paid fifty per cent more — a dollar and a half a day plus board — than the stookers. On the return trip to Toronto he served as a drover for some cattle on their way to market, and rode the train in the comparative luxury of the drover car's comfortable seats and pot-bellied stove.

In Toronto it was back to short-term factory jobs again and further experiences of the kind that would prejudice him against this kind of work forever. For a few weeks he toiled on a machine that bagged finished wooden rulers and yardsticks, breathing wood shavings and chewing snuff in an attempt to protect his throat and lungs. He briefly laboured as a pattern cutter in a button factory, but during his first week on the job lacerated his finger in one of the cutting machines and had to have it sewn up in hospital; the finger would have a permanent hook in it for the remainder of his life. When he applied to the Ontario Workmen's Compensation Board for help in getting his job back — he had been fired as soon as the accident occurred — he was refused any assistance and threatened with arrest if he continued to raise a fuss, an experience that further reinforced his already strong sense of the shabby way society treated its working-class citizens.

Although Garner met and talked with a number of socialists, communists and "wobblies" — members of The Industrial Workers of the World organization — on the road and in the relief camp at Kamloops, he was at first inclined to be suspicious of their interest in the working class. Many of them were university-educated, middle-class people of the type Garner considered natural oppressors of the workers, and he was particularly irritated by their "deification of the working man. I had been born and raised a member of the working class, and I knew there were just as many self-centered, mean, and petty workers as there were bosses or capitalists." Ken Tilling feels the same way about "the Reds:" "I believe a lot of what they believe in, but unlike most Reds I've talked to I don't put the working stiff up at the top of the noble pile. I'm a working stiff myself ... and I believe that some of the worst sons of bitches in the world are other working stiffs." This kind of no-nonsense, down-to-earth thinking is typical of Garner's suspicion of theories and his reliance on immediate experience. From a Marxist perspective, of course, attitudes such as Garner's are the result of what is conceptualized as "false consciousness," the product of a capitalist ideology that equates class position with intrinsic merit; we can only regret that there is no record of the mutually uncomprehending conversations which must have ensued when the as yet unconverted Hugh crossed verbal swords with left-leaning intellectuals. Garner's thinking in the summer of 1933, however, probably is accurately represented by that of Ken Tilling at about the same time:

> As a natural loner he sympathized with the friend-less and help-less, but refused to join any group. He had transferred his cynical distrust and hatred of the bureaucrat, the YMCA secretary, the Bible-thumper, and all their middle-class minions, into a distrust of politicians of all political hues and aims.

In that same summer of 1933, after his mother had moved to the 82 First Avenue address she would occupy until 1940, Hugh and his friend Howard "Skinny" Moore (who would later be killed in Spain) decided to travel south rather than west. Whatever their reservations about socialist theory, they certainly exemplified its practice: sharing their assets, which in total came to a package of cigarette tobacco, ten cents in cash and a bag of cucumber sandwiches donated by Annie Garner, they hitchhiked to Niagara Falls, Ontario. But Moore wasn't permitted to enter by the American immigration authorities, and so Garner found himself alone in a strange country with a nickel, the makings for a few cigarettes and the memory of his mother's cucumber sandwiches.

During the next two years Hugh would hitch-hike and hop freights from one end of the United States to the other. Since he never wrote a detailed account of this period of his life, it is not always possible to know exactly when or where certain events occurred. We do know quite a bit about what happened to him, however, and by putting together many scattered bits of evidence I think I have come up with a reasonably accurate chronicle of his travels.

In a 1976 radio interview Garner stated that he initially followed a New York-Philadelphia-Baltimore-Washington route, which makes it possible to date an earlier reminiscence of his first view of New York as having taken place in September 1933. The city made quite an impression:

My first sight of New York was from the brow of a hill near Patterson, New Jersey. ... I was riding with a man who had given me a lift an hour or two before. This man, a New Yorker himself, stopped his car on the shoulder of the highway, pointed ahead, and said, "There she is, son." In the distance stood the monolithic towers of Manhattan, separated from the earth by a thick blanket of mist, suspended in space like the cruel king's castle in a book of fairy tales.

But this was a very short visit, and before long he found himself headed out of New York on a western and southerly route.

Garner's fiction is once again a great help in establishing what happened next. He used his own travels as a model for Ken Tilling's movements in *Cabbagetown* and describes two of his short stories, "Another Time, Another Place, Another Me" and "No More Songs About the Suwanee," as being "about my hobo days in the United States during the Depression, and ... absolutely true." The stories recount experiences he had in the fall of 1933, when after about a month of bumming around the eastern U.S. he decided to make his way out to California.

October found him in Keyser, West Virginia, where he spent seven days in jail after being convicted of vagrancy. In *One Damn Thing After Another!* he describes how he was tormented by the other inmates, who made him do all the dirty work and generally made his life hell. But by chance he was given a perfect opportunity for revenge:

> On the morning of my discharge the turnkey's wife, who was also the jail cook, asked me to take the prisoners' breakfast out to the cell blocks. I carried a large tin platter of fried eggs and a pot of coffee into the jail yard, shouted the breakfast call to the prisoners, and — while they watched me in impotent rage and horror — I dumped the eggs on the ground, poured the coffee over them, and did a victorious war dance on the mess. Then despite the din I shouted a soldier's goodbye to the prisoners, walked back through the turnkey's house to the street, and hurriedly caught a coal truck out of town.

It perhaps goes without saying that "a soldier's goodbye," as one would expect from the context, is of the type expressed in the phrase "Goodbye and fuck you!"

"Another Time, Another Place, Another Me" begins the day after the protagonist has finished his sentence in Keyser and has made it as far as Parkersburg, West Virginia, just east of the Ohio border. On a cold, rainy night he takes shelter in a storage shed beside the railway line, where he encounters an elderly hobo who is very sick and about to die. As he observes the old man's laboured breathing and final death rattle, he is struck by both the horror of death and the wretchedness of this particular death, and continues on his travels with a new realization of the essential frailty of human life.

"No More Songs About the Suwanee" takes place in November 1933 in Jackson, Mississippi, where the protagonist and two companions have gravitated to a "jungle" — an area of waste railway land where the hobos were pretty much left alone. Here the clever tricks of a card-sharp lead to a shooting and a severe beating, and the narrator leaves town in a hurry on the next westbound train. The story is simply a slice of life, unadorned by any hint of moral or message but sharply evocative of a period when those who lived in hobo jungles might find themselves reverting to the law of the jungle.

Continuing on through Shreveport, Louisiana and Gladewater, Texas (where Hugh, lounging on a wooden sidewalk, was told to leave town immediately by a marshall in a ten-gallon hat), his next notable stop was Lordsburg, New Mexico. There he was allowed to sleep in the town jail where, he was told, Billy the Kid had once been kept in the same cell. On this trip both he and his fictional counterpart Ken Tilling made the acquaintance of two of the legendary railway policemen feared by the era's hobos:

> The worst railroad bulls in North America were Texas Slim in Longview, Texas, and Step-'n-a-Half in Marshall, Texas — both on the Texas Pacific Railroad. *One Damn Thing After Another!*
> I was chased by a lot of railroad bulls, including Texas Slim in Longview and Step-'n-a-Half in Marshall, Texas. They're two of the toughest railroad cops in the United States, on the Texas & Pacific. *Cabbagetown*

Yet another example of Garner's refusal to discard anything that might be literarily recycleable is his later use of "Step-'n-a-Half" as the title for a short story about a hippie hitch-hiker and his pregnant, crippled and eponymous consort.

The miles and experiences accumulated. The trains through Texas, New Mexico and Arizona were often stopped by U.S. immigration officers looking for Mexicans who had crossed the border illegally. A brief stopover at the Salvation Army hostel in Phoenix was memorable if only for the loss of his one suit, which was stolen when he turned it in for fumigation. After another night's free accommodation in a jail cell in Yuma, Arizona, Hugh made it to Fresno, California by Christmas. The Fresno YMCA was home for about twenty-five unemployed young men, who in exchange for light janitorial work received free room and board. The board, however, was rather unusual:

> Our meals were furnished us through the Seventh Day Adventist Church, which ran a tented cafeteria for the unemployed.... The arrangement was fine except for two things: the cafeteria was closed on Saturday [the Adventists' Sabbath] and they didn't serve meat. On Christmas Day we lined up as usual for our dinner, with some of the YMCA gang betting their packs of Bugler or Bull Durham tobacco that turkey would be served. Instead, we received the same vegetarian dishes as any other day, with the addition of a meatless mock-duck made of highly-seasoned poultry stuffing. It was like being late for a banquet and finding nothing left but the artificial insides of the fowl. In the evening we each received a free pass to a local movie, and we sat there with our mouths watering enviously at the sight of Charles Laughton tearing chickens apart with his teeth in *The Private Life of Henry VIII*.

From Fresno, Hugh backtracked south to Los Angeles, where he spent his first days in the city in the "vag tank" of the Lincoln Heights Jail. During part of the winter of 1934 he lived in a Figueroa Street rooming-house where his landlady, a spiritualist, held regular seances in her living room. She would be remembered years later in a magazine article on the oddballs who followed her profession, "Chatelaines and Charlatans." In Los Angeles he spent much of his time at the public library, where he "began by reading the books on abnormal psychology, including Krafft-Ebbing, moved on to Freud, Jung, and Adler, and from the psychologists on to the philosophers, Spinoza, William James, Schopenhauer, Descartes, and Nietzsche." As is typical of Garner in his autobiography, he provides no explanation for this striking change in his reading habits, but in a sense both abnormal psychology and philosophy were among the subjects he was studying on the road. Hoboing showed him humanity at its best and at its worst: he saw those who had very little share it with those who had nothing, and he saw people viciously beaten by policemen, railroad bulls and sometimes their fellow tramps. He also encountered sex in its rawest forms, including a "13-year-old prostitute in the Illinois Central Station in Cairo, Illinois, who offered herself for a quarter to all comers" and "two young homosexuals, one … who told me he had been raped by three old hoboes in a New Brunswick jungle, and another one … who lived for a while in the Y.M.C.A. in Fresno, California." It may have been these experiences which stirred a new interest in the farther reaches of human behaviour, and would ultimately be explored in several of his stories and novels.

After a brief visit to Ciudad Juarez in Mexico, he continued up the coast to San Francisco, where he lived in the YMCA on the Embarcadero and supported himself by stealing shirts from a nearby department store and selling them to his fellow residents. In the spring he decided to return east by a more northerly route than the one he had taken on his way out to California. On this trip Garner retraced his steps to Yuma, Arizona but then took the Southern Pacific-Rock Island route to Kansas City, existing primarily on oranges stolen from a refrigerated boxcar. In Tucumcari, New Mexico he shared a bug-infested bed with an unwashed sheepherder at a New Deal Transient Administration hostel. On the Kansas City-St.Louis leg of the journey he was taken for an escaped prisoner and arrested in Jefferson City, Missouri, although he was soon released. And if Ken Tilling's confession regarding the "chamois wind-breaker he had stolen from a car in East St. Louis, Illinois" is to be believed — which it probably should be, given Garner's description of himself as "wearing only a chamois windbreaker over a shirt" on a very cold day in Kankakee, Illinois on his way from East St. Louis to Chicago — he may have exacted a sort of revenge for the loss of his suit in Phoenix.

By the late spring of 1934, in any event, Hugh had made it back to New York, where during the next year and a half he would become deeply interested in the political and intellectual controversies that made the city's streets and meeting places ring with the voices of a revolution struggling to be born. New York in the mid-1930s was a highly politicized city that offered communists, fascists and just about everyone in between a wide range of organizations and forums for discussion. Both Garner and Ken Tilling spent a lot of time listening to the various speakers who made Union Square their headquarters; but as of the fall of 1934, both were still sceptical about the left-wing radicals they met there. Garner found their ideas "far-fetched and ridiculous," while Tilling confessed, "I don't like the Communists I've met."

At the same time as he was expanding his political horizons, Hugh held his usual bewildering variety of jobs. Much of his work, when he could find work, was as a bus-boy and handbill distributor, although he also toiled as a dishwasher (or "pearl-diver," as he often called it) and door-to-door salesman of soap products. As a bus-boy he worked mostly in cafeterias operated by the Exchange Buffet and Stewart's chains, and as the latter's "extra man" was sent all over New York's five boroughs to fill in where necessary; as a soap vendor he at first had a terrible time getting up the nerve to knock on suburban doors, but found that the sight of a co-worker fleeing from an ornery goat made the job so absolutely preposterous that he was able to settle down and become a fairly good salesman.

After leading an abortive strike against a Brooklyn shoe store that refused to pay its handbill distributors more than twenty-five cents an hour, he was labelled a trouble-maker and kicked out of his room at the Bowery YMCA. He moved to the nearby Hotel Majestic, which despite its name was in fact a flophouse, located at the corner of Bowery and Houston Streets. The Hotel Majestic's rooms were cubicles whose wooden partitions were roofed over with chicken wire; they rented for twenty-five cents a night, payable in advance. One of his fellow tenants was the legendary bohemian "Professor Seagull" Joe Gould, a Harvard graduate who had lived on skid row for years while compiling

his multi-volumed *History of the Modern World*, composed almost entirely of anecdotes about his day-to-day adventures as
one of New York's most public eccentrics. It was at the Hotel
Majestic during the summer of 1935 that two very significant
things happened to Garner: he took the first steps toward the radical political involvement that would lead him to Spain, and he
decided that he would seriously pursue a career as a writer.

Hugh attributed his conversion to socialist political views to
his friend "Slats" Fisher, a convicted safe-cracker from Utah
whom Garner considered a "criminal individualist." For this reason he was all the more struck by the way that Fisher, the most
independent and self-sufficient person he had ever met, was
nevertheless convinced that communism was the only answer
for the oppressed working class. Fisher, his nickname changed
to "Legs," also appears in *Cabbagetown* as the agent of Ken Tilling's political transformation:

> They had been talking about the young Jewish Communist agita-
> tors who held forth in Union Square every night, and whom Ken
> despised as he despised all true believers. Legs had said, "Maybe
> it's different for you an' me, Ken, but for the ordinary working stiff
> Communism seems his only hope."
>
> Just that. Nothing that would ever make Bartlett's, change the
> world, be quoted widely, or even be remembered by anyone else;
> yet this simple sentence of a professional criminal was to remain
> with him for the rest of his life.

Hugh now began to read heavily in the works of Marx, Engels
and Proudhon, although it was George Bernard Shaw's *The Intelligent Woman's Guide to Socialism and Capitalism*, encountered a year later in Toronto, that he considered the book
which "turned me into a social radical."

Garner's aspirations to become a writer were fired by the reading of second-hand copies of periodicals such as *Story* and the
era's literary quarterlies, which he found in the bargain bins of
New York bookshops. These introduced him to a kind of fiction
he had not encountered in his casual reading of mass-market magazines, one in which the realities he knew served as the basis

for narratives about the unemployed, the destitute and the desperate. Among the writers he most admired were Alvah Bessie, Albert Halper, I.J. Kapstein, Helen Hull, Rachel Maddux and Albert Maltz; of these, it was Maltz who most appealed to him with stories such as "The Jungle" and "The Happiest Man in the World."

Hugh twice singled out the latter story as a superb example of how to write about real people in an absorbing way. The protagonist of "The Happiest Man in the World" is an unemployed man so desperate to work that he begs for a job driving a nitroglycerin truck, despite the fact that every year twenty per cent of the drivers are killed. When he finally does get the job he tells himself, "I'm the happiest man in the world," while the man who hired him bitterly regrets taking on another future statistic. Garner would have been able to identify with Maltz's description of his main character after years of tough times:

> Jesse knew he looked terrible. ... nothing would get the red gumbo dust out of his suit even though he had slapped himself till both arms were worn out ...
> ... the face was too gaunt, the body too spiny under the baggy clothes ...
> ... He was ashamed of his shoes. They had come from the relief originally, and two weeks on the road had about finished them. All morning, with a kind of delicious, foolish solemnity, he had been vowing to himself that before anything else, before even a suit of clothes, he was going to buy himself a brand-new strong pair of shoes.

Hugh knew immediately that this was the kind of fiction he wanted to write; after many more years and a number of detours, he would eventually succeed in doing so.

But first he had to learn how to write. He purchased paper and pencil — this in itself, given his poverty, an indication of how serious he was about his new enthusiasm — and started trying to set down some of his own experiences in literary form. Initially, however, this was simply too difficult: neither imitating his chosen models nor just letting his thoughts flow freely produced anything worth saving. He even overcame, temporarily, his bias against formal education and enrolled in an English composition course given by a lower east side settlement house, but quit when this proved to be an English-as-a-second- language class.

With both his political and his literary interests defined in much sharper terms, Garner returned to Toronto in the fall of 1935, found a furnished room for himself on Langley Avenue and began to see what his home town had to offer a budding radical and writer. Politically, he became an active member of a Cooperative Commonwealth Federation youth group which met in an empty store at Logan Avenue and Gerrard Street, and after a few months was elected president. The CCF, founded in 1932, was still a loose coalition of disaffected groups rather than a cohesive political party and contained within its ranks everyone from discontented farmers to reformist ministers to radical union organizers. In joining the CCF, Hugh was in effect affirming that his political beliefs were still more socialist than communist: he was still dubious about the "doctrinaire Communist functionaries" who seemed to dominate the party, and suspected that they were more interested in wielding power than in bettering the lot of the working class.

The highlight of his CCF period was his attendance at the first Canadian Youth Congress in Ottawa in May 1936, where he encountered a true cross-section of the contemporary political spectrum: liberals, conservatives, communists and fascists were all represented at the lively and often disorderly sessions. Garner, as he had often done when crossing the U.S., bunked down in a cell at a nearby police station, got carried away on one occasion and delivered an impassioned plea for a revolutionary uprising to a public meeting. On this trip he also met CCF leaders J.S. Woodsworth and M.J. Coldwell, whom he liked, and Tommy Douglas, whom he found "supercilious."

A good job was still hard to find. In the early part of 1936 Hugh and his friend George Young, who went on to become an Anglican minister, worked part-time at the Gerrard and Broadview branch of the public library, reshelving books for fifteen cents an hour. From the spring of 1936 to January 1937, Garner was working steadily as a salesman of men's clothing, first in the wholesale end of the trade at Imperial Specialty Neckwear on Wellington Street, and then as a retail clerk at the Style Cravat Shop on Danforth Avenue. In the latter job he worked a sixty-two-hour week and was paid $10, exactly the same wage he had received during his brief career seven years earlier as a copy boy at the *Toronto Daily Star*.

The book-shelving job, although it only lasted a few weeks, symbolized how much Hugh had changed since the days when the library had primarily been a place for his gang to hang out. Although he had always been a reader and had his own library card at the age of twelve, it was the crystallization of his desire to be a writer that really started him reading in earnest. At the Gerrard and Broadview branch, he spent much of the winter and spring of 1936 devouring everything he could find on politics and economics, reading Marx and Engels dutifully and Shaw's *An Intelligent Woman's Guide to Capitalism and Socialism* with great pleasure. At the same time he applied himself to the serious study of contemporary fiction, adopting Dos Passos and Hemingway as his mentors in the writing of realistic narratives but reserving a soft spot for the sentimental effusions of J.B. Priestley and the didactic messages of H.G. Wells.

He was no more successful at creating his own fictional stories than he had been earlier in New York, but he did make a major breakthrough in the writing of non-fiction. In the spring of 1936 he printed, in pen and ink and on lined notepaper, an essay entitled "Toronto's Cabbagetown" and sent it off to *The Canadian Forum*. This journal was at the time under the control of the League for Social Reconstruction, a loose alliance of reformist intellectuals instrumental in the founding of the CCF. Someone at the magazine would likely have known of Garner through his presidency of the CCF youth club, or he may have mentioned the fact in a covering letter; but whatever the circumstances of his article's acceptance, he found himself being published in the same pages as the likes of E.J. Pratt, F.R. Scott, Frank Underhill and A.J.M. Smith.

"Toronto's Cabbagetown" is a very fine piece of work, understated and yet vividly graphic in a way that undoubtedly reflects the influence of the American realists Hugh so much admired. The generally matter-of-fact tone renders his periodic touches of sarcastic humour that much more effective:

> Cabbagetown lies a short mile below the homes which dot the hills of Rosedale. (Why is it that a house in Rosedale is called a 'home,' while a house in Cabbagetown is just a house, except in obituary columns when it is a 'residence'? But hardly anyone in Cabbagetown ever hits the obituary columns).
>
> The district is blocked off by streets running east and west, north and south. There are numerous little 'places' and 'lanes' interspersed among them, lined by blocks of red brick houses crowding the broken sidewalks into the narrow roads. They are five- or six-room houses, and are supposedly easy to heat. That is why the landlords refrain from the expense of a furnace to heat them.

The selection of particular details is also extremely impressive: itchy charity sweaters "slit in front with a pair of scissors" and kitchens furnished with "pieces of dry bread on tables, and filmy milk bottles half full of souring milk" etch a sharp portrait of what life looks like in the slums.

Perhaps the single most compelling aspect of "Toronto's Cabbagetown" is the dramatic tension generated by its seemingly straightforward recital of the district's everyday events. The kind of intuitive feel for the juxtaposition of complementary images that could be glimpsed in nascent form in his adolescent poem "Dawn" is here under firm artistic control and being used to make powerful effect:

> The people get orders for clothes at the relief office. These are taken down to the central clothing depot and are filled by a man behind a wooden partition, who glances at the order form and retreats behind rows of high shelves. The room smells like an army quartermaster's stores, and the recipients line up in front of the wicket. There are benches around the wall where shoes may be tried on. These are unnecessary as none of the shoes ever fit. The attendant ties up the order in brown wrapping paper and the recipient hur-

ries from the office and down the street, looking straight ahead until he is clear of the neighbourhood.

The old people sit on the front steps in the summer evenings, chatting and laughing across the small lawns or from step to step. The men wear blue work-shirts and wide suspenders, and smoke rank-smelling tobacco in their patched-up pipes. The women cover their ample figures with cotton house-dresses, and mend socks while they talk and joke with their neighbours. On Friday and Saturday nights the men retreat to the 'Avion' or 'Shamrock' beer-parlours, where they argue about the merits or demerits of the Conservative or CCF political parties. They are nearly all ex-soldiers, and when they get drunk they talk about the war. They don't usually speak of it when they are sober.

"Toronto's Cabbagetown" does include some more direct indictments of the evils of poverty, among them a very sentimental passage on the heartbreak occassioned by "the all-sacrificing love of a mother for her children," but the predominant mood is one of dispassionate observation enlivened by frequent bursts of rather subtle wit. And where did this sudden mastery of literary technique come from? In the absence of any hints from Garner, who treats its writing as the fruit of a momentary impulse rather than as the fulfilment of any sort of apprenticeship, a reasonable guess would be that "Toronto's Cabbagetown" represents a successful synthesis of his journalistic experience with his reading in the realistic fiction of the day.

Despite Hugh's insistence that he was lucky to have been fired from the *Star*, he did go so far as to admit that he "learned how to write sharp condensed prose" during his brief tenure there, and this talent is certainly evident in his essay for *The Canadian Forum*. Its content, of course, is taken directly from his own background, and even the one detail that may be pure invention — the use of "like an army quarter-master's stores" to describe the smell of the clothing depot — may have had a factual basis in his stays at relief camps run by the military. "Toronto's Cabbagetown" is an evocative slice of intensely experienced life that is the first significant expression of Garner's literary talents; when we consider that it was written by a twenty-three-year-old high school dropout without benefit of arts-council grants, crea-tive-writing courses or even one sympathetic mentor, it becomes that much more impressive an achievement.

In the same month that *The Canadian Forum* published Hugh's literary début, the military garrisons of Spanish Morocco rose in revolt against their homeland's left-leaning Popular Front regime. The conflict soon spread to Spain itself, which for the next three years would be the theatre where the world's major powers rehearsed the forthcoming global war. In faraway Toronto, Hugh Garner attended meetings in support of the hard-pressed Loyalists and read every word he could find about the escalating conflict. Soon he began to wonder if perhaps the time had come to test his growing political convictions on the battle-fields of reality.

Chapter Three

Spain and Radical Politics (1936-1939)

Writing about his radical years in a 1960 magazine series for *Liberty*, "Depression Memories," Garner stated that "The outbreak of the Spanish Civil War affected me more than anything else in my life, up to or since that time." He went on to describe his feelings as he read about the early defeats suffered by the Loyalist forces:

> I grew sick inside. I hated the fascists, the army generals, the Spanish Catholic hierarchy, and everything they stood for. I became maddened at the stories I read, in the Toronto daily papers, of the massacre of the Republican population of Badajoz in the bull-ring, of the murder of Federico Garcia Lorca, the famous Spanish poet, by the fascists, of [their] arrogance and surety of victory ....

As Ken Tilling put it in *Cabbagetown*:

> The last battle between the workers and the fascist reactionaries had begun. ... Those who *really* believed in a better world were already manning the barricades blocking the entrance of the ... fascists advancing on Madrid. (Garner's italics)

And because it was the "last battle," an apocalyptic struggle between the purely good and the thoroughly evil, there was no longer time to debate the finer points of sectarian political differences. For both Hugh Garner and Ken Tilling, now was the hour to make common cause with all those who actively opposed the Spanish Fascists.

In Canada, as in the United States and most European countries, this meant accepting the direction of the indigenous Communist Party. The Canadian government, although officially neutral, in practice inclined to be sympathetic with the Nationalist forces opposing the Loyalists. Mackenzie King's ruling Liberal Party drew much of its strength from Quebec, where many Catholics had been angered by the Loyalists' violent suppression of their faith: pictures of churches plastered with signs proclaiming "Now Under the People's Management" had been prominently featured in the province's newspapers, and there was no denying the fact that many priests had been murdered in the settling-old-scores atmosphere of the first days of the Civil War. By the summer of 1937 Canadian passports were being stamped as invalid for travel in Spain, and Canadian volunteers for the International Brigades fighting on the Loyalist side were told that jail sentences awaited them upon their return home. Even the CCF, which of all the other political parties was the most sympathetic to the Loyalists, hedged on the question of advocating military assistance and as a result lost much of its younger and more radical membership.

Hugh, never very good at accepting direction from anyone, continued to maintain his mental reservations about communist ideology: he considered its economic theories irrelevant, its view of the working class ridiculously romantic and its use of false, simplistic propaganda reprehensible. Still, it was the communists who were actually getting international aid to the Loyalists, and so it was to their meetings, sympathizers and party members that he gravitated.

By the end of 1936 Garner was desperate to get to Spain, even going so far as to place a notice in the *Star*'s "Personal" classified ads asking for assistance in paying his way there: "Young socialist, aged 23, wants fare to Spain to fight in loyalist militia. Information supplied. Box W1552." Nothing came of this, but a short time later his barber, whom he knew to be a Communist Party member, asked him if he was really serious about going to Spain.

Hugh's answer must have been the right one, because it wasn't long before he was contacted by the party and accepted as a recruit for the International Brigades. Although Garner managed to alienate the party official responsible for his passage — even his zeal to get overseas couldn't entirely suppress his natural insubordination — early in February 1937 he at last found himself on his way to join the Loyalist forces of the Republic.

Getting to Spain was an adventure in itself. Garner took the bus from Toronto to New York, telling U.S. immigration that he was a student on his way to Paris, and on his arrival was supplied with a First World War American army uniform and other war-surplus military kit. The next morning he boarded the *Berengaria*, a Cunard Line ship, and occupied a third-class cabin on the crossing to Cherbourg. During the trip he was grilled about his destination by a man he took to be an RCMP agent, who was told that Garner and his eight fellow volunteers were on their way to Europe for a series of ice hockey games. When the man asked him if they were going to play in Spain, Hugh replied, as deadpan as he could, "No. We'd like to, but there's a war on there."

After taking the train from Cherbourg to Paris, the volunteers were given a perfunctory medical examination and formally enrolled in the International Brigades. Asked to identify his *profesion*, Garner replied that he was a *journaliste*. He later remarked that he didn't know why he had done this — although it undoubtedly reflects his pride at being a *Canadian Forum* contributor — but he would later have cause to be grateful that he had told a bit of a white lie about his professional status. About three hundred new recruits then embarked on the train journey to Perpignan, near the border with Spain, from where a short journey by bus through the Pyrenees brought them into the country for which they would be fighting. Hugh spent his first night in Spain walking on the battlements of Figueras, where he felt he had reached another dividing point on his path to the future. It "marked an end and a beginning in my life," as he rather prosaically put it in his *Liberty* series on "The Spanish Civil War;" Ken

Tilling would wax more poetic in the concluding paragraph of *Cabbagetown*:

> The dawn can be seen to the east, but it really comes from the west. It comes across the watcher's shoulders and envelops him in its light as he watches for it. It starts as a narrow ribbon of lighter darkness, then squeezes together before it fans high into the sky. As the watcher looks for its birth it begins at his feet and lights him, so that he becomes a part of it. The dawn is in the crease of his trousers and in the ... eyelets of his shoes. The dawn is in the new shapes around him, and in the lighted fields. The dawn is a widened earth — a populated earth. The dawn is not only the beginning of the day, but the ending of the night.

For the raw recruits on their way to join the International Brigades the dawn also brought a new awareness of what it meant to be in a country at war. As their train to the Brigades' headquarters waited on a siding in Barcelona, they saw their first civilian victims of the conflict: "frightened little people, ... seemingly stunned," refugees from Malaga where, on February 8, 1937, Nationalist and Italian troops had occupied the city after heavy artillery and airplane bombardments had driven out the Loyalist defenders. Some of the refugee columns had been overtaken by pursuing Nationalist soldiers, who executed the adult men and spared the women and children so as to increase the already difficult food situation of the Republic.

The train continued along the coast to Valencia and then headed inland toward the International Brigades' depot at Albacete. The recruits spent their first night there sleeping in the arena where bullfights were held, and on the following morning officially became soldiers in the Spanish Republican Army. Garner surrendered his passport to the headquarters staff for safekeeping and became International Brigadier Number 13,005. Then he was issued with "a Loyalist woollen uniform with trousers that folded over the tops of my boots" and "a Basque beret with an infantry badge on its front," which he supplemented with the war-surplus sheepskin coat he had been given in New York.

The International Brigades, which had been created at the behest of the international association of communist parties, the Comintern, at this time consisted of five brigades numbered from the XIth to the XVth. Garner served in the last of these, which was made up of four battalions whose original members had been Yugoslavian, French, English and American volunteers. As the war progressed and recruits from all over the world joined the Republican forces, additional formations such as the Canadian Mackenzie-Papineau Battalion were established as part of the effort to maintain a national *esprit de corps* in each unit; but the "Mac-Paps" were not organized as a separate entity until September 1937, and so it was the largely American Abraham Lincoln Battalion in which Hugh served.

At their first morning assembly a call was made for specialists of various kinds: first cavalrymen, then artillerymen, truck drivers, medical orderlies, clerks and bandsmen by turn stepped out of the ranks of the recruits. When a request for signallers was made, Garner rushed forward despite the fact that he had no signalling experience of any kind. By this time, it had dawned on him that the men left over would be assigned to the infantry as replacements, and he had heard that replacements were now being thrown directly into the fighting without any training whatsoever. If he had not opted for a military specialty, he would likely have been sent straight to the Jarama front, where the International Brigades were at this time suffering very heavy losses in resisting a major Nationalist offensive.

The apprentice signallers, some thirty in number, soon had an object lesson in what it meant to be fighting in an inexperienced and ill-equipped army. Before they could learn how to signal, they had to have something to signal with, which meant that the "field-telephone course consisted mainly of filing the rust from thousands of water-logged army telephone sets that had been recovered from the bottom of Barcelona harbor following the sinking of a French supply ship." As Hugh laboured at this tedious task, so unlike his romantic visions of participating in a crusade for righteous victory, he realized that life was playing one of its periodic tricks on him: for all the satisfaction he was getting out of his soldiering, he might as well be back in Toronto slaving at some stupid factory job.

During his time at Albacete, Garner met another individual whose independence and strength of character reminded him of his old safe-cracking pal, "Slats" Fisher. This "little guy called Reid" (his first name never identified) was "one of the few men who helped to shape and alter my life." Reid had been an Industrial Workers of the World ("wobblies") organizer as a young man and still held to essentially anarchist beliefs that were the bane of the Communist Party members who officered the International Brigades. Reid refused to parrot the simplistic slogans and dogmatic doctrines with which they tried to indoctrinate the men under their command; and although Hugh thought that he was wrong to deny the communists credit for their role in organizing resistance to the Nationalists, he was tremendously impressed by Reid's courage in standing up for what he was convinced was right.

Reid was a voracious reader of literature as well as politics, economics and philosophy, and his self-taught erudition would certainly have reinforced Garner's already well-developed belief in the value of the library as a substitute for formal education. Garner later made fictional use of some of Reid's qualities when creating *Cabbagetown*'s "Noah Masterson," a free-thinking radical who becomes one of the major influences in the political education of Ken Tilling.

But it was Reid's tenacious adherence to his principles that most impressed Hugh, and would later help to sustain him on the many occasions throughout his life when he seemed to be in a minority of one. The following exchange with a senior Communist officer struck Garner as proof of Reid's integrity:

[the officer's speech] was full, among other things, of revolutionary urgings to fight to the death against world Fascism, to believe in the glory of the Soviet Union, and trust in the wisdom of Comrade Stalin. When he was finished he glanced at Reid and me for approbation. Reid shook his head from side to side in a gesture that is negative in all languages. ... the interpreter said to Reid, "Are you a member of the Party?"

"No."

"What are you doing here?"

"I'm a member of the world proletariat."

"But what party do you belong to?"

"None. I'm an anti-authoritarian."

I tried to pretend that I'd never laid eyes on him. Telling a Communist officer that you were anti-authoritarian was like telling your father confessor you didn't believe in God.

Although it is clear from this passage that Hugh did not at the time agree with Reid's idiosyncratic political views, he would later reflect that "He taught me two things which I still believe: to think things out for myself, and to stand up for my convictions." Events would soon give Garner ample opportunity to exercise his new ideals.

After a week of cleaning up old army telephones, Hugh was ready for almost anything else. He wangled his way into a detachment of trainees bound for the artillery school at Almansa, about thirty miles east of Albacete on the Valencia railway line. Here he once again encountered evidence of the difficult supply situation of the Loyalists: the artillery school did not have any artillery, because every available gun was needed at the front. The course necessarily consisted mostly of theory, with some practical work in map reading, surveying and — finally — signalling. But Garner was now beginning to feel that he was wasting his time at these supposed schools, and in characteristic fashion he managed to do something about it.

For a week or two he tried going by the book. He applied for transfer to the front, was told it was more important that he become a skilled artilleryman, and returned the next day to go through the same process again. Finally, he simply took off, and by train and truck made his way west to the Abraham Lincoln Battalion's positions near the town of Morata de Tajuna on the Jarama front. He was issued with a French tin helmet, a pair of cartridge pouches on a leather belt and his first rifle, a Russian-made firearm that represented the substantial quantity of munitions being supplied by the Soviet Union. He spent his first night as a full-fledged soldier on sentry duty in no man's land, where an enemy sniper periodically sent a disturbingly well-aimed round over the two sandbags that served as his only protection. He described his feelings in a letter to his American friend George Zoul:

> I tried to put more and more of me into the hole while I clutched my rifle and prayed that the sniper would go blind or something. The sweat ran cold over my face and my heart pumped jerkily under my tunic. When relief came I nearly tore all the buttons off my coat crawling back to our trench. I was scared!

The next morning he transferred to the battalion's machine-gun company, which contained significant numbers of Cuban and Irish volunteers as well as many Canadians and also included a large contingent of radical students from New York's City College. Garner found he had already met several of its members on the long train ride from Paris: Herman Katz, with whom he shared a dugout, Colin Cox and a former longshoreman named Greg Duncan. Together they would man a Russian Maxim machine-gun, a bulky, slow-firing but very accurate and reliable weapon mounted on a wheeled carriage shielded by a protective metal guard at the front, extremely effective against infantry. Even though their trenches were only about 100 metres from those of the Nationalists, the mutual deficiencies in artillery of the antagonists meant that the stalemate conditions of First World War trench warfare had in effect been re-created on the Jarama front.

The "Lincolns," as they were familiarly known, had been ordered into just such a hopeless assault on February 27, not long before Garner's arrival; and their heavy casualties — 120 killed and 175 wounded out of a total strength of 450 — had been a severe blow to their morale as well as a shocking revelation of the ineptitude of their officers. Ernest Hemingway's novel *For Whom the Bell Tolls* described the XVth Brigade's commander, Vladimir Copic, as "a stupid fool," a sentiment with which the men Garner talked to heartily concurred. Later they would sing, to the tune of "The Red River Valley,"

There's a valley in Spain called Jarama
It's a place that we all know too well,
For 'tis there that we wasted our manhood.
And most of our old age as well.

The Lincolns held their section of the Jarama trenches until late June. Both sides seemed to have been exhausted by the February fighting, and although there were sporadic exchanges of artillery, mortar and rifle fire, things were generally quiet. Every now and then they were visited by some of the many famous war correspondents who covered the Spanish Civil War. On one occasion Ernest Hemingway and John Dos Passos, both of whom Garner would later cite as significant influences on his writing, attended a ceremonial luncheon at XVth Brigades' headquarters in the Duke of Tovar's former castle near Morata de Tajuna. Hugh was up in the trenches when these festivities took place, but later he did meet Herbert Matthews, the *New York Times* correspondent who spent more time at the front lines than most of his colleagues combined. Matthews took down the names and addresses of the soldiers he talked to as "we each gave him some sort of message for posterity to be sent home to our hometown papers." A probe by a Fascist patrol on the evening of April 24 caused a brief flurry of excitement:

> As soon as their rifle volleys began cracking we were ordered to stand-to in the trench. I was reclining on my blanket in my dugout at the time, and when I heard one of our group shout, "Come on, boys," I rushed headlong into the rain. My tunic was off. I jammed on my helmet, picked up my rifle and ran up the communication trench to our machine gun ...
> After the attack had been thwarted I returned to my dugout, soaked to the skin, and with my boots and trousers caked with yellow clay. Consequently when I woke up I was very wet and cold.

Otherwise, Hugh and his friends on the machine-gun crew passed their time complaining about the stupidity of their officers, playing soccer on the slopes running down behind the trenches and making frequent trips to the latrine to ease their chronic dysentery. Tensions between the more outspoken non-communist enlisted men and "the Red Rotarians," as the hard-line ideologues who comprised most of their officers were called, resulted in a growing number of desertions and discipline problems; these were answered by ever-harsher penalties, including the execution of several deserters and terms in military prison for those convicted of lesser offenses.

Thus on a pleasantly warm day in the middle of June Garner and several other ideologically independent soldiers, his friends Cox and Duncan among them, were assigned to the *Corps du l'ingenieur*, the so-called engineering corps which was, in fact, a punishment battalion for recalcitrant troops. After sundown they were issued with picks and shovels and marched out into no man's land, where they were ordered to start digging a new trench line. The Nationalists could hardly help hearing them and would periodically open fire in the general direction of all this commotion, which was certainly not lessened by the fact that many of the men had fortified themselves for their ordeal by getting thoroughly drunk. Hugh, who at this period of his life was by no means a heavy drinker, often trading his wine ration for cigarettes or cheese, was unable to similarly blunt the reality of this unnerving experience: he was soon "so jumpy that I'd feel myself all over for wounds when a bullet cracked close by."

At the end of June the Lincolns were suddenly taken out of the line with great haste and secrecy. Garner and his companions in disgrace were left behind, but quickly decided they weren't going to hang around and wait for the bullet that had their number on it. The following day they technically became deserters: although they intended to find the Lincolns and convince their commanding officer of their desire to take part in fighting, if not trench-digging, they could well have been shot if their lack of proper travel documents had been seriously questioned. Since they had no idea of the Lincolns' whereabouts, they resolved to go to Madrid and report to the International Brigades' offices there.

Madrid in the summer of 1937 was a city under seige. The confident Nationalist assault of November 1936 had been valiantly thrown back by militiamen, ordinary citizens and a few Russian advisors, but with the enemy still at the gates the initial enthusiasm of its defenders had been replaced by a dogged determination to hold on until the Republic could organize an effective counter-attack. Garner was struck by the incongruity of waging war within a modern metropolis:

> Imagine if you can a city of more than a million people, with movie houses, museums, a subway system, beautiful parks, lakes, boulevards, shopping streets, grand hotels, buses and streetcars — all reduced, somehow, to a mixture of two colors, khaki and grey.
> …
> The streets, with their broken curbs, and filled-in shellholes, had a look of poverty about them. … The buildings looked drab and dusty, unkempt and uncared for, and at night under the blackout you walked along dim alleys in the valleys of the moon.

Madrid, along with Toronto and New York, was one of the cities Hugh found most fascinating, at least partly because when he revisited it in 1959 he could not decide whether it was the bustling modern version or its brooding 1937 persona that represented its essential character.

But no matter how khaki and grey it might be, Madrid seemed wonderful after months of desultory trench warfare and rigid military discipline. Garner and his companions decided that they deserved a bit of a vacation before trying to find their unit. There hadn't been much to spend their pay on at the front, and they had each accumulated a sizeable bankroll that went a long way in certain quarters of the city. The brothels, for example, charged the equivalent of a day's pay for their services, and Hugh had three months' worth of Bank of Spain currency burning a hole in his pocket. And since the brothels were organized along political lines, staffed by union members of anarchist, communist, republican and socialist sympathies, his determination to avoid partisan political affiliations required that he distribute his largesse in even-handed fashion. Twenty-three years later, happily married and no longer interested in their services, he still spoke affectionately of the prostitutes he had known during his hobo and soldier days: "We met as business acquaintances, and always parted as friends. I can't say the same for most women."

But this short interlude of rest and relaxation came to an abrupt end when he was closely questioned by the secret police as to why he was not with the Lincolns. After a brief visit to an Anarchist unit outside Madrid, where he for the first time realized that he had been a small-"a" anarchist all his life, he returned to the city and finally reported to the International Brigades' headquarters. Waiting to be seen by a senior officer,

> I sat down on a chair near the entrance to the dining room. When I peeked through the doorway I saw a long refectory table at which were sitting all the Communist commissars, functionaries and flunkeys eating fried eggs and steaks. We'd never even seen an egg at the front, never mind a steak.

Perhaps embarrassed by this inadvertent lesson as to the ubiquity of class distinctions, the officer Garner finally saw, the English novelist and staunch "Red Rotarian" Ralph Bates, threatened to have him shot for desertion. Doubtless well aware that members of the International Brigades had already been executed for this and lesser offenses, Hugh ran out of the office and escaped from the building before the startled sentries could stop him. Later that day he met a soldier from another XVth Brigade battalion who told him that the Lincolns were currently stationed near the village of Alcala de Henares, about twenty miles east of Madrid.

When he finally did report to the Lincolns' headquarters, he was placed under arrest and told that he would be charged with desertion. Fortunately, the officer who had originally singled out Garner as a malcontent deserving punishment was away at the time, and his more easygoing second-in-command reduced the charge to being absent without leave. He was sentenced to the one day's imprisonment he had already served and put back on the battalion's rolls, just in time for the International Brigades' next important engagement with the Nationalist forces. During the week Hugh spent in Alcala de Henares he introduced himself to the slight, bespectacled man who operated a mobile blood transfusion unit in the area, and was ever afterwards grateful that he had had the chance to meet Dr. Norman Bethune.

At the beginning of July 1937 the Loyalist high command attempted to relieve the siege of Madrid by initiating a major offensive against the Fascist troops to the west of the city. The XVth International Brigade, Garner's unit, was to be used as a shock force in this operation: the plan called for them to punch a hole in the Nationalist lines by seizing the three small villages of Villaneuva del Pardillo, Villafranca del Castillo and — as if in acknowledgement of the Canadians among the Lincolns — Villaneuva de la Canada. The Loyalist reserves would then pour through the gap in the Nationalist lines and seize the town of Brunete, whose position astride the main western approach to Madrid made it a key factor in any attempt to deliver the city from its besiegers. When they were issued with Swiss Cheese, Dutch chocolate and French cigarettes (their normal rations included no cheese, no chocolate and the cheapest Spanish cigarettes), the Lincolns knew they would soon be asked to go on the attack.

On July 5 the battalion began its drive on Villaneuva de la Canada, and Hugh saw his first serious action of the war. He was the first to admit that he did not cover himself in glory. Of the three autobiographical stories he wrote about the Spanish Civil War — "The Expatriates," "The Stretcher Bearers" and "How I Became an Englishman" — it is the last, which he incorporated with very few changes in his 1960 *Star Weekly* series about the conflict, that most graphically conveys the extreme nervous tension and mood swings that combat brought out in him. Suffering from badly blistered feet, the protagonist feels that he is "the luckiest man in the brigade" for having a legitimate excuse to remain behind when it is the Lincolns' turn to attack; but the next day, July 6, his pride in his national origins is stirred by the singing of the XVth Brigades' English Battalion as it marches into battle, and he impulsively leaves his safe rear-echelon post to rejoin his unit at the front. His description of this epiphanic moment makes it clear that it was English spirit rather than Communist Party fervour which spoke to him:

> Something happened to me then that all the Communist propaganda and all the Communist songs had been unable to bring about; I felt a warmth towards these unseen men marching past me through the darkness, and I knew I had to go where they were going. I could pick out the accents of the singers: the Cockney, Scots, Welsh, Lancashire, and the broad West Country voices. They rose from the ranks of marching men and hung in the air, the words clear and resonant against the darkness. Theirs was no Communist Revolutionary song; there was no vain promise of valour or hate or self-abasement in their words. Although most of them were Communists now, they were Englishmen first.

The irony, of course, is that it was the Communist Party's decision to organize the International Brigades by national groupings that made such an occurrence possible and, in the process, helped to confirm Hugh's conviction that he would never be able to unreservedly embrace the Party's ideals and methods.

When he caught up to the Lincolns, they were moving into position for the assault on Villaneuva de la Canada. Garner resumed his normal responsibilities as part of a Maxim crew, which involved carrying the machine-gun mount — which weighed about 80 pounds — as well as his other gear. Today, however, the Maxim was knocked out of action, and Hugh's section was ordered into line with the attacking infantry. They stumbled over the rough terrain separating them from the village, bullets whining through their ranks and periodically finding a human target; it was here that Garner for the first, but not the last, time "felt the taste of fear on my tongue, as if I were sucking a copper coin." In a field overlooked by the village church they were pinned down by enemy machine-gun and automatic rifle fire, and Hugh discovered that in the face of death he suddenly regretted not having any children:

> I dreamed up visions of girls I had known at home, and wished I had impregnated one of them before I left. I felt the urge to leave something behind, so that all of me would not come to an end in

that wheatsheaf-strewn field under the boiling sun that afternoon. I felt that I had not rounded out my life, and I wanted so much to do so.

In his later years Garner would become a staunch defender of the traditional nuclear family, something which might primarily be attributed to the "broken home" that he remembered from his childhood, but must also reflect this dramatic revelation of his own strong desire to become a father.

When there was a pause in the firing he made his way to the rear "in a daze, dragging my rifle by the barrel." His story "The Stretcher Bearers" recounts what happened next: assigned to help carry an apparently lightly wounded casualty to the rear, the protagonist and three other men lose their way and, their tempers frayed by the realization that they are more afraid of dying than of being labelled cowards, begin to bicker among themselves while the wounded man gradually weakens and dies. This story (also almost literally incorporated into his 1960 *Star Weekly* articles) is brutally candid in recounting its protagonist's profound shock and dismay when confronted with the reality of warfare. Immediately after the events described in "The Stretcher Bearers," Hugh was resting at a first-aid station in the rear when shock and dismay turned to horror:

A small group of Spaniards were taunting a wounded Moor, whom they were slinging across the back of a mule. They were shouting "Moro! Moro!" and the Moor was crying, wiping his tears on his sleeve. He wore a dirty bandage around his head, and another thicker one around his knee.

… There was a young Spanish kid lying nearby, and his left arm ended about three inches below the shoulder, in a thick bundle of bandage and batten. His eyes were open and his face was very wet with sweat.

From the direction they had taken the Moor on the mule we heard the sound of a single rifle shot. Then the mule, its eyes staring from the scent of death, was led back around a bend in the road. I thought, I no longer believe in the brotherhood of man. It's all balls, and this whole stinking war is all balls.

Garner went back into action the following day and learned that Villaneuva de la Canada had finally fallen after fierce hand-to-hand fighting, and that Spanish Republican troops had then gone on to take Brunete. The International Brigades tried to continue their advance in an effort to turn this tactical victory into a major defeat for the Fascists, but the latter quickly brought up reinforcements and began a series of strong counter-attacks; these regained Brunete and left the Loyalists with a small increase in territory at a terribly high cost in casualties: about 25,000 dead and an unknown number wounded, as opposed to about 10,000 dead on the Nationalist side.

The International Brigades' losses were also very heavy, and there was widespread insubordination among the men. The XII-Ith Brigade mutinied and had to be withdrawn to the rear, and the English Battalion of the XVth Brigade, its strength reduced to fewer than ninety men, had to be reassured that it would not be used in frontal attacks. In the aftermath of the bloody stalemate that followed the taking of Villaneuva de la Canada, which seemed to make their sacrifices completely pointless, Garner found that his fears had completely overwhelmed his ability to function as a soldier. He was sent to hospital in Albacete along with several other men considered to be suffering from "shell shock."

He stayed at the Gota de Leche hospital from July 10 to August 12, where the treatment for problems such as his was somewhat less than sophisticated: "In the mornings a Polish doctor used to sit on the edge of a bed and talk to us nerve cases. Then he would ask us to open our mouths and look at our tongues. Then balance pieces of paper on the backs of our hands. There was really no treatment he could give us, I suppose." The theory behind the diagnosis of "shell shock," a term that had come into general use during the First World War, was that the shock waves generated by exploding ammunition produced a disruptive effect on the nervous system. It was only during the Second World War that this condition was identified as a form of psychoneurosis that had nothing to do with exposure to exploding shells but was the result of the sufferer's inability to tolerate the stresses of combat. Garner simply needed to go home. After being discharged from the hospital and hanging around Albacete for several more weeks, his orders finally came through: he would resume his *profesion* as a *journaliste* and return to Canada to write propaganda for the Republican cause. He had no passport but was not about to go back to the International Brigades' headquarters and ask for it; he had last left there as a fugitive facing a charge of desertion and was not going to take the chance that some zealous bureaucrat might still have it in for him. One unanticipated consequence of this decision was that his passport probably ended up in the the hands of the Soviet Union's intelligence operatives in Spain, since as a matter of policy "the passports of all dead (and some alive) members of the International Brigade ... were dispatched to Moscow ... Then new bearers were issued with these, and entered America as, apparently, reformed citizens. One of these was the Catalan Mercader, the murderer of Trotsky."

The train journey from Albacete to Valencia provided Garner with the material for the last of the stories he would later identify as autobiographical accounts of his experiences in Spain — and which, like "How I Became an Englishman" and "The Stretcher Bearers," he used almost verbatim in a non-fictional journalistic piece. "The Expatriates" describes how a group of nine departing soldiers, four discharged for medical reasons, four as "undesirables" and one returning to the U.S. for a propaganda tour, react to a communist newspaper correspondent who tries to turn the medical dischargees against the "undesirables." The soldier bound for the propaganda tour, a"Red Rotarian," agrees with the journalist; but the others submerge their disagreements about the war and band together against the two, in the process learning that the similar things which happened to them are of more significance than their differing political views. Although not intended as a summation of Hugh's experiences in Spain, "The Expatriates" might well serve as one. Its message that only those who have seen war can comprehend the behaviour of soldiers is a reaffirmation of Garner's lifelong preference for experience rather than theory; and it may also be a kind of plea for understanding from those who might consider him a coward because he succumbed to the stresses of combat.

From Valencia they took another train to Barcelona, where they spent the night in the empty cages of the city's zoo; the former occupants, unlike their Madrid counterparts who had been eaten during the food shortages of November 1936, had been killed because of the danger of their being released by the frequent bombing raids. In Barcelona he went to see the British consul, who provided him with a temporary passport that would enable him to get into France, and then continued his journey up the Costa Brava to the French border. Here Hugh walked through a long tunnel to Cerbere, where the immigration officials allowed him to enter, and he boarded the train for Perpignan and then Paris. He stayed at the Hotel Minerva on the Rue Louis Blanc for six weeks while waiting for a new passport to be issued, and when he finally obtained one went on to London. There he spent a week at a boarding-house just off the Waterloo Road, where the landlady's demeanour had him imagining he was back under military discipline: "Not only did she make us rise and shine and attend breakfast to the numbered strokes of a gong, but she was as adamant as a regimental sergeant-major when she refused victuals to those unfortunates who were a minute late for morning parade."

Back in Toronto, Hugh was asked by Roy Davis, an organizer for the Young Communist League, to become involved with the youth-oriented publication *New Advance*, which had been founded in 1937 as part of the Canadian Communist Party's efforts to follow the "Popular Front" strategy advocated by the Comintern. In line with this policy, *New Advance* cultivated ties with YMCAs and YWCAs, church groups and university student organizations, and featured stories on popular science, the current cinema and notable athletes as well as more political subjects. Hugh was listed on the masthead as a member of the editorial board for the five issues produced between March and July of 1938. Earlier, he had contributed two articles that illustrate the range of *New Advance*'s content: his December 1937 "Salute to a Hero" was a conventional denunciation of fascism in general and Italian aggression against Ethiopia in particular, but his January 1938 description of what was happening to the Gerrard Street West "Village" area, "You're Telling Me," was a spirited harbinger of his later assaults on his home town's snobs and renovators:

> A few years ago the members of Toronto's artist colony, intelligentsia, lunatic fringe or what have you, decided that what Toronto needed was a district given over to the Bohemian. They settled on a slum area. Almost overnight the shabby, smelly, rickety frame houses were transformed into creations of pink and white, green and gold, blue and yellow. What had been a dismal slum was now a rendezvous for the elite. It was the Mecca for aesthetes who sipped Chinese tea and had their cup read by Madame Zozo. The houses boasted tiny, slanting floor restaurants named "Ye Tiny Tea Roome" in synthetic Shakespearean English. Hat shops were housed in broken down cottages with a large window built into the front, adorned with one hat. Woodcarvers, metal artisans, portrait painters and curio shops lined the narrow streets. We have visited Bloomsbury, the Quartier Latin and Greenwich Village, but never have we seen a Bohemian quarter quite so Bohemian.

This combination of acute social observation and acerbic social commentary is very characteristic of Garner's writing about the middle and upper classes and is significantly different from his accounts of working-class or proletarian life. In the latter, as in "Toronto's Cabbagetown" or another essay for *The Canadian Forum*, the December 1938 "Christmas in Cabbagetown," his evident sympathy with his subjects sometimes produces an almost elegiac account of the way they live:

> I would rush into the kitchen-living room in my underwear to see what Santa had brought me. There stood the 25 cent Christmas tree (if you waited until late on Christmas eve you could buy one of the skinny ones that were left for a dime), hung with the familiar ornaments that were hoarded from year to year, some of which were still in use when I had become a man.
> Below the tree stood the tied-up Christmas box that my maternal Grandma had sent to us from Yorkshire, and beside it, tagged

with our names, stood a toy for my brother and me, that my mother had scrimped to buy us. Mine might be a small toy tin train with a 48-inch circular track, a Sandy-Andy, or the smallest and cheapest Meccano set (No. 00), but there was always something. It wasn't what I had asked Santa to bring me, but I was always grateful to Santa no matter what it was.

Here the tone of the narrative is much more relaxed, perhaps because Garner need not be so alert for signs of the follies perpetrated by the monied classes; on the other hand, it also comes pretty close to being stickily sentimental, a generally ignored facet of his writing which often goes hand in hand with both social realism and protagonists who see themselves as tough, cynical he-men.

During his association with *New Advance*, Hugh worked as the janitor and furnace tender of a building at 929 Bay Street, which housed the offices of the popular-front group The Canadian League for Peace and Democracy, an organization that before the Comintern's softening of Stalinist orthodoxy had been known as the more militant-sounding Canadian League Against War and Fascism. Here he discovered what he would later describe as the real meaning of the communist catch-phrase "the downtrodden, toiling masses:" it meant being paid "at the munificent proletarian wage of $3 a week" while taking orders from your supposedly revolutionary bosses.

One of the non-communist political groupings in which *New Advance* showed a strong interest was the co-operative movement. Based on the example of the Rochdale Society of Equitable Pioneers, which had been founded in 1844 not far from the Yorkshire mining country where Garner was born, co-operatives offered their members financial savings, a thoroughly democratic system of organization and a tradition of interest in the broader principles of socialism. The Depression spurred the formation of co-operatives throughout Canada, particularly in the western provinces and Ontario, and many communists were excited by the prospect of becoming involved with a movement that appealed to both the urban working class and rural farmers.

New Advance therefore included a "Co-operative News" section in its early issues, although this was really something of a misnomer. It did not, as one might expect, concern itself with what particular co-operatives were doing, but instead offered simple descriptions of what such groups were all about and how they might grow and develop. A November 1938 article on "Purchasing Power" is typical:

> members increase ... until the amount of business is too large to be handled any longer by a part-time unpaid staff. At this stage the turn-over will usually be sufficient to carry the expenses of a paid manager and a rented building, and the buying club develops into a cooperative society in the full sense ...
>
> As the number of members increases, various commodities other than groceries might be bought or ordered through the store, such as — meat, baked goods, milk, coal, dry goods, gasoline, oil and motor accessories, etc.

How or why Hugh Garner became interested in co-operatives is one of the few subjects about which his autobiographical writings are silent, but whatever his motivation, by the summer of 1938 he was managing such an enterprise in Port Credit, a small Lake Ontario community about ten miles west of Toronto. He shared a house with the president of the society, George Randerson, and learned "how to keep books, bag sugar, slice ham and turn down members who asked for credit." We do know that this was one of the few jobs from which he was fired, as opposed to quitting after a short period of employment, and perhaps this is the reason why he seldom mentioned it; or it may be related to his more general reticence about the period between his return from Spain and his enlistment in the army, which he skips over in one paragraph in *One Damn Thing After Another!* without mentioning his connection with the *New Advance* or Canadian League for Peace and Democracy at all, although he did write about them elsewhere. Since these two "front" organizations were about as close as Garner ever came to formal affiliation with the Communist Party of Canada, he may well have felt some embarrassment at an association that does not seem to have had much relevance to, or influence on, his subsequent career.

In any case, the beginning of 1939 found Garner back in Toronto, broke and staying at his mother's flat at 82 First Avenue, picking up odd jobs such as selling ice cream cones in Riverdale Park during the royal visit of King George VI and Queen Elizabeth. Bruce West's *Toronto* describes this part of their tour:

> After the ceremonies at Queen's Park, the Royal couple proceeded to Riverdale Park, escorted this time by the mounted soldiers of the Governor General's Horse Guard, resplendent in their scarlet tunics, their pipeclayed gauntlets and their burnished helmets. In the vast natural amphitheater formed by the surrounding green hills of the park there extended a sight the like of which had never before been seen in Toronto. Down on the flat, where ancient guns had been fired in the early part of the century to celebrate "old battles" every May 24, were assembled 75,000 Toronto school children. Sitting or standing on the grassy slopes were 100,000 more of Toronto's people. As the glittering cavalry accompanied the Royal car into the great bowl of Riverdale, a thunderous cheer arose from the assembled throng.

Garner, always a lover of parades and always sentimental about his ties with England, recalled, "that day I was a bigger royalist than [Lord] Beaverbrook."

That July he hitch-hiked to south-western Ontario's tobacco belt, where he arrived a bit too early for the harvest and in the interim picked apples and berries while living in an abandoned boxcar near the town of Simcoe. When the tobacco was ready he got a job as a primer (the person who strips the prime leaves from the plants), for which he was paid $3 per day. These experiences gave him the material for two later short stories, "The Conversion of Willie Heaps" and "Hunky." "Hunky" provides an evocative description of his surroundings:

> It was a hot August morning. The sun, still low against the horizon, was a white-hot stove lid that narrowed the eyes and made the sweat run cold along the spine. The sky was as high and blue as heaven, and the shade-giving cumulus wouldn't form until noon.

Before us lay the serried rows of tobacco, armpit high and as dull green as bile.

Into this rural backwater, where on the morning of Sunday, September 3 Hugh was enjoying a leisurely breakfast with his employers, came the radio announcement that Great Britain was at war with Germany. Although it took until the following Saturday for the Canadian Parliament to assemble and declare the country officially a party to the conflict, there was no doubt in anyone's mind that Canada would be involved. And for a twenty-six-year-old man with no settled occupation, few responsibilities and still-vivid memories of "How I Became an Englishman," there wasn't much doubt as to how he would respond to the wave of patriotic sentiment that swept the nation.

Chapter Four

At War in the Atlantic (1939-1945)

On Saturday, September 9, 1939 Garner's employer drove him to the bus depot in Simcoe. After buying a pint of rye Hugh boarded the bus for Hamilton, opened his bottle and, not yet being much of a drinker, quickly became intoxicated. This premonitory experience — in years to come he would exhibit a strong compulsion to combine drinking and travelling, often with disastrous effects — almost got him thrown off the bus by the driver, but in due course he arrived in Hamilton and changed buses for Toronto. On the following Monday he went to the University Avenue Armories and enlisted in the 23rd Medium Battery of the Royal Canadian Artillery, convinced that he now knew how a by no means heroic but in his own way patriotic citizen could best serve in his country's armed forces. As usual, there would be a detour or two before he found his appropriate place in the military world; and during this conflict he would face the enemy under conditions far more hazardous than those posed by the amateurish soldiering of his Spanish Civil War days.

The Royal Canadian Artillery was in some respects an odd choice of military specialties for Garner. Having learned that he was not cut out to be an infantryman, it was certainly sensible to opt for a more behind-the-lines role; but his brief period of attendance at the International Brigades' artillery school at Almansa had given him only a slight and entirely theoretical acquaintance with the ancient French 75-mm. guns that made up the bulk of the Loyalists' armament and would, in any case, not have been of much use in dealing with the very different 6-inch howitzers used by the RCA. The artillery was also a highly technical section of the armed forces, demanding a degree of mathematical aptitude far greater than that exhibited by Garner's dismal high-school grades in the subject.

There was a social-class aspect to the situation as well. With the replacement of mounted cavalry by the tank, the artillery had become the most desirable branch of the service for officers concerned with fighting as gentlemanly a war as possible: if one could no longer ride down the enemy on horseback, one could at least kill him at a distance rather than while mucking about in the mud with the "P.B.I." ("Poor Bloody Infantry"). Another Toronto-based formation, the 30th Battery of the Royal Canadian Artillery, was commanded by Major Conn Smythe, M.C., who temporarily gave up the direction of Maple Leaf Gardens and recruited so many athletes and sports personalities that the 30th soon became known as the "sportsmen's battery." At a time when the number of willing volunteers far exceeded the military's capacity to absorb them (artillery recruiting offices were closed two weeks after Canada's declaration of war because of the sheer volume of applicants), even the enlisted men in the more desirable units tended to be of middle or upper-class origins.

In these circumstances a person from a background such as Garner's, who at the time of his enlistment was sleeping on the floor of his mother's kitchen because there was no unoccupied bed in the flat at 82 First Avenue, could not have felt terribly at ease; and if we add in the fact of his service with the Loyalists, which was known — and very much frowned on — by several of his officers, it is not hard to see why he spent a pretty miserable six months in the Royal Canadian Artillery. When their makeshift barracks in the Canadian National Exhibition's Government Building were finally ready at the beginning of October, the 23rd Medium Battery drilled at the complex routines of the gunner's art and prepared to be shipped overseas; but for Hugh, who had been told to his face that as a suspected communist sympathizer he could not be trusted in action, the absence of any incentive to do well resulted in very low grades on his examinations and efficiency ratings.

He stuck it out until the 23rds actually received their orders to embark, hoping that he might still be allowed to go, but when it became official that he would be remaining behind he knew his career in the artillery was over:

> In March [1940] I had myself paraded before the colonel of the No. 2 District Depot and told him I wanted a discharge or I'd go over the hill; I hadn't joined the army to stay in Toronto. I was given a "Services No Longer Required" discharge and found a job putting up wooden hangars at Malton Airport.

On his army discharge certificate Garner was described as being five feet, five-and-one-half inches tall and having brown hair and eyes as well as a "medium" complexion. Somewhere along the line he had picked up a tattoo of the skull and crossbones on his upper chest, thus manifesting a penchant for bodily decoration that he would later indulge more seriously in the navy.

Hugh gave up the hangar-erecting job after four or five weeks and went back to hanging around his mother's flat at 80 Caroline Avenue, where she had moved at the end of 1939. He devoted much of his time to further attempts at writing fiction and produced two stories that he would later polish into publishable form. One, "A Couple of Quiet Young Guys," is a competent low-life vignette clearly indebted to Hemingway's "The lowlife Killers;" but the other is the first of his stories to exhibit an imaginative comprehension of characters who are not thinly disguised likenesses of their author. One evening, sitting at the kitchen table after everyone else had gone to bed, he wrote a story called "The Conversion of Willie Heaps," which struck him as by far the best thing he had ever done. But he wasn't entirely satisfied with it — he would later make a few minor changes to its first two pages — and so he put both stories away in an old suitcase, where they remained until he returned home from the war in the fall of 1945.

"The Conversion of Willie Heaps" was inspired by the "apple and berry-picking jobs plus a stint on a haying crew" that Garner had worked at during the summer of 1939. The story begins as a bucolic interlude in the life of a twelve-year-old boy and his thirty-year-old friend Willie, a fundamentalist Christian who is "a little simple" but nonetheless skilled at gelding colts. When Willie is frustrated by a neighbour's failure to keep an appointment, however, he begins to systematically castrate all of the man's livestock on the grounds that both they and their owner are sinners; then, completely in the grip of this frenzy of blood lust, he tries to do the same to the narrator before mortally wounding himself in a final paroxysm of passion. The story concludes with an attempt by the Reverend Blounsbury, the minister of Willie's church, to comfort the boy:

> "Poor child, to be bereft of a friend so soon in life," he said. "But don't grieve, lad. Willie now sits at the right hand of his Maker. He had been saved, you know."
> My mother nodded again.
> "And how about you? Have you been converted yet, young man?"
> "No!" I cried, shaking his hand from me and edging to the door.
> "My, what's come over that boy!" exclaimed my mother.
> I ran out of the house and down the road towards home. I hated them all: Willie, Mr. and Mrs. Heaps, my mother and father, and especially the Reverend Blounsbury. Why couldn't they have left Willie alone, I asked myself. Why couldn't everybody in the whole wide world leave everybody else alone?

The story's movement from rural nostalgia to stark sexual pathology to the final indictment of evangelical religion is skilfully managed, and the very effective description of Willie's castration mania undoubtedly reflects its author's familiarity with Krafft-Ebbing's *Psychopathia Sexualis*, that exhaustive catalogue of esoteric sexual practices which Hugh had first encountered in the Los Angeles public library and would often use again, most notably in *The Sin Sniper*.

The poignant question with which the story concludes is particularly affecting in the light of what we know of Garner's background. This is no mealy-mouthed call for toleration, that characteristic and all too often condescending middle-class virtue, but rather a plea to be literally *left alone*: it is the cry of a man whose life has always been meddled with, most recently by military authorities ignorant of the idealistic impulses that led a kid from the slums to affiliate himself with communist-controlled organizations, but before that by all the social workers, teachers and other do-gooders who bedevilled his childhood. When Hugh began submitting this story to magazine editors in the late 1940s, many were afraid that its overt anti-fundamentalist message would alienate some of their readers; if they had been aware of the profoundly anarchical sentiments "The Conversion of Willie Heaps" more covertly expressed, this very fine story might never have seen print. In fact, "The Conversion of Willie Heaps" would not be published until 1951.

May 1940 found Hugh Garner once again at loose ends as to what to do with his future. He finally decided that if the Canadian armed forces would not have him, he would try his luck with those of the land of his birth: in late May he hitch-hiked to Halifax with the intention of working his way to the U.K. on a freighter, after which he would enlist in the "Koylies," the King's Own Yorkshire Light Infantry, the regiment in which previous generations of his ancestors had served the cause of king and country.

But he was unable to arrange a working passage, even though he made himself a nuisance on the Halifax waterfront with his daily visits to each shipping office. Passing the naval dockyard one day, he saw posters announcing a new recruiting drive by its supply services branch, and with characteristic impulsiveness he decided he might as well try to join up. On June 2, 1940 Garner enlisted in the Royal Canadian Navy, which seemed to have no reservations about letting a former member of the International Brigades train for the post of "victualler's assistant" aboard its ships. Gentlemen were definitely not lining up to shift crates of provisions and keep accurate inventories of naval supplies, but for a former "Journalist and retail store manager" — as he described himself on his service record — the navy must have thought this a reasonable choice of specialties.

First, however, Garner had to go through his basic training, which took place on HMCS *Stadacona* in Halifax. After being issued baggy coveralls, upon which they stencilled their names with paint, the recruits began a course that included field training and gun drill as well as classes on ammunition, fire control, torpedoes and anti-gas routines. Then three weeks of concentration on the basics of seamanship were followed by a week's practical work at sea, following which they were deemed ready to serve on one of His Majesty's Canadian Ships.

The great majority of the supply branch's personnel occupied shore-based posts. But Garner's inability to accept authority and fit into the military bureaucracy meant that, as usual, he was in constant conflict with his superiors, who were thus usually quite happy to put his name forward whenever a shipboard opening had to be filled. As a result, he spent much of the war as a member of the crew of various combat ships, where he would both appreciate the somewhat looser discipline and see more sea duty than many of those specifically trained for such a role.

His first such assignment, in fact, was to a ship that was still under construction. And when this new corvette was finally completed by the Quebec City shipyards, the ice buildup on the St. Lawrence River in the winter of 1940 kept it in port until the following spring. Thus he was posted instead to a small patrol boat, the former RCMP launch *Eileen*, whose armament consisted of an ageing Vickers machine-gun, a handful of rifles and two depth charges that had to be physically manhandled over the side. Following this he was posted to the converted yacht *Ambler*, a similarly lightly armed vessel of the kind that early in the war was being pressed into service until new warships could be built.

While staying at a small Quebec City hotel waiting for the *Ambler* to be repaired, he agreed to go on a blind date with the sister of one of the hotel's employees. On a chilly evening in December, perched on a garbage can at a street corner in the Lower Town, he waited for the date he knew only as "Alice."

When she arrived, he quickly discovered that Alice Gallant, a twenty-five-year-old hotel worker from the Gaspé, was in more ways than one the woman for whom he had been waiting. After a week's whirlwind courtship, Hugh was convinced that he was madly in love, and when he was ordered to report to Halifax for reassignment, he told her he would write often and would not let the war come between them.

Alice wasn't quite so certain that this was the ideal man of her dreams. Her friend at the hotel told her that everyone there thought Garner was crazy: he said all kinds of strange things, and when asked about his religion replied that the only thing he believed in was slitting the throats of priests (this having occurred all too often during the atrocities committed at the beginning of the Spanish Civil War). She found him attractive but so different from the other men she knew that she was also a bit apprehensive of him. One thing she did like was his *joie de vivre*, expressed in spontaneous exhibitions of tap-dancing or bursts of song; his penchant for falsetto renditions of popular tunes such as "I'm a Millionaire" made just walking down the street with him a pleasure. But at the time Alice had another beau whom she very much liked, and she parted from Hugh without having definitely made up her mind as to whether their relationship had a future.

Given the state of the world at the end of 1940, a Canadian sailor slated for corvette duty wouldn't have been the choice of anyone who wanted to immediately settle down in a conventional marriage. The war was not going well: the evacuation of Dunkirk and the capitulation of France had cost Great Britain both its major ally and most of its modern military equipment, and it was only its air force and navy that barred the way to a successful German invasion. Desperate for additional ships to protect its endangered supply lines, Great Britain urged its allies to take all measures possible to increase their ocean-going fleets. As a result, Canadian shipyards began to concentrate on the small but extraordinarily efficient vessels known as corvettes.

In the aftermath of the Munich Crisis of 1938, when it became clear that a global war was inevitable, the British Admiralty had devoted a good deal of thought to the question of how it could protect the Empire's sea lifelines. The traditional naval escort vessel, the destroyer, was the ideal choice, but the length of time it took to build one and the relatively small number of shipyards capable of constructing them argued for some other alternative. Eventually the Admiralty settled on the corvette, a smaller, simpler and much cheaper craft designed along the lines of modern whalers. Fast, maneuvrable and durable, the corvette would prove to be the only Allied escort with a turning radius superior to that of a submarine, which meant they could track and destroy U-boats better than any other warship.

What this meant for Hugh Garner was that ship's crews were being hurriedly put together and thrown into action, and with service on the corvettes HMCS *Fennel* and HMCS *Collingwood* in the immediate future, his next shore leave would not be until July of 1941. In the interim, he wooed Alice with three and four letters a week, to which she at first responded with at most one of her own. But as the correspondence continued, she was gradually won over by Hugh's eloquence as well as his persistence: anyone who wrote this beautifully would surely be able to fulfil the ambition to write he was always talking about. They were married in Halifax on July 5, 1941, in St. Mark's Anglican Church; four days later his new ship, the corvette HMCS *Arvida*, hoisted anchor, and Alice returned to Quebec City. For the next three years they would see each other only for short periods of hectic shore leave, but their relationship endured and even strengthened as two children, Barbara Ann and Hugh, Jr., were born to them in 1942 and 1944. This very gradual introduction to marriage was probably a good thing for Hugh, since the transitory nature of his previous love affairs would have made a more conventional settling down very difficult.

Arvida was part of the Canadian Escort Force based in St. John's, Newfoundland — quickly dubbed "Newfyjohn" by the sailors stationed there — that had been created in June 1940 to serve as the Western link in the chain of convoy protection stretching across the Atlantic. At what was known as the "Mid-Ocean Meeting Point," about 500 miles east of St. John's, the

Canadian escorts handed over their charges to their British counterparts and returned to their home bases. The average convoy included five escort vessels and forty merchant ships and was spread out in a formation that created a perimeter of more than thirty miles to defend. Since the "Asdic" apparatus, which detected submarines by means of underwater radio pulses, swept through an arc of only one mile, the escorts had to dash up and down the length of the convoy in an effort to keep the U-boats at bay.

Hugh was on convoy duty with *Arvida* from June to September of 1941 and then spent most of the following winter on the armed yacht *Moose*, patrolling the upper St. Lawrence and the Bras D'or Lakes for the German submarines that were beginning to be reported in the area. In February 1942 he was transferred to the corvette HMCS *Lunenburg*, which then escorted the troopship *Lady Drake* to Lake Melville in Labrador, where Goose Bay Airport was under construction. Here he delighted his ship's cooks by trading 100-pound bags of sugar to the Indian and Eskimo fishermen in exchange for the equivalent weight in fresh lake trout, and for a time enjoyed the increased prestige earned by this welcome addition to conventional naval fare.

The entry of the United States into the war at the end of 1941 meant that Canadian ships were now welcome to refuel and refit in American ports. Early in 1942 Garner's escort group put in to Newport, Rhode Island for fuel and supplies, where its battered vessels and haggard crews were regarded with distaste by the as yet unblooded U.S. naval trainees. Since they were manned almost entirely by young recruits rather than old salts, corvette crews tended to appear sloppy and undisciplined by regular navy standards, but their performance in combat was so remarkable that they were able to largely escape official censure.

But even the corvettes had certain minimal disciplinary requirements, and it wasn't long before Garner was demonstrating that his nose for trouble had not deserted him. Two incidents that occurred in mid-1942 brought him uncomfortably close to a dishonorable discharge. The first was more humorous than serious: on a less-than-sober return from a provisioning expedition

Garner, having somehow lost the civilian driver of his horse-drawn cart, decided to see how fast the elderly animal could make it back to the ship. Thundering up the *Lunenburg*'s gang-plank like some demented Ben Hur, he managed to get the horse wedged into a space between one of the corvette's lifeboats and its forward davit, which brought about the following exchange:

> The captain turned, blinked, and asked, "What the hell are you doing, Garner?"
>
> "Bringing our mascot aboard, sir," I answered, giving him a snappy salute.
>
> He turned away, whether to laugh or cry I don't know.

Everyone had a good chuckle and Hugh received only a token punishment. But if the treatment of this incident suggested that he could get away with almost anything, his next brush with naval authority brought about a rude awakening.

It all started with a telegram from Alice announcing the arrival of their daughter, Barbara Ann, who was born at the Hotel Dieu Hospital in Campbellton, New Brunswick, the town closest to the Gallant family farm where Alice was now staying. Hugh was ecstatic; after the members of his shipboard mess had presented him with their collective rum rations — the customary method of celebrating momentous occasions — he also became thoroughly intoxicated. And in the sentimental mood that often overtook him when he was drinking, he decided to go into town and buy his new daughter a pair of baby shoes.

Unfortunately, he did not go about this in anything resembling the proper military manner. When he left the *Lunenburg* he simply ignored the usual business of reporting to the officer of the watch and obtaining a pass to exit from the dockyard area. Even this might not have been viewed too seriously if he had made an appropriately penitent return, but instead he got into a shouting match with the dockyard guards and was placed under arrest. When his alleged offenses were added up, they made a rather impressive collection: Leading Hand (a naval rank corresponding to that of a corporal in the army) Garner was charged with being drunk aboard ship, leaving ship illegally, breaking into ship illegally and using abusive language to the officer of the guard.

Hugh pleaded guilty and was sentenced to the loss of a good conduct badge and fourteen days detention. His two weeks were served at Point Edward Detention Barracks near Sydney, Nova Scotia, which was run by the army in a manner that made the hill-billy residents of Keyser, West Virginia's jail seem like gracious Southern gentlemen. Garner devoted seven pages (out of the book's total of 354) to this experience in *One Damn Thing After Another!*, and it is clear that despite his efforts to shrug it off as one more brush with stupid authority figures, he realized he had gone about as far as he wanted to go in bucking the system:

> Everything in a detention barracks ... is meant to punish physically and insult, humiliate, and psychologically "break the spirits of" the prisoners inside them.
>
> Each morning, after we had sand-scrubbed our slopbuckets to a mirror-like shine with handfuls of sand ... we would double to the washroom, mark time while we shaved ourselves with laundry soap and a communal safety razor, mark time while we washed or showered ourselves, and even keep marking time while we defecated in an outdoor privy containing three seatless toilet bowls. ... you were forced to evacuate yourself at that specific time each day, and do it while moving your feet "at the double." Not only that but you had only a certain time on the toilet bowl, and had to get off when the guard shouted, "You three bastards next!"

Hugh would do his share of carousing during the remainder of his naval service, but he never again did anything that might have resulted in another term in a detention barracks.

When he was released from Point Edward he was ordered to travel to St. John's, Newfoundland to serve on the corvette HMCS *Battleford*. The day after his arrival the ship left to join a convoy forming up for the run to Londonderry in Northern Ireland; on this trip there would be no handing over of merchant vessels to British-based escorts in the middle of the Atlantic. The

Newfoundland Escort Force, of which the *Battleford* was a member, was now shepherding its sea-going flocks right to their ultimate destinations; and this meant that they would be drawing closer to both the U-boat bases and the continental airfields from which the German air force mounted attacks against Allied shipping.

The passage to Londonderry was relatively uneventful, and there Garner discovered that he could indulge in some useful petty larceny by trading pound casks of navy tea for a pound of civilian cash, which he immediately invested in pint glasses of Guinness stout at Cassidy's Railway Bar on the waterfront. A more serious note was struck by anti-aircraft practice at "the dome," where crew members were taught the proper angles and distances at which to fire at attacking planes. From Londonderry the *Battleford* received orders to join a convoy headed for North Africa. On October 26, 1942 she became part of the protective screen for the troop-ships and supply vessels that carried the components of "Operation Torch," a joint British-American assault on Casablanca, Oran and Algiers. They were attacked by planes as well as submarines, and at his "action station" — the combat role that he fulfilled in addition to his supply duties — Hugh had his first crack at the enemy when a Junker 88 bomber came into view. Firing his twin Browning .5 machine-guns at maximum elevation, he hit nothing but clear blue sky but at least had the satisfaction — very uncommon in anti-submarine warfare — of actually seeing what he was shooting at.

The convoy passed through the Straits of Gibralter on November 5, and there they were met by a powerful British task force intended as insurance against any intervention by the nearby Italian fleet. After an interlude of comic-opera negotiating with the French garrisons of the three cities, which were rent by arguments between those loyal to the pro-German Vichy regime and those supporting neutral or pro-Allied factions, the invasion was launched against sometimes heavy resistance. On November 8 there was a serious scare when a strong Vichy French naval squadron almost succeeded in getting in among the unarmed transports off the coast, but they were turned back by the last-minute arrival of part of the covering task force.

After Operation Torch had been successfully concluded, the *Battleford* returned to St. John's for more cross-Atlantic convoy duty. The next Londonderry run was a quiet one, but on the passage back Convoy ON-154 suffered severe losses from an unusually heavy concentration of U-boats. On December 24 it entered the area known as the "black pit," a 300-mile stretch in the mid-Atlantic where air cover could not be provided by land-based aircraft, and on Christmas afternoon it was spotted by one of the long-range reconnaissance planes used by the Germans. Everyone knew that their position was now being reported to the submarine packs, but on the *Battleford* the crew refused to let this dampen their celebration of the holiday:

> The Sick-berth Attendant put on his female impersonation act, we sang our complete repertoire of bawdy songs, there was an orchestra which consisted of a mouth-organ and two spoon-on-table virtuosi, the officers dropped in to pay their respects, and we played our favorite phonograph record, *She Said No, I Said Please*, over and over on the ship's communication system. It was a wonderful night, but it was also the last one for a week that we didn't spend at action stations.

As if they didn't already have more than enough to worry about, on December 26 a severe gale scattered merchant ships and escorts to all points of the compass just as the U-boats were preparing to attack. On the following day all hell broke loose: while the gale still raged, four merchantmen were torpedoed along with the convoy's fuel tanker; the escorts now faced the impossible task of rounding up the convoy's ships and fighting off submarines while at the same time trying to conserve fuel.

The 28th was relatively quiet, as the U-boats probed ON-154's defences and planned a concerted attack with their rapidly increasing numbers; meanwhile, the escorts did what they could to herd the merchant vessels back into a defensible formation. By the evening of the 29th the submarines were ready. Joseph

Schull's *The Far Distant Ships* provides a graphic account of what happened next:

> U-boats bored directly in among the columns, firing salvoes of torpedoes from all their tubes. Streams of tracer fire from merchantmen criss-crossed in the night to indicate the many sightings ... and behind the convoy, as it struggled on, the sea was dotted with the wrecks of blazing ships and the multiplying light of rafts and lifeboats.
>
> Within two hours nine ships had gone down.

ONS-154 had now lost a total of fourteen ships out of its original complement of forty-six; the last to be torpedoed was the rescue vessel *Toward*, carrying the survivors from the first thirteen ships lost, only a few of whom were rescued a second time. The submarines disengaged at first light, but no one thought the battle was over. The convoy was still well short of the point at which air cover could be provided, and of the four remaining escorts one, HMCS *Shediac*, was out of fuel and had been taken in tow by the *Battleford*. Under these circumstances the convoy commander reluctantly issued the order that signalled the end of ON-154 as an effective naval force: if individual ships saw an opportunity to escape independently, they might do so.

But help was, in fact, on the way. A squadron of British "Fleet" destroyers — fast, experienced submarine hunters — had been dispatched from Gibralter on Christmas Day, and they arrived just in time to rout the unsuspecting U-boats. The *Battleford* was ordered to tow *Shediac* to the nearest oiling facility, the port of Ponta Delgada on the Azores island of Sao Miguel, where they arrived on the afternoon of December 31. Having been dramatically rescued from almost certain disaster and finding themselves in the momentary haven of neutral Portugal, the order was given to "Splice the main brace — doubled:" translated into English, this directed the issuing of a double ration of rum to each member of the crew and ensured that the *Battleford* would be *hors de combat* for the remainder of 1942.

Garner later maintained it was in the navy that he first became a heavy drinker, and given the way in which rum was issued it's a wonder that all naval veterans aren't chronic alcoholics. Every day a two-ounce ration of rum, called a "tot," was distributed to each member of a ship's crew — officers excepted — thus carrying on a British naval tradition that seems to have begun early in the eighteenth century. According to a 1740 regulation introduced by Admiral Sir Edward Vernon, the rum was to be diluted with twice its volume of water; this produced a beverage dubbed "grog" after the grogram — a material composed of silk, worsted and mohair — coat favoured by the Admiral, who was not surprisingly doomed to be remembered by posterity as "Old Grog."

On a combat ship such as the *Battleford*, where any moment might bring the need for quick and decisive action, the men tended to save their rum rations for a thorough drunk when they were next docked in port, which led directly to the kinds of escapades that had gotten Garner thrown into a detention barracks. As a supply rating, Hugh was usually in full or joint charge of the preparation and distribution of the rum, which took up several pages in the bible of his profession, *The Manual of Naval Storekeeping*; the making of bread, by way of contrast, was disposed of in two paragraphs. Those sailors too young or too seasick to drink — and in the early years of the war this would have constituted a substantial proportion of any corvette crew — had their rum rations emptied into a large jug, which by custom became the private and abundant stock of the supply ratings. Thus in June of 1945, when Garner was assigned the task of inventorying the beer stocks remaining in St. John's' naval canteens, he remarked that this was "like sending Jack the Ripper to run a girl's school;" his years of officially sanctioned abuse of alcohol in the navy had left him with a permanent drinking problem.

When they weren't experimenting with new methods of pickling their systems with rum, the crew of the *Battleford* did its best to indulge in the other traditional activity pursued by sailors on leave. Garner's years of knocking about the world had accustomed him to satisfying his sexual needs with prostitutes, and his new role as a husband was both too recent and too unreal — Alice Garner estimates that she saw her husband for a total of less than three months during the first three years of their marriage — to cause him to alter this pattern. When he had been stationed in Halifax and Quebec City, he and Alice had been able to spend many of his leaves together; but when he was based in St. John's and making frequent voyages to foreign ports, they were for all intents and purposes separated, especially since Alice soon had a young child to look after.

Two of his erotic adventures had humorous consequences. The first occurred during a short leave in Belfast, Northern Ireland, just before sailing on the North African voyage described above. One of the tried and true methods of finding a brothel was to make use of young waterfront layabouts, who were usually happy to serve as native guides in exchange for a small tip; but in this case their young tout led them to the gates of a suspiciously magnificent-looking building where Garner, not in his most sober condition, told the woman who answered the door, "Honey, we've come to see your girls." He was somewhat taken aback when she laughingly replied "You've come to the wrong place, me boyo," at which point he took a closer look and discovered that he was speaking to a nun.

Another sort of misunderstanding occurred at Ponta Delgada, where January 1, 1943 found the hungover crew of the *Battleford* suddenly aware that they had just one more day to relax in a neutral port. Once again Garner and some of his buddies accosted a young quayside lounger. After he had impressed his friends with his fluent command of pidgin Spanish and Portugese, Hugh and his friends were directed to the type of female companionship they desired. There they had an absolutely wonderful time, treating themselves to everything the establishment offered and running up a gigantic bill. It was only when Garner remembered that he was completely broke and announced this fact to his associates that a stampede ensued: apparently everyone else had assumed that he was paying, and during the post-mortem it turned out that he had drunkenly — and with no memory whatsoever of it — assured them, "Don't worry boys, it's all on me." The result, in any case, was a wild scramble back to the *Battleford*, closely pursued by women un-derstandably outraged at such flagrantly immoral behaviour.

The winter months of 1943 found them back at the convoy-escorting business, this time without serious incident, as the "Ultra" interceptions of German communications and the new allied 10-cm. radar tipped the scales against the U-boats. One voyage took them to Gibralter, where another member of the crew took the opportunity to catch up on his accumulated rum ration. Unfortunately, he did so while from the bridge a British officer graciously pointed out Gibralter's sights to the *Battleford*'s captain, both of whom were shocked to discover a tipsy sailor perched high upon the foremast; even more shocking was the fact that the sailor was completely naked and refused to come down until the bottle of rum had been completely consumed. Perhaps encouraged by this exhibition of drunken bravado, Hugh became similarly inebriated on his shore leave in town and had to step lively to avoid the bread knife of a Spanish baker, whom he had unthinkingly called — in a phrase that he had not too long ago used in the trenches at Jarama — a fascist bastard.

Home port was still St. John's, the only North American city to be blacked out for the duration of the war, where an English colonial culture not far removed from Victorian times continued to flourish: tea-rooms and unarmed policemen were among the sights that surprised Canadian sailors, who also found its residents far friendlier than their counterparts in Halifax or Quebec City. At the Seagoing Officers Club, known informally as "The Crowsnest," the upper ranks dozed in leather armchairs and warmed their feet at a large open fireplace; at the Chief and Petty Officers Wet Canteen a group of serious drinkers that included Garner formed their own exclusive society under the rubric of "The Gag and Vomit Club," and did their best to live up to its name. Elsewhere in the city, Canadian, British, American, Polish, Norwegian and French sailors mingled with their host New-foundlanders in an atmosphere that seemed curiously genteel in comparison to the rougher waterfront areas of most of the other major ports.

By the fall of 1943 Hugh had served the three years of sea duty after which the navy permitted its supply services personnel to opt for shore-based jobs, and he promptly did so. He was transferred to Halifax and put in charge of "mess traps," the nautical term for the equipment of a naval establishment's mess and galley. Christmas brought a two-day leave and a welcome opportunity to see his family at the Gallant farm. The train to Campbellton was met by one of their neighbours driving a horse and cutter, into which Garner was bundled, snuggly swaddled in a buffalo robe, after the necessary visit to the local liquor store. From there it was an eight-mile drive back into the hills, singing and yelling "Merry Christmas!" to everyone they met on the way, with Hugh waving his bottle of rum and enjoying the white, frosty twilight that illuminated this memorable journey.

He remained in Halifax until early in the winter of 1944, when he was assigned to the supply depot in Quebec City and lived in a rooming-house on the Rue St. Jean. Here he experienced a rekindling of the desire to become a writer that he had expressed to Alice but had otherwise done little about since mid-1939, and made an attempt at a novel about his naval experiences. These five or six pages, tentatively titled "Convoy," were the first intimation of the book that would later surface as *Storm Below*, although at the time Hugh was so dissatisfied with them that he threw them away and would not make another attempt at a naval novel until after the war.

Garner spent the February 1944 to May 1945 period in Quebec City, where he was eventually joined by Alice, Barbara and the newest addition to the family, Hugh, Jr., in the fall of 1944. Alice now discovered that Hugh's madcap shore leaves in foreign ports had resulted in some highly visible additions to the skull and crossbones tattoo she had always considered one of his least desirable features: he had really had a job done on himself in Gibralter, starting with a coiled mass of rings and serpents on his upper arms and shoulders and culminating in an immense battleship that completely covered the previously unadorned area of his chest. Alice, who was generally able to mask her displeasure at her husband's sillier escapades, must not have been able to suppress her feelings about spending her nights with snakes and a battleship as well as the skull and crossbones; Hugh, much abashed, went through the painful process of having his tattoes removed, which left him with large masses of white scar tissue as well as a lifelong aversion to being seen in anything other than a high-buttoned and long-sleeved shirt.

On May 8, 1945 Germany surrendered, and Hugh was sent to St. John's to close down the "wet canteens" operated by the navy. Given the amount of time he had spent in them while stationed there, this was certainly a reasonable assignment, if not one calculated to ease his drinking problems. While he was in St. John's, one of the clerks at the naval barracks tried to pressure him into prolonging his enlistment, but Garner was having none of that: he had signed up to fight the Germans, and now that they were defeated he had other plans for the remainder of his life.

In August 1945 he travelled to Quebec City aboard the destroyer HMCS *Saskatchewan* and from there proceeded to Toronto to be discharged. At the end of the month he travelled by train to the Gallant family farm in the Gaspé, where Alice and their two children had spent the summer. Here Hugh Garner's young family awaited the final return of their sailor, home at last from the sea.

Chapter Five

Reckoning with Toronto (1945-1952)

When Hugh and his family returned to Toronto at the beginning of October 1945, they discovered that the post-war housing shortage made it almost impossible to find affordable accommodations. Their economic situation was very simple: they had almost no money — the one hundred dollars Hugh had received as his "Rehabilitation Grant" on being discharged was almost entirely gone — and regardless of how much money they had, Toronto had almost nowhere for them to live. It was estimated that the city had about 30,000 families doubling-up in houses built for single-family occupancy, and the newspapers were full of stories about people living in tar-paper shacks or even out in the open.

But whereas Annie Garner and her boys had had to manage as best they could by themselves in 1919, this new batch of Garners at least had some help from their families. For almost four months they stayed with Hugh's mother in her small cottage at 21 Winnifred Avenue, but that was "like living in a phone booth:" its two small bedrooms didn't go far when shared among Annie, her teen-aged daughter June and Hugh's family, and when Ron Garner returned from the army conditions became intolerably overcrowded. To make matters worse, Alice was having some health problems: a medical examination had discovered spots on her lungs, which it was initially feared were tubercular. Although they turned out to be benign, it was still necessary for her to take a week's rest in a convalescent home.

With homesickness and concern about her health adding to their already difficult living situation, Alice finally suggested that it would be a good idea for her and the kids to go back to the Gallant farm. Hugh at first wouldn't hear of the idea, but since the only work he could find was as a construction labourer at eighty cents an hour, he eventually, if reluctantly, agreed with her. Just before Christmas he put Alice and the children on the train to the Gaspé and resolved to make the optimun use of this temporary bachelorhood by taking a serious approach to his still persistent ambition to become a writer.

Garner planned his attack on this objective with the meticulous care that, along with learning how to become a serious drinker, was the navy's major contribution to his future. He had always, when in funds, been a "snappy dresser" — part of his attraction for Alice was that, unlike the other *maudits Anglaises* who moped around the streets of wartime Quebec City, "He always looked sharp" — and the navy brought out this love of neatness and order that had had little chance to flourish during his childhood. Although he was still in social terms something of an anarchist, never comfortable for long in any limited or sharply defined role, from now on Hugh would increasingly attempt to control the circumstances of his life rather than ignore or run away from them.

Thus by the end of December 1945 he was ensconced in a rooming-house at 8 St. Joseph Street, equipped with notepaper, fountain pen and pencil — but not with typewriter, eraser or dictionary — some mostly second-hand civilian clothing and a box of books: the fifty or so titles that he had accumulated included Hemingway's *The Fifth Column and the First Forty-Nine*, Dos Passos's *U.S.A.* and "a veritable bibliophile's nightmare of English and American fiction, biography, naval manuals, old school textbooks, and some that defy description." He had signed up for a course in "Cooperative Management" with the Department of Veterans Affairs, which paid him just enough to live on, and the course conveniently covered material with which he was already largely familiar.

On New Year's Day, 1946, he took a sheet of notepaper and in his firm, neat hand printed "Cabbagetown" at the top and under it "by Hugh Garner." During the next three months he would write, entirely by hand and in printed rather than cursive script, six hundred pages of manuscript; he would do this while spending his weekdays attending a vocational course; and, most importantly, he would do it without drinking.

This established a pattern that Garner would, with few deviations, follow for the remainder of his writing career. Although he discovered that he could write journalistic pieces and commercially oriented short stories while indulging his usual moderate to heavy drinking habits, his more serious fiction was written during rigidly enforced periods of almost complete abstinence. For his first draft of *Cabbagetown*, for example, Hugh enforced this regimen so diligently — permitting himself not even a single beer — that in combination with the avoidance of fattening foods he managed to lose forty pounds off the rather corpulent frame he had inherited from his naval imbibing.

He had a pretty good idea of what he wanted to do in *Cabbagetown*. It was going to be an autobiographical novel that would follow the outline of his career from his last day in high school to his arrival in Spain:

> the protagonist would be me as regards age, dates, schools, jobs and so forth. It is very important that dates and ages be familiar ones, for it saves a lot of unnecessary re-reading, checking and note-making throughout the book. When the character you are writing about does a certain thing, at a certain date, when he is of a certain age, it is far easier to write about him doing it without having to resort to notes to make sure your timing is correct.

This is the sort of artlessly honest statement that made it difficult for many critics to take Garner seriously, but at the same time it puts its finger on the pulse of truth in a practical if inelegant way. Although Marcel Proust or Thomas Mann would never have put it so directly, both in fact did precisely what Hugh is advocating in this passage; and if he had ever bothered to learn the jargon of contemporary literary criticism, he could have enhanced his reputation by tarting up this homely credo in cant phrases such as "the transformation of experience into art" and "the encounter between objectivity and subjectivity." But Garner always disdained anything smacking of an academic approach to authorship, and as a consequence he was sometimes inaccurately stereotyped as a simple and crude writer.

In keeping with his characteristic determination to waste nothing that he had written, he also planned on working in some of the short-story ideas he hadn't been able to nurse into independent life. The initial chapters of *Cabbagetown* came easily as childhood memories flooded in on him, and later he would fondly remember the incredible sense of accomplishment he experienced as the book progressed:

> The deeper into the book I got the better it began to read back to me. I found a tremendous satisfaction in a phrase or sentence that sprang full blown with beauty or skill from my thoughts. I began to feel that I was omniscient, a little creative god who could make his people live, love, hate and act foolish as real people did. I became interested in their lives, and looked forward from one chapter to the next to see what they would do. I found a payment for my hours of loneliness, my writer's cramp, my self-imposed hunger, in a psychological satisfaction that only a creative person knows.

He finished both book and course at the end of March, and perhaps his unaccustomed sobriety was beginning to tell on him: after his class' horrifying tour of a slaughter house, which left him with permanent memories of screaming animals and callous workers, he got roaring drunk, told his Co-operative Management teacher to go to hell and went from valedictory student to ignominious failure. But the course had served its purpose in helping to get his first important literary effort off the ground; now all he had to do was find someone willing to publish his novel.

He started by dropping into the offices of J.M. Dent & Company where, "like an unmarried girl seeking an abortion," he explained that he had a friend who had written a novel and wanted to know how it should be submitted. C.J. Eustace, a senior editor who must have been used to such furtive inquiries — novels and abortions being on roughly the same plane of immorality for those dour Protestant fundamentalists who were still a significant force in Toronto — gave him the information he needed, of which the most important conditions were that it be typed in a double-spaced format on white bond paper. What seemed like elementary requirements for an editorial department, however, turned out to be major stumbling blocks for an impoverished young writer. After he had wasted both time and money having it incorrectly typed by an amateur, it would take Garner several months of his own unskilled hunting and pecking to put his manuscript into the form in which it would be taken seriously by a publisher.

In the meantime, he had managed to find an inexpensive rental home in a veteran's housing project in the western suburb of Etobicoke, which meant that Alice and the children were able to rejoin him after he got a job as a clerk with the War Assets Corporation (WAC). They moved into 109 Uno Drive in April, Hugh rented a typewriter for five dollars a month and the family began what everyone hoped would be a more settled kind of existence. Hugh went off to work in the morning to WAC's downtown office, Alice looked after their two pre-school children and Hugh came home at night to type away at his manuscript:

> Every evening after supper I would retire to our unfurnished dining room, close the door so as not to awaken the children who were sleeping upstairs, and place my typewriter on the top of our treadle sewing-machine. On my left would be the slowly diminishing pile of the original typescript, and on my right the slowly thickening pile of revision, this time double spaced on white bond paper. I worked on it most evenings, and always tried to do twenty pages before quitting for the night. It was sheer bull labor now, for there was not the elan of creation that had carried me through the winter before.

For the next two years or so, things seemed to have fallen into place for the Garners. The WAC job was fairly interesting, involving as it did the disposal of the varied manufactured goods, buildings and other materials now surplus to the government's peacetime needs, and after *Cabbagetown* had finally been properly typed there began that alternately hopeful and depressing cycle of submission, waiting, rejection and submission to a different and perhaps more appreciative publisher which almost every apprentice writer experiences.

The first publisher he tried was the Macmillan Company of Canada, where editor Peggy Blackstock gave it a "page by page constructive review" that he later described as "of tremendous help to me." Blackstock thought she discerned a worthwhile novel lurking within the pages of *Cabbagetown*, but found it "at least a third too long and too verbose," and concluded by saying, "It may be true, but it hasn't been translated into art." Macmillan had recently come under the new and vigorous management of John Morgan Gray, who would eventually build the firm into an important literary publishing house, and this may have had something to do with the unusual amount of attention devoted to a sprawling manuscript from an unknown writer; but whatever the reasons, they set in motion a process of multiple revisions and rewritings that would eventually result in a publishable book, even though it would be another firm that would finally benefit from them.

The next Macmillan editor to have a go at his manuscript was Ellen Elliott, who in January 1947 advised him that further pruning was necessary, since "your descriptions of places particularly are too meticulously done and create photographs in the mind of the reader rather than real pictures." Hugh, understandably, was not sure that he knew exactly what she meant, but he pared away some more descriptive writing and submitted it again. This time Elliott found that the book "while realistic is so in a photographic rather than in an artistically impressionistic way," and suggested that he put the book aside for six months and then have another look at it.

The response of a young writer with no time to waste was to take it to his old acquaintance C.J. Eustace at J.M. Dent & Co., who took eight months to respond with moderately encouraging praise and a vague offer to try to arrange joint Canadian-U.S. publication. Less than impressed by Dent's business acumen, Garner then submitted his manuscript to William Collins Sons, who liked it but thought it required substantial revision. At this point, Hugh was ready to unburden himself of some of the accumulated frustration created by these developments. In a letter to Collins editor Robin Taylor he expressed himself in a manner that would soon earn him the reputation of being the scourge of publisher's row:

> I am unwilling to go ahead with the amount of work involved in carrying out your suggestions unless I receive more assurance than I have of your intentions toward it.... During my sojourn among the publishers I have built up a protective screen against the things they say and write to me, so that sometimes it is hard for me to distinguish between a pat on the back and a kick in the nuts.

This might seem rather tame by current standards, but in the still cozy and gentlemanly atmosphere of Canadian publishing circa 1948 it was the sort of thing that got you immediately stereotyped as one of the world's wild men.

After another series of revisions and rejections — Taylor's reply must have been a model of diplomacy — the fall of 1948 brought a different sort of frustration. Having disposed of Canada's surplus war materials, the War Assets Corporation was being shut down, which meant that Hugh had to find a new job. First, however, he took his one month's severance pay and treated himself to a month of uninterrupted writing, working on some short stories and making an encouraging start on the novel about his navy experiences that he hadn't been able to get under way in Quebec City. But none of this was bringing money into the household economy, and he was down to his last dollar when he managed to get a position as a punch press inspector at the Massey-Harris plant on King Street.

Unfortunately, this turned out to be a less than ideal job for an aspiring author. It required shift work, which completely messed up the schedule he had become used to, and he soon learned that coming home with the sound of punch presses reverberating in his head wasn't the best preparation for a productive writing stint. Frustrated with both his job and his inability to write, he realized that he simply could not support his family while trying to prove that he had the makings of a professional author somewhere within him. It was time for another serious talk with Alice, and after a discussion that must have left both of them feeling depressed about the future, she agreed once again to take the children back to her parents' farm.

Living in cheap hotels and rooming-houses in downtown Toronto, working at poorly paid clerking jobs at a succession of different firms, he plugged away at his writing. Collins gave *Cabbagetown* a final brush-off but seemed interested in the uncompleted navy novel that he had put aside after the latest break-up of his family. When he picked it up again, Hugh was surprised by how good it seemed, and he spent all of the next weekend writing the final quarter of what he now called "Landlubber Lying Down Below," a title evoked by memories of a favourite song from student days at Queen Alexandra School. Expecting nothing more than another series of disappointments like that he had endured after finishing *Cabbagetown*, he dropped off his manuscript at Collins' Avenue Road office one October morning before going to his clerking job at the British-American Oil Company.

Two days later Collins editor Robin Taylor phoned him at work, said they were very excited about the book, and asked if he could come in at the beginning of next week and sign a contract that would include a five-hundred dollar advance royalty payment. Totally stunned by this sudden change in his fortunes, Hugh hesitated a moment before replying that yes, he supposed that he could. Then he put down the phone, walked out of the oil company's offices without a word to anyone and went on a monumental drunk that left him still somewhat hungover when he kept his appointment at Collins. The contract signed, a cheque for five-hundred dollars in his pocket and a genteel lunch with his publishers at the Park Plaza Hotel's roof-top restaurant under his belt, he wasn't at all upset by their suggestion that the novel's title be changed to *Storm Below*: "I didn't care if they called it

Little Women as long as it was to be published." What he did care about was finally being able to afford a typewriter, and with $128 of his advance he purchased an Underwood Noiseless portable that he used for the remainder of his life.

Storm Below takes place on "HMCS *Riverford*," a fictional corvette that is a composite portrait of the similar vessels Garner served on during the Second World War. Given the alacrity with which the book was accepted and rushed into print, Collins obviously considered it a likely commercial success; and when it was published in March 1949, its reviews were generally favourable and it did sell quite well. The book's treatment of its subject-matter elicited a number of fan letters from the likes of former war correspondent Leslie Roberts and H.W. Patterson, managing editor of the *Winnipeg Citizen*. Patterson lauded it for its "honest, yet dramatic picture of the Canadian sailor," and it was clear that with *Storm Below* Hugh's career as a writer had been successfully launched.

Although *Storm Below* does impress as a realistic documentary of life aboard a combat ship, it is otherwise a pretty rough piece of work that attempts to cram too much plot and too many characters into its 224 pages. The dialogue, despite being full of salty sailor's slang, often seems awkward, and the narration is burdened by the frequent use of melodramatic clichés such as "for the first time in his life" and "there was a tension in the air." Garner's depiction of the corvette's officers suffers badly from his typical inability to fashion believable middle and upper-class characters, as this stiff-upper-lip description of why the *Riverford*'s captain prefers to eat alone painfully illustrates:

> If he had been asked why he preferred to eat alone, he would have replied, "Well, it's hard to say. It's not snobbishness exactly — although I'd have a hard time proving it to the others — but it is something which I believe is necessary for the discipline of a ship. I may be wrong, but I believe it because I was brought up to believe it."
>
> If pressed further he might have continued, "You know, what people fail to realize is that I am the chief sufferer from my self-imposed anti-gregariousness. Suppose, now, that I were sitting

here with the other officers, and they were skylarking and having a good time — which they certainly would not, were I here — and in order not to be a boor I joined in the fun. Do you know what would happen? Well, I'll tell you: there would be an immediate rise in their friendliness towards me, but a distinct slackening in their respect. In order to keep their respect — which I believe is vitally necessary out here — I will forego their deeper friendship.

Whether these sentiments come from dim memories of his childhood reading of G.A. Henty or more recent viewings of Hollywood films, their stilted expression is characteristic of *Storm Below*'s generally tentative prose style.

Its publication did, however, give Hugh instant credibility as a writer. Magazine editors who had previously rejected his stories without a word of encouragement were suddenly interested in seeing his work, and he made his first sale of a short story, "Some Are So Lucky," to *Canadian Home Journal*. He also discovered that his work had to be tailored to match the requirements of particular publications. When *Journal* editor Mary-Etta Macpherson suggested changes in the story's title, protagonist's name, season of the year, negative treatment of a character and number of "I"s, Garner complied with all her requests — taking out more than one hundred "I"s from what must have been a somewhat excessively first-person narrative — and made a $250 sale as a result. He also sold his first magazine article, a satirical send-up of "Toronto the Terrible," to that city's *National Home Monthly*, where editor Jake Thomas earned his gratitude by paying promptly — if not particularly well — for several journalistic pieces accepted during the next year.

This new willingness to consider criticism and advice on some — if by no means all — matters, which would have been unthinkable for the pre-war Hugh Garner, represented the conjunction of several important developments. For the first time in his experience the navy had, in sometimes forceful fashion, shown him that keeping things in order could give him a sense of creating order in his personal life; the responsibility for the support of a family meant that he couldn't disregard any opportunity to sell his work, no matter how it might be changed in the process;

and he had been genuinely impressed by the improvement in *Cabbagetown* that had occurred as a result of Macmillan's editorial advice. He was now becoming an author in fact as well as fancy, and in the decade to come he would use these new insights and motivations to make himself into one of the most widely read and admired writers in Canada.

For the moment, however, it was time to renew his acquaintance with Alice and the children. He spent the summer of 1949 on the Gallant farm, where he was a particular favourite of Alice's mother. Although she was unilingual and he spoke very little French, they enjoyed being together on her weekly excursions into nearby Campbellton, New Brunswick, where Hugh acted as her chivalrous escort on the sorts of leisurely promenades from shop to shop that his own mother had never had time for. But he got along well with everyone there, as his sister-in-law, Irene Parker, remembers:

> He was such a handsome man that he really caused a commotion in Campbellton. The first time he visited us he was introduced to everyone, and then he saw a statue of St. Theresa in the corner and said "I haven't been introduced to *her*," and made us all laugh. Then he took a big bottle of rum out of his coat and put it on the table, and by the time he and my dad finished it they were good friends. We all loved him, especially the way he liked to laugh and tell little jokes.

The farm also seemed to relax and refresh him, and while he was there he spent much of his time writing a few stories, among them "One Mile of Ice" and "Red Racer," as well as the short novel *Present Reckoning*. He described his working conditions in a letter to *Canadian Home Journal*'s Mary-Etta Macpherson:

> My desk is an old trunk, upon which I place my portable; and my chair is one that I filch from my daughter's kindergarten set. These arrangements work out all right, except that I should have come fitted with a built-in hinge in the region of my seventh vertebrae.
> Most of my day is taken up with anguished runnings between my typewriter and the door to see which of my children was decapitated at the time of the most recent scream. Between trips

downstairs, and time off every five minutes to roll a smoke, I manage, somehow, to end the day with a fair pile of typewritten paper.

What he didn't mention was that he helped to earn his keep by looking after the Gallants' large kitchen garden, which he both enjoyed and, to everyone's surprise, was quite good at.

In September 1949 he returned alone to Toronto, still not confident that he could support a family on what he would be able to earn as a writer. During the summer several of his stories had been rejected by *Chatelaine*, *The Star Weekly*, *National Home Monthly* and, to his chagrin, *Canadian Home Journal*'s Macpherson, who kept asking him for something similar to "Some Are So Lucky" while turning down everything he sent her: obviously he wasn't quite at the point where he could work to order. He also submitted several stories to Robert Weaver at the CBC, who in his rejection letter advised him that shorter fiction about fifteen minutes in broadcast length was what the network needed. Several rejections, many letters and half-a-year later, Weaver would buy "Our Neighbours the Nuns" and eventually become Garner's most important contact with the upper echelons of the literary establishment.

Weaver, born in 1921 in Niagara Falls, Ontario, came from a solidly middle-class background that included several writers as well as many avid readers. He served in the air force and the army during the Second World War and then graduated from the University of Toronto with a degree in English in 1948. His first job at the CBC involved working on a variety of literary and other programmes, which eventually led to the creation of Anthology, the network's major literary showcase from 1953 to 1983. He also founded *The Tamarack Review*, which from 1956 to 1981 was one of the most important Canadian literary periodicals, and edited important collections such as (with Helen James) *Canadian Short Stories* (1952) and (with William Toye) *The Oxford Anthology of Canadian Literature* (1973). But at the time Hugh met him Weaver was, like himself, just getting started on a long and productive career, and for the remainder of his life

Garner would rely on Weaver's knowledgeable advice and quiet encouragement.

At this time Hugh also acquired a New York literary agent, Willis Kingsley Wing, who he hoped would help him break into the lucrative American markets. In the late 1940s and early 1950s, when he often despaired of finding Canadian buyers for his best work, Hugh seriously considered moving to the United States, and he once went so far as to inquire about immigration procedures at the U.S. consulate in Toronto. He abandoned the idea when he learned that International Brigade veterans were automatically rejected, although he continued to submit his books, stories and articles to American publishers until the mid-1950s, by which time their uniformly negative response permanently discouraged his efforts in this direction.

His brief career as one of Wing's authors sparked an exchange of letters that throws some light on Garner's growing awareness of the realities of authorship. On the one hand, he was anxious to make money. In October of 1949 he wrote Wing that

> Right at the moment I am desperately short of money, and this factor is coloring my point of view.... My wife and children are still down in Quebec, because I cannot afford to bring them back here; and though I do not like crying poverty, I want to make you acquainted with this so that you will know my eagerness to sign anything that will get me a few hundred dollars *fast*.

And in January 1950 he thanked Wing for "letting me know about the plethora of teen-age stories, I will avoid them like the plague," with reference to his story "Coming Out Party."

On the other hand, Hugh was also concerned about gaining literary recognition for his more serious work. He wrote Wing that he considered stories such as "One-Two-Three Little Indians" "prestige pieces" which, "though they may not make me much money they may help to build me a reputation." During 1949-1952 he often sent his less commercially saleable stories to magazines which paid very little or even nothing at all — usually after first submitting them to the better-paying markets — simply in order to maintain his credentials as a literary writer.

Still doubtful of his ability to pay the monthly rents being asked for even the cheapest apartments, and anxious to bring his family back to Toronto, he borrowed three hundred dollars from his mother and made a down payment on a home-made house trailer parked on a lot at 492 Danforth Road in the eastern suburb of Scarborough, "really just a long single room on wheels," into which the now reunited family moved in November 1949. Alice was less than delighted with the plumbing arrangements — an outdoor privy supplemented by a chamber-pot for the children — and the kitchen consisted of a cold-water sink and a two-burner hotplate. But they only had to pay five dollars a month for the rental of the lot, which did make it possible for them to get by on Hugh's income from writing. Here the Garners spent what he would later describe as undoubtedly the worst Christmas of his life, with the family shivering in the cold, leaky trailer because he had decided to splurge on a duck — rather than some extra bags of coke for the stove — as a treat for their holiday dinner.

His earnings slowly inched their way upward as he began to get a better idea of what editors really wanted. He sold stories to *Chatelaine*, *Liberty* and *National Home Monthly* and, through no fault of his own, sold his first story to Robert Weaver at the CBC in March 1950. Having not heard from him about his decision on "Our Neighbours the Nuns," Garner telephoned Weaver from a tavern and poured forth several minutes of inebriated abuse. Weaver, at the time a young and by no means self-confident editor who certainly did not want to offend anyone, even an abusive drunk, waited for a pause in this tirade and interjected, "But Mr. Garner, I don't think you've read my letter."

"What letter?" Hugh yelled.

"The letter in which I said that I want to buy your story if you'll make a few changes in it," Weaver replied. He had written to the 21 Winnifred Avenue home of Annie Garner, which Hugh was using as his mailing address until his family found more permanent living accommodations; the letter was sitting there unopened.

There was a long period of silence at the other end of the line. Finally a much softer and apologetic voice asked, "Do you still want to talk to me after what I've said to you?"

The much-relieved Weaver answered, only partially in jest, "Of course, Mr. Garner, I'm an editor, and editors have no feelings."

A much-abashed Garner soon appeared in Weaver's office to apologize and make the necessary revisions, thus beginning a relationship that would become an important element in his career as a writer. From now on he would offer his stories to the CBC before submitting them to magazines, and would in this way earn at least two cheques for most of his shorter fiction.

There was a more serious misunderstanding with *Maclean's*, which had commissioned him to do a piece on the stately mansions and sinful flesh-pots of Toronto's Jarvis Street. The magazine's new managing editor, Pierre Berton, was less than enthusiastic about Hugh's impressionistic approach to what he thought should be a solidly factual treatment, and the article was finally published pseudonymously and Garner's fee cut in half. This left him with a permanent grudge against *Macleans's*, Berton and the excessive respect for facts, with this last prejudice steering his journalistic efforts toward essays and "think pieces" rather than investigative reporting.

The year 1950 also saw the publication of two more novels, although for completely different reasons he was unsatisfied with both of them. Collins offered to bring out *Cabbagetown* as a paperback and, by now sick to death of revising it, Garner let them publish a much-abridged version in which he had made major changes in the book's content and message. The novel was nonetheless a big hit with the public: it wasn't long before it sold 45,000 copies and, most unusually, was receiving feature reviews in publications that ordinarily disdained to notice original paperbacks.

The 1950 edition of *Cabbagetown* leaves out most of Ken Tilling's political experiences and ideas, omits the episode with the overly friendly social-work volunteer, and ends when he is shot to death by the police after a bungled attempt at an armed robbery. It does, however, contain some added dramatic and humorous passages that Collins had asked him to work in, such as this comic account of an attempted eviction, which was dropped when Garner's original version appeared in 1968:

> The bailiff ... made another attack on the door with the axe, helped this time by Corrigan who had his own dignity to regain. When it seemed that the door must give way, the two heaving and tugging figures were suddenly drenched with the contents of a pail of water emptied on their heads by a mop-haired virago who had returned, unnoticed, to the battlements above. With gasps and sputters of surprise the attacking force again retreated.
>
> "That's the stuff, Mrs. Gaffey," cried a voice from the audience, "but next time use the other pot." Mrs. Gaffey accepted the applause like a trouper, smiling at the audience through her teeth.
>
> "I'll get the police!" shouted the bedraggled bailiff, his dignity running down his back in rivulets. He shook his fist at the upstairs window.
>
> "That'll help to cool you off, but the next time the water might be hot," warned the victorious Mrs. Gaffey.

The bantering tone of episodes such as this and the more melodramatic accounts of Ken's criminal activities produced what is in many respects a livelier portrayal of Cabbagetown than the more autobiographical novel Hugh originally wrote. But regardless of the intrinsic merits of the 1950 version, he was always dismissive about what had happened to a book that was really a part of himself rather than anything as objectively distanced as a "novel," and it was a great day in his life when the original manuscript was finally published eighteen years later.

An entirely different set of circumstances surrounded the production of *Waste No Tears*, released under the *nom de plume* of "Jarvis Warwick" (derived from one of his favourite watering holes, the Warwick Hotel on Jarvis Street) for a fly-by-night company called Export Publishing Enterprises Limited, which also commissioned pseudonymous quickies from "John Holmes" (Raymond Souster) and "Alice K. Doherty" (Ted Allan). This "Novel About the Abortion Racket," as it was subtitled, was issued just in time to be almost completely destroyed when Export's warehouse burned down in the fall of 1950; as a result, it is by far the rarest book in the Garner canon. Since it was also written for a publisher whose sole editorial concern was that sex be prominently featured, it is also by far the raciest, as this extract — the first time any portion of the book has been reprinted — demonstrates. The protagonist, "Tom Matterson," has just been seduced by his landlady, "Nora Ranning:"

> During the next few months I practiced, with some of the young girls of the neighborhood, all that Nora Ranning taught me of the art of love. I began to feel like a regular Don Juan, and that every young woman I met was a potential mistress. Things went their merry way until the evening Nora came home early from a party and found me in bed with a girl who lived down the street.
>
> The girl and I were so engrossed with one another that we were unaware Nora was in the house until she opened the bedroom door and looked in on us.
>
> "So this is what goes on, is it?" she asked. Her question was almost a snarl.
>
> Neither the girl or I answered the woman's question.
>
> "Who is this dirty little slut?" she shouted, advancing across the floor.
>
> The girl hid her head beneath the covers.
>
> "Get her out of here!" Nora screamed. "You're not making a whorehouse out of my home!"
>
> I laughed then. It sounded funny coming from her.

Although it has few other points of interest, *Waste No Tears* is certainly proof of its author's increasing professionalism, since he was paid four hundred dollars for writing something that took little of his time and amply fulfilled its publisher's admittedly less than exacting requirements.

In the fall of 1950 the Garners moved to what would be the first of three flats they rented on the Toronto Islands, where the residents prided themselves on being "the damndest gang of nonconformists ever gathered together," as he later described them. For the next three years they lived the moderately "bohemian" life of the Islands community, taking the ferry across the bay to downtown Toronto when necessary but also enjoying a small-town atmosphere where the local police were known as "the Keystone Kops" and the Manitou Hotel operated "the only beer parlour in Ontario where the patrons have to watch out for kids on tricycles riding around the tables."

Garner was one of the regulars, and with fellow Islands resident Ollie Plunkett was part of a group that enjoyed playing word games such as "Ghost," with the losers contributing a quarter to the communal beer-buying fund in the middle of the table. Plunkett remembers him as

> a heck of a nice guy, full of stories about where he'd been and what he'd done, always good for a laugh. He loved to play those word games, and he was really good at them, too. When it was closing time at the Manitou he often invited the bunch of us back to his flat, where we'd carry on until all hours. I used to wonder when he did his writing.

The Garners, children and all, also went to the movies two or three times a week, spurred on by the free chinaware given away at each performance, and eventually accumulated enough dishes to ease Hugh's guilt about his tendency to drop them when he was on one of his periodic binges.

The year 1951 saw Garner publish the remarkable total of seventeen short stories, several of them among his best. "The Conversion of Willie Heaps" finally found a home in the prestigious literary magazine *Northern Review*, was a co-winner of its annual prize for the best short story and in the following year was selected for inclusion in Martha Foley's *Best American Short Stories, 1952*. Three more titles received honorable mentions: "The Yellow Sweater" from *Chatelaine*, "A Couple of Quiet Young Guys" from *The Canadian Forum* and "Our Neighbours the Nuns" from *Northern Review*. With a track record such as this, a writer would now be assured of getting some financial help from the Canada Council and probably a provincial arts council as well; but in 1951 there were still six years to come before the establishment of the former, and it would be even longer before the provinces began to take an interest in supporting their indigenous artists.

The year 1951 was also marked by the publication of his fourth novel, *Present Reckoning*, which Collins brought out as an original paperback in the same "White Circle Pocket Edition" line that had hosted *Cabbagetown*'s début. *Present Reckoning* is a much less polished narrative of a returned war veteran's tragic involvement with a now-married old flame, and lumbers to a melodramatic climax in which their adultery is punished by the death of her baby. There are a number of autobiographical aspects to the story — the protagonist bones up on psychopathology in the library and later concludes that he is doomed to superficial relationships with women — that make it still of interest to students of Garner; but on its own terms the novel is basically a pot-boiler that, like *Waste No Tears*, exhibits little more than the ability to write quickly while maintaining a certain minimal standard of professional competence. Its opening pages may catch something of Hugh's feelings about Toronto upon coming out of Union Station in 1945:

> Letting his gaze take in the shortened view of the city he felt again the involuntary hatred of it that he had almost forgotten; remembering it as it had been, something that he had to fight, an enemy of brick and stone and smug condescension.
>
> It had not changed; the same dull, black taxis stood against the curb, the same dirty streets were at his feet, the same welter of poles and wires fenced in the new buildings that stood like interjections between the old, baroque business houses of the century before. The hotel — Largest in the British Empire — squatted sullenly against the opposite sidewalk, daring those leaving the station to pass it by without a glance.... To him it symbolized the city: smug, part good taste and bad, a brave thing formed of a maladmixture of decency and sham.

Perhaps the single most impressive demonstration of Garner's new-found facility for rapid writing took place on a summer's evening in 1951 when he realized that he was broke and the rent about to come due. The first thing that occurred to him was to write a short story, and he didn't have time for anything too fancy. As he would often do even when not under severe time pressure, he used someone he knew quite well as his protagonist: his mother, whom he imagined taking a very short rail journey that was nonetheless a great adventure for her.

"A Trip for Mrs. Taylor" — the choice of name no doubt largely determined by its alliterative echoing of "Trip," but perhaps also a subconscious remembrance of his mother's Yorkshire employers, Taylor's Woollens — was written in less than a day and immediately purchased by *Chatelaine*. The real Annie Garner, who had crossed the ocean in 1919 and found herself condemned to a hard struggle for survival, may well not have recognized herself in the mousily genteel Mrs. Taylor; but by this time Hugh had learned that it was sentiment, not sense or sensitivity, that sold stories to the glossier magazines, and he provided it in spades in this well- crafted bit of fictional fluff.

Perhaps buoyed by this proof of his capacity to please at least some of Canada's magazine editors, he did not attempt to control his indignation when the *Family Herald & Weekly Star* of Montreal turned down the story "One Mile of Ice." Complaining to editor H. Gordon Green about the accompanying rejection letter from an anonymous subordinate, he once again exploded — as he had with Robin Taylor at Collins — with the kind of outburst that was already earning him a reputation for excessive pugnacity:

> Perhaps the story does finish disappointingly to one whose obvious brush with literature has consisted solely of the Pollyanna books, but what is he, she or it doing in an editorial office?
>
> This story was sent to you because you said that you would like to have a Garner story to put into your pages, and I resent very much that it should come back with such a puerile criticism from an obvious moron. He, or she, should be left at their usual task of rejecting articles on making black-currant jam sent in by farm housewives in Pincher Creek, Alberta, and not let loose to vent their old-maid spleen on professional writers.

A more tough-minded editor might have had some fun responding in kind to this presumptuous missive from a "professional writer" of barely three years standing. Green, however, replied apologetically and asked Hugh to submit some other stories, an action he probably regretted when Garner responded to editor R.S. Kennedy's rejection of "The Old Man's Laughter": "I find it impossible to be charitable to Mr. Kennedy, for he, and the other Rover Boys of the Canadian Authors Association, have too long tried to stifle anything that rose above their own mediocrity in Canadian literature."

When the stories he was writing during this period were collected in *The Yellow Sweater and Other Stories* in 1952, many critics found it difficult to understand how the fierce psychological realism of "The Conversion of Willie Heaps" and the cloying sentimentality of "A Trip for Mrs. Taylor" had originated from the same writer. From the standpoint of the cloistered academic, accustomed to thinking of serious authors as dedicated artists immune from anything as mundane as commercial considerations, this was indeed a puzzling phenomenon; but from the perspective of someone with mouths to feed and a small number of very different sources of income, it was the most natural thing in the world. George Woodcock was just about the only reviewer of *The Yellow Sweater and Other Stories* who understood this disparity. He observed that "Mr. Garner is a man with a curious kind of virtuosity which enables him to write up and down the scale of fiction, apparently at will," and even this eminently just assessment occurs in the context of a review which suggests that this sort of verbal legerdemain is not necessarily a good thing.

But the publication of his first short-story collection did help to consolidate Hugh's reputation among his fellow authors, several of whom had by now written to express their enthusiasm for his work. Scott Young had been very impressed by *Storm Below*, and Raymond Souster described *Cabbagetown* as "the most thrilling work of fiction ever written by a Canadian," adding that it even surpassed Morley Callaghan's *Strange Fugitive*. Callaghan himself offered a very encouraging reply when Garner sent him a copy of *The Yellow Sweater and Other Stories* and asked for a recommendation for a Guggenheim Fellowship:

about a week ago I wrote a long piece to the Guggenheim people about your work. ... if there are three good writers of fiction in this country you are certainly one of them, and I couldn't imagine a writer more deserving of a fellowship than you. ... I got a comforting feeling out of your book. I had always felt in my sublime egotism that as a short story writer I had no contemporaries in this country, and now there you are large as life, and twice as contemporary. ... you have about everything you need as a story writer....

This was one of the few times when Hugh's abilities were acknowledged by a writer he respected, and it meant a great deal to him. A quite different form of recognition came his way when in April of 1950 he was invited by D.M. Le Bourdais to serve on the Executive Committee of the Canadian Authors Association branch in Toronto. He declined on the perfectly accurate, if somewhat understated, grounds that "I am not the Executive Committee type, as anyone who knows me will vouch."

Such recognition was all very nice, but it wasn't doing anything for the hand-to-mouth existence that he and his family were leading. Many factors contributed to his decision to concentrate on more remunerative journalistic work, but one of the immediate causes was the failure of *The Yellow Sweater and Other Stories* to earn back its advance from Collins, which as a result declined to publish it as a paperback. With events conspiring to point out to him that even an author of four novels, more than twenty pieces of short fiction and a hard-cover collection of stories still couldn't earn enough to provide for his wife and children, Hugh decided it was time to pursue some of the many journalistic contacts that he had made during his first three years as an active — and by now both fiercely proud and defensive — professional writer.

Chapter Six

Selling Everything You Write (1952-1957)

One of the editors with whom Hugh had become friendly was *Liberty*'s Keith Knowlton, who had bought non-fiction pieces such as "Are Women People," "Don't Send Them to College" and — perhaps the most ridiculously titled article in a career well supplied with them — "The Boom in Bush-League Be-Bop." To be fair, Knowlton had also enthused over the much more substantial short story "One-Two-Three Little Indians," but he was nonetheless most interested in Garner's ability to rapidly churn out readable journalism on an extraordinarily wide range of topics. Knowlton listened to Hugh's description of the hard times he was having and said that he would speak to *Liberty*'s owner, Jack Kent Cooke.

Cooke, even then a wealthy man who would go on to amass a multimillion-dollar fortune in the United States, was in the middle of dissolving his partnership with newspaper mogul Roy Thomson; but it is an indication of his fabled attention to detail that he still took the time to consider how he could make use of Garner's abilities. It was rumoured that Cooke actually preferred employees with drinking problems — 'Always hire drunks, they don't last long but they're grateful for the work and don't ask for much money,' was one widely circulated version of this policy — and it was certainly true that Hugh was grateful for the job, although as far as he was concerned, he was very well paid by the standards of the time.

Cooke's growing corporate empire, which included *Liberty*, radio station CKEY, the Toronto Maple Leaf baseball franchise in the International League and an advertising company, was in need of a jack of all trades to handle its varied public-relations duties; for eighty dollars a week — soon raised to one hundred — Hugh agreed to take them on. Part of his conversation with Cooke summed up his situation as of 1952:

COOKE: What can you do?
GARNER: I can write.
COOKE: I know that; I've read some of your stuff. Can you sell?
GARNER: I have to sell everything I write.

Hugh spent the next year functioning as the "Public Relations Director" for Jack Kent Cooke's various enterpises. This entailed supervising the public-relations people who worked for separate branches of the organization, such as *Liberty*, CKEY and the baseball club, and dealing with his opposite numbers in the media and advertising world. Much of the latter was done at the Toronto Men's Press Club, the favourite watering-hole and social centre for the at the time almost exclusively male members of this profession, where Garner's inability to control his fondness for alcohol soon got him into trouble.

With the steadying influence of his periods of serious novel writing — and rigidly enforced sobriety — no longer a counterbalancing factor, Hugh would have started drinking more heavily no matter what his new occupation; but since he was now dealing with people for whom a couple of drinks were a normal accompaniment to transacting business, he was in effect being encouraged to start his days doing something that he was frequently unable to stop. It didn't take long before even the members of the Press Club — the majority of them newspapermen quite as familiar with tippling as they were with typing — were shocked by his alcoholic antics.

His first brush with the management of the Press Club took place when he passed out after an evening's drinking and was locked into its premises for the night. This wasn't a totally unknown occurrence and would in itself have occasioned only a mild reprimand; but with his by now well-developed nose for making mountains out of molehills, Garner was discovered the next morning sitting in the bar emptying an overlooked bottle of vermouth and was suspended for a short period of time when a perhaps over-zealous employee made a formal complaint to the management.

A few months later he made the mistake of getting drunk while attending the Club's annual family Christmas party and went home with absolutely no memory of the occasion's final hours. The next time he tried to enter, however, he was told that he had been barred until his case could be considered by the membership committee. When he asked what he had done, he was informed that he had loudly and persistently addressed the member acting as Santa Claus by his real name, thus ruining the party for its younger participants. This serious breach of etiquette led to his suspension "forever and a day;" from now on, Hugh's serious social drinking would have to be done at public bars and taverns.

At the beginning of 1953 Cooke, probably not overjoyed at the public behaviour of his Public Relations Director (he once ushered a distinguished visitor into Garner's office only to find its occupant snoozing away happily on the floor), shifted him to his new acquisition, *Saturday Night*, which he had purchased along with the other holdings of Consolidated Press. Here Hugh was dubbed an "Associate Editor," although his main function was to contribute an article to each issue of the then-weekly magazine on a subject of his choice.

Shortly after assuming his new position, he was asked to help select the winner of the 1952 Ryerson Fiction Award. With Lorne Pierce and A.W. Trueman, two charter members of that "establishment" Garner often excoriated, he served on a committee that inexplicably failed to find a sufficiently distinguished title in a year when both Ernest Buckler's *The Mountain and the Valley* and Ethel Wilson's *The Equations of Love* were published. Although the Ryerson Fiction Award wasn't all that prestigious a prize — it was only given on an average of every other year and then often went to mediocre books such as Evelyn Richardson's *Desired Haven* and Jeann Beattie's *Blaze of Noon* — being asked to serve as one of its selectors was a minor honour that Hugh was perfectly happy to accept.

The staff of *Saturday Night* soon learned that their newest addition was not going to be just another garden-variety magazine editor. It was Jack Kent Cooke's often expressed opinion that Hugh was "a genius," and he treated him more like a friend than an employee: during the summer months they tooled all over town in Cooke's snazzy white Cadillac convertible while they joked around together like a couple of high-school kids. This unusual relationship between a magazine owner and a staff writer had two important consequences: the "genius" didn't bother to come in to the office for increasingly long periods of time, and his nominal superiors at *Saturday Night* knew they would be in effect contradicting the head of the organization if they tried to do anything about it.

When Garner was there, his co-workers never counted on him being around for long. His second-floor office offered a view of Richmond Street, on the other side of which was a Liquor Control Board of Ontario store. The office's French windows opened out onto a small balcony, and in good weather Hugh could stand out there and keep his eyes peeled for any of his drinking buddies who might appear. When they did, often lurching down the street as they tried to make it to the liquor store, he would bellow something along the lines of "Hey you bum, so you're going to get smashed again eh, wait a minute, I'll be right down," and disappear for the rest of the day.

James Bacque was at *Saturday Night* for a few months as a junior editor while Garner was there and remembers being totally in awe of him; so awed, in fact, that he found communication very difficult:

> When he finally did appear in the office — he hadn't showed up for about a month — I was too naive and thunderstruck to realize that he was drunk. I tiptoed into his office and there he was, sitting behind his desk and looking pretty sick. "Mr. Garner sir, Mr. Garner

sir," I said to get his attention, and asked him some inane question about Dostoevsky, because I thought I had noticed some similarities between his writing and Dostoevsky's. He said something like "Oh, fuck off," and I did.

So much for literary chit-chat, at least when Garner was drinking. A couple of months later, when Bacque was cleaning out his desk after a sharp disagreement with Cooke, Hugh stuck his head through the doorway and said, "I hear you've been fired. It's a good thing." What Bacque remembers most clearly about this is that it wasn't said maliciously, but more in the manner of someone who had noticed something interesting and felt compelled to verbalize it. Years later he and Garner would meet fairly often and get along very well, and Bacque would realize that what was often taken as evidence of his abrasiveness was actually a combination of a droll sense of humour and a lack of conventional social inhibitions.

At *Saturday Night* Hugh did, in between drinking bouts with his cronies, write many of the autobiographical pieces that would eventually turn up as component parts of *One Damn Thing After Another!*, among them the description of the stubbornly independent International Brigades soldier Reid, previously referred to in Chapter Three. This was a favourite of his — he also used it almost verbatim in the 1960 *Star Weekly* series on his Spanish Civil War experiences — and unlike most of his *Saturday Night* writing, there was nothing the least bit facetious about it. A more typical approach for him would be to angle for a humorous or nostalgic slant on matters about which he could be somewhat more serious in other contexts.

As an example of how he could create contrasting treatments of the same experience, it is interesting to compare his two versions of the episode with the horse that represented his initial brush with authority on the *Lunenburg*. In *One Damn Thing After Another!*, published in 1973, he blames these shennanigans on his getting drunk while on a supply detail, and although the approach is certainly humorous, it concludes by admitting that he was given a mild punishment. In a *Saturday Night* piece written some twenty years earlier, "Let's Splice the Brain Mace" (a play on the expression "Splice the main brace," the naval term for a double issue of rum), he makes the protagonist an unidentified shipmate and adds a prelude in which this person cruises the Nova Scotia countryside in a vain effort to find the crew a new mascot. On his way back to the ship he spies the supply wagon horse and goes into his Ben Hur routine, after which the same exchange with the captain occurs. There are no serious consequences at all in this version, but only a humorous coda focusing on the wagon's civilian driver, who deplores the "strange whirl of chance that had brought him into contact with such an irresponsible outfit as the navy." Where the 1973 account, although certainly intended to be amusing, leads up to the more serious charges for which he was sentenced to the detention barracks, the 1953 version is played strictly — and anonymously — for laughs.

Something much less funny occurred while the Garners were still living on the Toronto Islands. The heavy rains of the spring of 1953 overwhelmed the community's septic tanks and polluted its drinking water, as a result of which Hugh contracted hepatitis. Thinking at first that it was just another symptom of his frequent hangovers, he ignored the illness until one of his *Saturday Night* co-workers told him his face was turning yellow. After following doctor's orders and taking a rest from both work and drinking, his hepatitis cleared up and he went back to his usual lifestyle. From this point on, however, he began to experience a number of recurring medical problems: stomach troubles and headaches, at first mild but gradually becoming more annoying over time, would bother him for most of the remainder of his life.

In the fall of 1953 he made his first appearance on the Toronto airwaves in the role of distinguished author, although it was only in the early 1960s that he became a familiar figure to radio and television audiences. A CJBC reporter interviewed him in an Adelaide Street coffee shop, and the two simply didn't hit it off; it may have been the fact that the reporter fancied himself more interesting than his interviewee, or it may just have been that during this period Hugh needed something more than coffee to get through the day. In September and October he appeared on CBC Radio's Court of Opinion, a rather stuffy panel show which debated non-burning issues such as "Do universities need more characters among the student body?" and "Has present-day living reduced the number of lasting friendships?" To the first, Garner answered, "They need more radicals such as Jesus Christ and Freud;" as for the second, he described himself as a man with "thousands of acquaintances but no friends," a sentiment repeated in his autobiography that suggests his many statements about how he loved being a loner should be taken with several grains of salt. Both his speaking tone and his choice of words seemed hesitant on Court of Opinion, and he was not asked to become one of its regulars.

Toward the end of 1953 the Garners moved into an apartment at 474 Kingston Road, where they would live for the next eleven years. Here Hugh could simply hop on a streetcar and go downtown, and Alice would not have to worry about him falling off one of the Islands ferries during their sometimes rough crossings. They now acquired their first television set, and for the next month watched everything from Dragnet to quiz shows to The Lone Ranger before beginning to make more discriminating choices. Garner was very impressed by the quality of some of the dramatic productions he saw on TV Playhouse, Fireside Theatre, Ford Theatre and Medallion Theatre and often wrote about them in the "Television" column he wrote for *Saturday Night* once or twice a month.

One of their apartment's features was its very long hallway, down which he often had difficulty navigating when returning home after a hard day's drinking. His daughter Barbara has vivid memories of listening to him slowly and profanely negotiate his way down the hallway one evening, after which a loud crash and a violent outburst of swearing announced that the bottle he had brought home was no more. But by this time Hugh had acquired his very own personal bootlegger, who for a fee approximately double the retail cost made deliveries at all hours, and thus the loss was soon made good.

By the late spring of 1954 Garner was spending almost all of his weekdays drinking with his friends, many of them *Toronto Telegram* journalists, at the Savarin Hotel on Bay Street, which became the very lightly disguised "Safari" in his story "Losers Weepers:"

> We used to have a table near the service bar at the rear of the men's beer parlor at the Safari, up against the dropped partition that separated the Men Only section from the Ladies & Escorts Room, as they used to call it then. This open-topped partition inhibited the sober customers at our table, but I was constantly getting myself cut off or kicked out for too-loud swearing. One time the whole table, around which we'd often crowd seven or eight chairs, was cut off because we were singing dirty wartime lyrics to the tune of *Sing Us Another One Do.*

The CBC's Robert Weaver once met him there for what was supposed to have been a luncheon date, and was put through a kind of initiation rite aimed at discovering if he was a regular guy or just another one of the "matriarchs, spinsters and fruity young men" Garner thought of as dominating the Canadian literary establishment:

> We had originally arranged to meet at a restaurant, but that morning he phoned and asked if I could meet him at the Savarin. When I got there, he was sitting in the men's beverage room with a table of his friends. He introduced me in not very flattering terms — "a snob editor from the CBC," I think it was — and got me a couple of draft beers. Then he disappeared into the bar next door, where he was buying shots of rye and getting progressively drunker, and came back once in a while to see how I was getting along. I sat there talking to his friends for over an hour, and eventually I realized we weren't going to have lunch and went back to my office. By surviving this I think I passed what had been a little test, and our relationship went on from there.

Such a behaviour pattern, of which this episode's failure to eat was typical, couldn't help but have serious consequences. During a drinking bout at the Kingston Road apartment Hugh suddenly started vomiting blood and was rushed to Sunnybrook

Veteran's Hospital. There he also had an alcoholic seizure, at first misdiagnosed as an epileptic fit, and spent some time in the psychiatric wing where he was given a battery of tests that proved largely negative. What was clear was that his drinking was completely out of control: Alice told her children that from now on they would have to realize that their father had a serious illness, and they would simply have to try to put up with it as best they could.

Life now took on something of a Jekyl-and-Hyde character around the Garner household. When Hugh was on a binge, which could last as long as a month, he became a boorish slob who made everyone's existence hell; when he was sober, which was still the majority of the time, he tried to make up for this by being a delightful and considerate father. As his daughter Barbara describes it:

> When he wasn't drinking, he was totally straight and meticulous and organized. When he was drinking, he was so belligerent and mouthy that he just made a complete ass out of himself. But we couldn't stay mad at him, because when he got over it he would be a great father again, lively and happy and full of fun. Until the final years of his life he would try to fight off the urge to drink in other ways, often by going for long walks. He used to set off whistling, and we knew that if he came home still whistling everything was going to be o.k.

As Barbara and Hugh, Jr. grew older, their father began to enjoy playing games such as Scrabble and Monopoly with them, entering into these contests with a childish enthusiasm that didn't entirely mask his fundamental competitiveness: he always played to win, and he wasn't the sort of parent who let you take back your mistakes.

But while his family was able to make allowances for the possibility that today's jovial joker might turn into tomorrow's depressed drinker, it had become obvious to everyone at *Saturday Night* that Hugh's increasingly disruptive influence could no longer be tolerated in its offices. Together he and Cooke worked out an agreement, dated June 21, 1954, under which Garner was guaranteed his current salary in the form of a drawing account but would work at home and have the fees for his articles and stories chalked up to the credit side of the ledger. This theoretically sound arrangement unfortunately proved to have one fatal flaw: the editors of Cooke's various publications were under no compulsion to accept Hugh's stories and articles, and it wasn't long before some of them — quite possibly in revenge for the inebriated hijinks to which he had subjected them — were rejecting many of his submissions.

Perhaps somewhat sobered by the realization that he had been just as much of a flop as an associate editor as he had been as a public relations director, Hugh spent much of his last two weeks at *Saturday Night* working on a new novel. His brushes with evangelical religion as a child had left him with a permanent dislike for those who claimed to have found God and were anxious to convert others to their views, and "The Conversion of Willie Heaps" had by no means been his last fictional word on the matter. He called the new novel "The Legs of the Lame", a title that reflected his love of alliteration as well as his choirboy's familiarity with biblical passages such as *Proverbs*, xxvi, 7: "The legs of the lame are not equal: so is a parable in the mouth of fools."

Garner unfortunately destroyed the manuscript of "The Legs of the Lame" in the early 1960s. For a writer who tried to waste nothing and recycle material wherever possible this was an extravagant thing to do, a fact that would come home to him when he later decided to write a short story — making use of the same title — about religious mania. But this was his most frustrating failure as a writer, a major novel on a subject about which he felt strongly and thought he had something of importance to say, and he was both baffled and disheartened by its failure to find a publisher.

Initially, remembering how much help Peggy Blackstock had given him when he first submitted *Cabbagetown* to Macmillan, he asked her to look at it and also get the opinion of an outside reader. Both her response and that of the reader were negative, although for quite different reasons, but this time Hugh ignored her suggestions for revision and submitted the manuscript directly to Macmillan. The publishing house rapidly turned it down without any encouraging words, as did the several other firms to which he sent it during the next few years.

Although *One Damn Thing After Another!* contains a concise plot summary of the book, Garner included a more reflective description of its contents in a letter to the firm of Longmans, Green and Company, one of the many publishing houses who rejected "The Legs of the Lame:"

> The theme of the book ... is that a young man, not stupid but emotionally and socially beaten by both himself and society, is taken up by a group of evangelists, and for a short time is on the way to raising himself from his psychological inertia. Then, due in part to the nature of the evangelical group and in part to his own warped suspicions, he breaks off from them and goes back to being what he was.
>
> My protagonist is not a "nice guy" nor is he a heel. He's one of the fellows ... you can see any day of the week in beer parlors or bars, standing on corners watching kids play ball, sitting waiting for a train to carry him somewhere, any bloody where, to escape from himself.

As outlined here, it sounds like a not very promising combination of *Present Reckoning* and "The Conversion of Willie Heaps," and it's not surprising that publisher after publisher turned it down.

There was trouble on another front as well. After a year of his special arrangement with Cooke, June of 1955 found Garner in the position of having drawn $2,500 more in salary than he had been credited with for his work, as a result of which Cooke told him he was no longer on the payroll. Freed from what had turned out to be an unworkable system, Hugh resumed selling his work on a free-lance basis to other publications beside Cooke's, and finally made up the deficit in 1958. It was a point of honour with him not to owe money to anyone, particularly Cooke, to whom he was always grateful for giving him a job at a difficult time in his life. In the letter that accompanied his last payment Garner observed: "I am very meticulous about paying my debts. This is probably a fear-inspired bit of behaviorism stemming from a proletarian background. Whatever it is, I have always believed that nobody who owes money is ever really independent — and independence is something I cherish." The persistence of such attitudes despite his interest in socialist ideas — he encountered Proudhon's catch-phrase "Property is theft" many times during the 1930s, for example — goes some way toward explaining why Hugh always had problems reconciling his instinctive hatred of class-based distinctions and injustices with the strictures about fulfilling your part of the social contract that he inherited from his forebears. Others might want to make a revolution *for* the proletariat, but if you already *were* a proletarian, you knew that staying out of debt was one sure way of keeping the bourgeoisie from bothering you. As Garner's dislike of the middle class grew stronger — he actually developed a kind of grudging respect for the upper class as he grew older — his determination to have as little as possible to do with it turned into what can only be called working-class chauvinism, and manifested itself in some strange literary and social occurrences in the years to come.

Hugh's output during this period included a great deal of work that was written strictly for the money. He wrote five entries for the *Encyclopedia Canadiana*, boning up on the subjects of burial grounds, cremation, undertaking, embalming and — a somewhat livelier topic — the Toronto Stock Exchange. He also made quite a bit of money writing some public relations and advertising copy for British-American Oil, the John B. Smith Lumber Company and Ed Provan, "the custom tailor."

His best market during this time was *Liberty*, where as "Dr. E. Jackson Francis" he proferred advice to *Liberty*'s readers about their marital problems, a subject he also addressed in its pages with pseudonymous articles such as "My Wife Is Frigid" and "My Husband Is Impotent;" as in this case, Garner often wrote on both sides of the issue in question. Frank Rasky had taken over the magazine's editorship in 1954, and he found Hugh a valued if occasionally unpredictable contributor:

He'd usually check with me before writing an article, but one time he didn't. He brought in a piece that just wasn't right for a popular magazine, and I had to say "I'm sorry, but I can't use it." He said "What!?" in that growly voice of his, took the article, tore it up and threw it in the wastebasket. That made me upset, and I said "Wait a minute, take it back, you can sell it somewhere else." But he just stomped out the door. It was only much later that he told me he had a carbon copy of the article at home.

Garner would later become the talk of Toronto's journalistic community when he had six articles published in the December 1958 issue of *Liberty*. One, "Deal Me Out of the Xmas Card Game," was actually attributed to Hugh Garner, while the other five were psuedonymous: "Murder by Manitoba's Praying Zealots" by "Morgan Winters;" "How You Can Ease Migraine Headaches" by "E. Jervis Bloomfield;" facing pieces entitled "I'm Sorry I Married an Older Woman" by "Trevor Gamble" and "I'm Glad I Married an Older Woman" by "Peter Thurston;" and "Canada's Unguided Missiles — Drinking Drivers" by his favourite *nom de plume*, "Jarvis Warwick."

At the Kingston Road apartment he worked in the master bedroom at a large oak desk, next to which stood a four-drawer filing cabinet and a steel typewriter table for his Underwood "Noiseless." As an apprentice author he had usually hand-written his first drafts, but by now he was such a proficient typist that he did them directly on the typewriter, after which he made the necessary corrections by hand and then typed a final draft. Those who actually saw him type were struck by his fierce concentration as he hunched over the machine, swinging his shoulders at it almost like a boxer working on a punching bag.

He had no hard and fast rules regarding hours of work or number of words written — he might skip several days and then spend a week hard at it from early in the morning to late at night — but he did try to observe a few basic principles of preparation: he always shaved, bathed and brushed his teeth before starting a stint at his desk, and when writing a novel tried to end the day in the middle of a difficult section rather than at the end of an easy one.

He allowed himself one cup of coffee in the morning and another in the afternoon, and also drank copious amounts of tea while he chain-smoked the unfiltered cigarettes that quickly turned the bedroom's atmosphere into a murky haze. But if he didn't get started in the morning, that would usually be it for the day; eating a normal, sit-down lunch, as opposed to the snacks he would grab when hard at work, meant that there would be no further attempts at writing.

The summer of 1955 brought an invitation to attend the Canadian Writers' Conference at Queen's University in Kingston, Ontario, held from July 28 to 31. This major literary event, funded by the Rockefeller Foundation, brought the period's most prominent authors — Earle Birney, Morley Callaghan, Irving Layton, Dorothy Livesay and Miriam Waddington among them — together with academics, publishers and other media people to examine the theme of "The Writer, His Media, and the Public." Given that he was a relative outsider among the assembled guests, many of whom represented the "matriarchs, spinsters and fruity young men" he had already managed to alienate in his short but turbulent career as an author, an observer familar with Garner's past history might have made two predictions: he would drink too much and he would at some point make a public spectacle out of himself.

He did his best to live up to the first of these by immediately searching out the serious drinkers among the delegates, and discovered that Vancouver lawyer and short-story writer William McConnell had come prepared with his own bottle. After assisting in the emptying of this, Hugh wandered around chatting with everyone from F.R. Scott to a group of *Maclean's* writers and then went to his room for a nap. Before passing out on his bed he learned that his room-mates were "two quiet academic types" from the University of New Brunswick, Fred Cogswell and Desmond Pacey, who for the remainder of the conference had to put up with his late hours and booze-befuddled preparations for retiring. Pacey may have been getting his own back when in the 1961 edition of his *Creative Writing in Canada*, at the time the standard work on the subject, he made only two brief mentions of Garner in a book that contains extensive discussions of authors of the calibre of Mazo De la Roche, Thomas Raddall and Will R. Bird.

That evening Hugh revived and went on a pub crawl with some of the other attendees, Morley Callaghan among them, and ended up at a party at the home of Queen's professor Malcolm Ross, where his vocal complaints about the inadequate supply of beer probably did not endear him to his host. He carried on in this manner for the rest of the conference, attending its morning sessions but often adjourning to Kingston's beer parlours thereafter, and is seldom referred to in *Writing in Canada* (1956), the permanent record of the conference's proceedings that George Whalley later edited. The one context in which his name does appear, however, suggests that he may have made a verbal as well as a visual impression on some of his fellow delegates.

In a discussion of the writer's relations with the media — which included Pacey, F.R. Scott, Ralph Allen and John Gray and was chaired and summarized by Henry Kreisel — the conversation turned to the subject of government subsidies and endowments:

It was felt that additional subsidies were needed, and Mr. Scott said that magazines were in fact subsidized by the Post Office. Mr. Allen denied this, although he said he didn't have the exact figures; in fact, he thought the Post Office was making money from magazines. Scholarly books certainly have been subsidized for some time and the results were good. But Mr. Garner said that creative writing could not be subsidized, that the wrong people would be subsidized. That, said Mr. Scott, was a defeatist attitude. Who would be on the committee? asked Mr. Garner. They wouldn't choose anything of Hugh Garner's. They'd subsidize people who were safe. Then what about Garner? "The hell with that mob." I asked Mr. Allen to clarify his remark made yesterday that he did not think subsidies were now right, that they would be right again ten years hence, but that now there should not be any hand-outs from the government. I asked him to clarify the point, but back came the answer from Mr. Garner that during the last ten years Allen had got a steady job.

Although a few sharp disagreements had occurred in the course of the conference's proceedings — Irving Layton had been in characteristically argumentative form — the general tone was certainly quite genteel. Thus the interjection of "The hell with that mob," a phrase which would have struck many of those present as proof that a time warp had deposited them in the middle of a 1930s gangster film, probably had quite an effect amid this sedate atmosphere of civilized discussion among gentlefolk; it certainly had an effect on Kreisel, who otherwise reports his group's conversation through paraphrase rather than direct quotation. It should also be noted that Garner's rejection of the idea of government subsidy certainly did not deter him from making several applications for such assistance a few years later.

As the weekend drew to a close, Hugh spent more and more of his time in communion with a bottle, and by the final day of the conference he was in very bad shape. An *ad hoc* group that would also be returning to Toronto by train took responsibility for getting him back home, and everyone had assembled at the Kingston railroad station when a series of events right out of a slapstick comedy made the day one that they would all remember.

The train *en route* to Montreal pulled into the station just after the train bound for Toronto, which led to a certain amount of bustle and confusion. In the midst of this, Hugh suddenly disappeared from his group, and total panic ensued: fearing that he might have wandered onto the Montreal train, his companions went racing through its cars, looking under and over seats as well as in them, barging into lavatories without regard for sexual distinctions and generally creating total havoc. When this failed to reveal his whereabouts, they turned their attentions to the Toronto train and finally discovered Garner sleeping peacefully in a corner seat.

Much relieved, they all sat down to enjoy a relaxing ride home. But Hugh woke up when the train made a short stop at Trenton, and it was only with the aid of Earle Birney's bottle of tequila and the sympathetic attentions of Robert Weaver and Morley

Callaghan that their now-boisterous charge could be kept in his seat. They couldn't keep his mouth entirely shut, however, as two priests who got on at another stop soon learned. "Hey you guys," he yelled as he pointed to a by now thoroughly embarrassed Callaghan, "I bet you don't know who *this* is!" When the priests politely admitted that they did not, Hugh announced to everyone within earshot: "This is Morley Callaghan, and he's done more for you guys than any writer in Canada!"

If Garner's main accomplishment at the Canadian Writers' Conference had been to reinforce the growing body of opinion that considered him a public nuisance, he had while in Kingston spoken to a group with which he felt much more comfortable. Invited to address a journalism class at Kingston Penitentiary, Hugh found them familiar with his work — especially *Cabbage-town* — and a serious and attentive audience. In years to come he would often speak to prison groups, especially after the acquisition of his papers by Queen's meant that he made at least one trip per year to the Kingston area.

One of the issues that had been addressed at the Canadian Writers' Conference was the declining quality of, and prospects for, the nation's magazines. Many authors had decried the increasing difficulty of selling their best short stories to consumer magazines, which were declining in numbers, profitability and intrinsic quality as the impact of television and American competition began to be felt. Beginning in 1954, the percentage of total advertising revenue directed to magazines fell steadily; the market share of Canadian consumer magazines went from 28.8 per cent in 1950 to 23.3 per cent in 1959; and the 1950-60 decade was the first one in which the number of magazines going out of business exceeded the number being founded.

The 1959-60 Royal Commission on Publications, more familiarly known as "The O'Leary Commission" for chairman Grattan O'Leary, identified these problems accurately and suggested that magazines be treated as an endangered species; but although some of its recommendations were implemented, periodicals continued to bite the dust. *Canadian Homes* ceased publication in 1962; *Liberty*, after desperately experimenting with a true-confessions format, gave up the ghost in 1964; and by the mid-1960s, *Playboy* took in as much money in Canada as did the seventeen largest English-language domestic consumer magazines combined. In the context of these developments, it was obvious that a writer depending on magazine sales had better add another string to his bow.

Since part of the reason for the decline of magazines was the advent of television, and since Garner was already selling his work to its sister medium, radio, it didn't take him long to begin investigating the possibilties of the new medium. He went to the library, made some notes from a book on television play-writing, and adapted one of his stories into a TV script. Although Hugh was not a superstitious person, his choice of "Some Are So Lucky," his first story to be sold for publication, perhaps indicated that he had faith as well as confidence in the sentiment expressed in its title.

Once again, the story didn't let him down. The CBC TV drama department bought it immediately and was happy to do the same for his adaptation of "A Trip For Mrs. Taylor" a week later. This was obviously an important new source of income for a writer whose productivity had been adversely affected by the onset of his serious drinking problems, not least because it involved the adaptation of existing material rather than the creation of original work. Just as he had often sold the radio rights to his stories to the CBC's Robert Weaver before selling them for publication, so now he would be able to benefit from a second resurrection of some of his strongest stories with a minimum amount of effort.

Hugh had always considered the ability to write convincing dialogue as one of the things that separated the literary sheep from the goats, and in studying the work of John O'Hara he had been fascinated by the way that dialogue alone could convey the essence of a fictional scene. Having striven for this effect in many of his short stories, it now required very little revising to present them in the form of a TV script. A comparison of parallel passages from the short story and TV-script versions of "Some Are

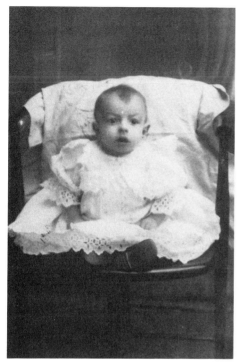

Hugh, six months old, in England

Annie Garner with Ronald and Hugh, 1919

Hugh in his militia dress uniform, *c*. 1930

With his sister June, *c*. 1933

Passport photo, on the eve of departing for Spain, 1937

Taking time out for a haircut in the
trenches during the Spanish Civil War, 1937

Alice in Rivière-du-Loup, *c.* 1941

Hugh and Alice, 1942

In the navy, 1942

The writer hard at work, early 1950s

Hugh and Alice visiting the CNE in the mid 1950s

Hugh and, from left, Alice, Hugh Jr. and Barbara, 1962

As tourists in London's Trafalgar Square, 1970

The author in a pensive mood, 1976

Last photo taken of Hugh, surrounded by his grandchildren, 1979. From left: Robbie, Dean, Carrie, Lana and John

So Lucky" demonstrates the relative ease with which he made this transition.

In the short story, Ethel Blanton is talking with Rod Murphy:

"I guess it's not so lonely for a man. You can always get a girl when you want one, can't you.?"

It sounded like a dirty joke. I nodded my head.

"What business did you say you were in, last night?"

"Insurance," I answered.

"You look pretty prosperous. I guess a lot of people have bought insurance since the war? Of course there's a lot of walking in it — ringing doorbells and things."

"I'm not a salesman," I said, laughing.

"Oh!"

She told me that her insurance collector had a hard time finding her in when he called.

"How much do you carry?"

"Oh, let me see. I never was one for that sort of stuff. I guess it's ten thousand dollars."

I guessed that it would be more like a quarter of that amount.

"What does your husband do, Ethel?"

"He works for a packing company," she answered. "They wanted him to go on the road — selling, you know, but he'd sooner stay in the plant. He's got a good job — they only work a forty hour week."

This translates easily into television terms:

Ethel: I guess it's not so lonely for a man. You can always pick up a girl when you need one, can't you? *(Rod nods but straightens back in his chair.)* What business did you say you were in?

Rod: Insurance.

Ethel: You look pretty prosperous. I guess a lot of people are buying insurance these days? Of course, there's a lot of walking in it — ringing doorbells and things.

Rod: I'm not a salesman. Anyway, things have changed today. There's not so much door-to-door selling as there was when we were kids. Or weekly collecting either.

Ethel: There isn't? An insurance man'd have a hard time finding me in.

Rod: How much insurance do you carry?

> *Ethel: (Places a finger to her lips.)* Let me see. I never was one
> for that kind of stuff. I think it's fifteen thousand dollars. Ernie has
> some group insurance from his union too.
> *Rod: (Stares in disbelief.)* What does your husband do, Ethel?
> *Ethel:* He works for a packing company. They wanted him to
> go on the road — selling, you know, but he'd sooner stay in the
> plant. He's got a good job. They've got a forty hour week and a
> pension plan.

After updating Ernie's insurance and job benefits and translat-
ing a few descriptive phrases into stage directions, there isn't
much else that has to done in order to turn the story into a teleplay.

Hugh was very pleased with the productions of "Some Are So
Lucky" and "A Trip For Mrs. Taylor," not least because very few
changes were made in the scripts he submitted, but he soon found
that there was more potential for trouble in this new medium.
His next several scripts were severely mauled in the production
process, which he described in some biographical notes made in
1960 under the heading "What Do You Dislike Writing Most?":

> The author of a TV play ... is not a person placed in the sink-or-
> swim position of a novelist or short story writer. The play is his
> baby only while it is being written, but as soon as it reaches the tel-
> evision corporation it is taken over by more foster parents, and
> sillier ones, than the Children's Aid Society would ever come up
> against in a thousand years. The dramatic editor is usually a hack,
> and at best is a frustrated author in his own right, who would starve
> to death trying to write for publication. Above him is some s.o.b.
> who represents the advertising agency, whose knowledge of litera-
> ture ends with writing such deathless prose as "the jar with the stars
> on top" or "mild, pink, liquid Vel." The sponsor, whether he sells
> soap, automobiles or fertilizer, is a complete ass. Then there is the
> executive producer who has to be sold on the play. ... Then there
> are people such as floor directors, actors, set designers, lighting
> and audio men, and so on who can make or break any play ever
> written. The author becomes only a minor member of the whole
> shebang, and as such his role is a pretty stultifying one.

The equation of the television corporation with social-work agencies, given Garner's contempt for the latter, is in itself a sufficient indication of his obvious disgust with what sometimes happened during the transition from script to completed production.

This process did, however, pay very well if you could put up with its sometimes farcical and even contradictory demands, and so Hugh did his not always sufficient best to suppress his feelings about the people he had to deal with. One of the things script editors wanted to see was an outline of the projects writers had in mind. At first he found it easy enough to comply with this: since he was merely adapting existing stories into a different format, all he had to do was make an outline of something he had already written. But when he began trying to create original teleplays, this became an onerous requirement that interfered with his usual way of working. In a letter to script editor Nathan Cohen, he complained that

> Giving away my stories beforehand destroys the *fun* of creating them, hems me in with artificial fences, and makes me hesitate to change them as I go along. There may be mechanical and editorial benefits to submitting detailed outlines, but I don't think they work as well for me, creatively, as going ahead and writing whatever piece of fiction it is, by myself and in the way I want to do it.

There is a certain amount of simple self-interest involved here — Garner never liked to waste time on work that would be both unpaid and superfluous from his point of view — but it is also undoubtedly true that some of his best fictional ideas occurred while he was improvising rather than following predetermined patterns.

Complain, bitch and moan though Garner might and would, by 1957 it was becoming obvious to him that magazine writing was both economically and creatively a losing proposition. Hugh did get along well with Frank Rasky at *Liberty*, who until he left the magazine in 1961 was a major source of support, but the situation was otherwise pretty bleak. The number of publications was declining, their rates of payment weren't keeping up with inflation and some of them were now being run by younger editors whose journalism-school backgrounds weren't necessarily good preparation for dealing with a crusty old pro like Garner. With the brave new world of TV offering a potentially less exacting way of earning a living, Garner prepared to launch himself into a field where the medium in many respects *was* the message.

Chapter Seven

The Play's the Thing
(1957-1962)

The ease with which Hugh's first adaptations of his short stories had been accepted was matched by the excellent press notices their filmed versions received. "Some Are So Lucky" and "A Trip For Mrs. Taylor" were even picked up by the BBC for 1957 airings, and the English reviews were likewise very favourable. In quick succession the CBC purchased outlines of his short stories "A Couple of Quiet Young Guys," "Father's Day," "The Old Man's Laughter" and "Tea at Miss Mayberry's," and it certainly looked as though Garner had finally stumbled on the free-lance writer's equivalent of Easy Street.

But in a life whose course never did run smooth, such a deceptively encouraging prelude simply had to be followed by some disappointments and discouragements. Of the four adaptations purchased after his two initial successes, only one, "A Couple of Quiet Young Guys", was ever produced, and then it turned out so badly that it had to be recast and reshot before it was finally broadcast in 1958. As he learned about the many different things that could go wrong between the acceptance of a script and the completion of a satisfactory filmed version, Garner's initial exultation at how easy it was to write for television rapidly turned into frustration, and two incidents that took place in 1958 turned his frustration into rage.

The first incident involved an original script entitled "Aftermath," which Nathan Cohen had bought while he was still TV script editor at the CBC. It then became the responsibility of a new executive producer named Esse Ljungh, who for reasons that he never satisfactorily explained to Hugh decided to cancel a lucrative sale to an American TV network. Although Ljungh subsequently bought "Aftermath" for a CBC Radio production — at less than a third of what the Americans had offered — Garner was not mollified, and remained convinced that the whole thing had occurred because he was not part of the "clique" of more established radio and TV writers.

Garner found the treatment of his adaptation of the short story "The Magnet" equally infuriating, although for somewhat different reasons. After his outline had been purchased, he was asked to make major changes in its plot, which he did with the predictable amount of grumbling and mumbling. But when he was told that at least one more rewrite would be necessary, he decided to favour script editor Robert Orchard with a candid piece of his mind:

> Let us get a few things straight right now.
> The writing of TV dramas ... has become a medium for third-class writers to collaborate with story editors and TV producers to produce plays which are innocuous enough to satisfy everybody from the old lady in Dubuque to the old lady in BBD and O. (the best-known advertising firm of the period — author's note) ...
> The TV drama called THE MAGNET was ... an adaptation of an original and powerful story of a middleaged woman who fell in love with a young hired hand, after feeling nothing for him ... You asked me to change it, and I did, no longer caring what sort of an ordinary, two-for-a-quarter piece of crap came out. Now we have a young man, full of youthful disdain for women, being slightly snubbed by the middleaged woman, then changing his mind and trying to get next to her, but being thwarted by having placed a younger woman in a family way in the meantime. That is the plot of a soap opera, not a piece of literary art.
> ... I do not intend to become a hack in the field of drama, like most of the bums who are members of the same union I belong to. Good drama is a one man creative process, as is good painting, novel or short story writing. When a writer begins fitting in other people's ideas, like pieces in a jig-saw puzzle, he sacrifices two things (which most never had anyway), his creative integrity and

his right to be called a writer. Strangely, these things mean quite a
lot to me.

This combination of spleen and idealism seems to have
succeeded in cutting through the accumulated red tape, since
"The Magnet" was finally produced in 1960, although with a
male lead — Don Franks — who in Garner's opinion "hoked it
up and blew the whole play."

As indicated in the above letter, Hugh had by now become a
member of ACTRA, the Association of Canadian Radio and Television Artists. This was one of the few organizations he ever
joined in which he actively participated over a long period of
time, and it soon came in handy when he had to threaten a CBC
drama editor with a union grievance for not paying promptly
enough after a script had been accepted. Garner loved to use the
letter of the law to get what he believed was rightfully his. He
would later teach an editor something about the advisability of
paying free-lancers promptly and successfully take his son's
landlord to small-claims court, actions which convinced his
daughter Barbara that he would have made a ferociously competent, if totally unorthodox, lawyer.

Hassles and all, writing for television had increased his income and to some extent freed him from the constant grind of
magazine journalism, and so he began to think about beginning
a serious novel. The Canada Council had been established in
1957, and although Hugh doubted that an official part of the literary establishment wanted anything to do with him — not an
unreasonable assumption, given his performance at the Canadian
Writers' Conference — he decided to cross his fingers and apply.
In retrospect, he should have been much more confident; he was,
after all, an established novelist and short-story writer, and with
letters of recommendation from bona fide members of the establishment such as Robert Weaver, *Maclean's* editor Ralph Allen
and McClelland and Stewart's Jack McClelland — who had told
Hugh that he wanted to publish a book of his — he must have
been an uncontroversial choice for that year's judges.

On April 3, 1959 he was notified that he had been awarded a Senior Arts Grant of $4,500 (he had requested $7,200), and in May he began to work on the book that would become *Silence on the Shore*. His first problem was finding an appropriate title for what he had already decided would be a novel about the varied inhabitants of a Toronto rooming-house in the Annex neighbourhood. Like many an author before him, he began by leafing through the Bible and *Bartlett's Familiar Quotations* in quest of just the right striking phrase.

The Bible yielded "What profit hath he that hath laboured for the wind?," (*Ecclesiastes*, v, 16), and for a while he toyed with "Profit the Wind" before deciding that there were already too many "wind" titles (W.O. Mitchell's *Who Has Seen the Wind* was the clincher). Then he expanded his search to an anthology of Canadian poetry, in which a line from Bertram Warr's "Working Class," "For we are walkers on pavement, who go grey-faced and given-up through the rain," suggested "Walkers on Pavement" as a good proletarian title. But in a decision that symbolized how removed he now was from his 1930s radicalism, he finally concluded that "Walkers on Pavement" was *too* proletarian.

Finally, *The Oxford Dictionary of Quotations* caught his ear with a verse from Lord Byron's "On Hearing Lady Byron Was Ill:"

> It is not in the storm nor in the strife
> We feel benumb'd, and wish to be no more,
> But in the after-silence on the shore,
> When all is lost, except a little life.

Garner sensed that his title was in there somewhere, but he was still uncertain as to its exact wording. He drew up a list of possibilities that included "The Lost Ones," "Nor in the Strife," "Benumbed No More," "The After Silence," "All Lost But Life," "Not in the Storm" and "The Silence on the Shore," and eventually settled on the last after "The Lost Ones" had spent a few months as the favourite. Nor was this the last bit of strife to affect the book's title: originally published as *The Silence on the Shore*, the paperback reprint dropped the *The* for reasons unknown — but almost certainly attributable to sheer human error — and gave the novel the final form of its name.

The difficulties Hugh had in deciding on a title were an indication of the problems he would have in writing the book. He wrote steadily for a week, but in the middle of the first chapter became dissatisfied with both the woodenness of his prose and his middle-aged protagonist, "Walter Fowler." So he started to tinker: he exchanged his protagonist's persona for that of a much younger character and tried to add a racier tone to what he had already written. But this didn't seem to work either, and he finally put the novel aside for what would turn out to be the remainder of 1959.

Perhaps looking for someone on whom to take out his frustrations, he got into a public brouhaha with *Mayfair* editor Jeann Beattie in the fall of 1959. In the interval between the commissioning of an article entitled "The Canadian Woman, 1960" and the magazine's acceptance of it, *Mayfair* was sold to new owners. Beattie made the mistake of telling Hugh that the transfer of ownership made it impossible to pay him right away. She might as well have waved a red flag in front of a bull: he immediately swore out a summons against the publication in Division Court, which had the desired effect of forcing *Mayfair* to pay him what it owed him. Beattie responded by complaining to one and all about how profoundly this uncivilized beast's ungentlemanly behaviour had shocked her, and he received several phone calls, including a very irate one from *Maclean's* articles editor Ian Sclanders, demanding that he apologize. Garner, however, was in no mood to back off from anybody: "I told him the same as I'd told the others, it wasn't *I* who had stolen seventy-five lousy dollars from *her*, but *she* who had tried to steal it from *me* for a job I'd done." This conflict between wounded gentility and outraged professional pride nicely symbolizes the divergent standards of conduct that separated Hugh from many of the editors and publishers with whom he had to deal.

Part of his difficulty in getting on with *Silence on the Shore* was that for the first time in his life he could accurately describe himself as "a victim of prosperity." Besides the lucrative TV scripts, he was still writing for many of the remaining consumer magazines, and he understandably hated to give up these sure sources of income to work full-time on a novel that might suffer the fate of "The Legs of the Lame." With this marked improvement in his finances had come a corresponding increase in expenditure, as the Garners began to acquire some of the trappings of middle-class status.

One of the banes of Hugh's existence was that he had never learned how to drive, and in 1958 he resolved that the time had finally come. When he informed family and friends of his decision, there was near-unanimous agreement that this would end in some unimaginable new disaster. But he went ahead and took lessons, overcame what at first seemed to be a mental block regarding the intricacies of parking and passed his driving examination with little difficulty; and to almost everyone's surprise, he proved to be a cautious and careful motorist who never drove when intoxicated.

With their children now teenagers, Hugh and Alice began to take advantage of the chance to go out in the evening. They subscribed to a series at the O'Keefe Centre, sometimes dined at a downtown restaurant beforehand and got back into the habit of at least one weekly trip to the movies. Their children were developing along normal adolescent lines. Hugh, Jr., the quieter of the two, occupied most of his free time doing desperately secret things with his buddies, while Barbara spent so many hours on the telephone talking to friends that her father once ripped it out of the wall when she refused to hang up.

In the fall of 1959 the *Star Weekly* asked him if he would be interested in doing a series called "A Loyalist Soldier Returns to Spain," for which they would guarantee his expenses up to one thousand dollars and pay him three hundred dollars each for three articles. This had the irresistible attraction of proposing to pay him well for something he had always wanted to do anyway, and with only a few misgivings about his abandoned novel he accepted the magazine's offer.

He crossed the Atlantic on the *Queen Elizabeth*, thoroughly enjoying the difference between its amenities and those of the *Berengaria* and the corvettes on which he had served. He arrived in Cherbourg on November 23, and retraced the route he had taken on his 1937 journey to join the International Brigades: by train to Paris, then south to Perpignan and across the border at Port Bou, then onward to Barcelona, Valencia and Madrid. He got a taste of what Franco's Spain was like when a young Frenchman carrying a large wrapped parcel was closely questioned by soldiers and police, whose swarming numbers made the phrase "police state" a highly visible reality.

In Madrid Garner hired a taxi and had himself driven to the Franco government's memorial to the war dead. This massive mausoleum, in theory dedicated to the fallen on both sides, was in fact the sort of egomaniacal monument dictators erect to their imagined greatness: when Hugh asked where the Loyalists were buried, he suddenly became an object of great interest to the shrine's uniformed guards. Realizing that this wasn't where he wanted to be, he told his driver to take him to Brunete, where he knew that some of his fellow soldiers *were* buried.

On the way they stopped at Villaneuva de la Canada, the village outside which the Abraham Lincoln Battalion had been chopped up by fascist machine-guns. Garner walked around the small, sleepy community, chatting with its inhabitants, chucking a baby under the chin and donating five hundred pesetas to the fund for a new church, on the grounds that during his last visit he had helped to burn down the old one. He had a couple of glasses of the local brandy and thought about the men who had died in this quiet corner of the world, motivated by the same burning idealism that he too had once shared and now found himself touched by again.

Hugh had been drinking steadily throughout the trip, but toward the end of his three weeks in Spain, steadily turned into heavily. He had decided to return home via Portugal, and on the train to Lisbon passed out after working his way through a bottle of Dom Pedro brandy. He spent most of his time in the Portugese capital alternating drinking bouts with frenzied interludes of sightseeing, and finally had to cable the *Star Weekly* for air fare home when his traveller's cheques ran out. Wisely, *Star Weekly* did not send money and instead booked him on a CP flight to Montreal, and for your normal human being this would have been the end of the matter.

Garner, however, had an astonishing ability to foul up even the simplest travel arrangements with some ridiculous piece of drunken misbehaviour. Carrying his by now almost destroyed suitcase, which was tenuously held together by assorted pieces of rope and string, he left his hotel "completely blotto" and grabbed a cab to the airport. Here the security guards took him aside and gave him a thorough grilling, apparently convinced that any foreigner making such a conspicuous ass of himself must be some sort of extraordinarily clever secret agent; Hugh, who had had more than enough of the Spanish police already and wasn't about to put up with any nonsense from Portugese dictator Antonio Salazar's minions, threatened to call in the British fleet and have Lisbon shelled to the ground. Finally, the officer in charge of the interrogation lost his temper and ordered him deported on the first plane to the United States, which happened to be flying to New York.

In New York, he was rapidly passed through customs — no one wanted to have anything to do with his suitcase, which by now was bearing a more than passing resemblance to the Gordian knot. After a thorough search of his pockets, he came up with enough French, Spanish and Portugese loose change to make up his plane fare to Toronto. This search also revealed that he had not yet exhausted his supplies of liquid currency, and he spent the flight to Toronto boring the daylights out of a Newmarket, Ontario poodle breeder with his well-lubricated theories about the care and handling of dogs. When he arrived at the Kingston Road apartment, his family took one look at him — his daughter remembers that he looked something like a door-to-door salesmen who had lost a battle with a steamroller — and bundled him into bed for several days of enforced rest.

Hugh had made it home in time for a somewhat subdued Christmas, after which he worked on his *Star Weekly* articles, making things easier on himself by incorporating wholesale chunks of previously published material. He had already made short stories out of some of his Spanish Civil War experiences ("The Expatriates," "The Stretcher Bearers" and "How I Became an Englishman"), and he worked these in with very few changes, as he did with a 1953 *Saturday Night* piece on his friend Reid's uncompromising integrity ("The Tired Radical"). When combined with a humorous account of his misadventures as a middle-aged tourist, the result was a superb journalistic series that he quite rightly used without change thirteen years later — and with an acknowledgement of its *Star Weekly* origins, at least — in *One Damn Thing After Another!*

January of 1960 was also enlivened by a humorous epistolary exchange with Ontario MPP John White. Responding to Garner's essay on "Why Are Canadians So Slow to Anger?" in what White identified as *"McLeans,"* the politician sent him a brief note: "Dear Hugh: Bullshit!" Garner's riposte was both longer and wittier:

> Dear Mr. White:
> How nice of you to write me such a charming letter. ...
> Your criticism of my magazine article, summed up so succinctly in your word, "Bullshit!," is political and literary criticism at its best. We need more of this in the legislature, and I only hope that you will have the guts some day to startle your friends in the back benches with its counterpart. ...
> One thing to remember, sir, in letters of this kind, is to make sure that all your facts, spelling, etc. are correct. A stupid mistake only points up the writer's hysteria and disregard for research. I have never written anything for a magazine called *"McLeans'* in my life, although I am a frequent contributor to *Maclean's.* ...
> In the meantime, onwards and upwards with the arts, if not politics.

When Garner finally got around to taking another look at the manuscript of his novel he found, as he had with the first two-thirds of *Storm Below*, that he felt much more positively about what he had written than when he last put it down. As he resumed working on it, he began to feel that its many characters were assuming lives of their own: "Aline Gellman", a sexually molested girl of Lithuanian ancestry, became the Welsh-Canadian virgin "Aline Garfield," and "Pearl Adamsky" insisted that her name had to be changed to "Sophia Karpluk." The eight major actors in his drama all asserted themselves in the sense that they suggested additional experiences which would help readers understand them better; by mid-February it became evident that the book was going to be about twice as long as he had originally thought.

In the background as he worked on *Silence on the Shore* was his anxiety about the book's eventual reception by McClelland and Stewart. After he had received his Canada Council grant he had offered the firm a new collection of short stories, which was rejected with nary an encouraging word; the firm also declined to publish a paperback edition of *Storm Below* in its New Canadian Library series and showed no interest in issuing the unexpurgated version of *Cabbagetown*, even though Hugh agreed to make good any losses. With these disappointments fresh in his mind and no recent evidence of interest from McClelland and Stewart in *Silence on the Shore*, he did something he knew wasn't strictly ethical: although Jack McClelland had made it clear when he agreed to write the letter of recommendation for a Senior Arts Grant that he would like first crack at the resulting manuscript, Garner nonetheless offered it to another publisher before submitting it to McClelland and Stewart.

Tempted by Doubleday Canada's announcement that it was giving ten thousand dollar advances on royalties to authors of publishable Canadian novels, Garner finished yet another rewrite of *Silence on the Shore* in December of 1960 and presented it for their assessment. It didn't take them long to say no, and for a while he toyed with the idea of submitting it to other publishers while making a few desultory revisions. But early in the summer of 1961 Jack Rackcliffe, a McClelland and Stewart editor, phoned and asked how the new book was going. Thankful that at least one of the company's employees was interested in what he was doing, Hugh decided to swallow his misgivings and submit the manuscript for Rackcliffe's consideration, after which he prepared to fly to Vancouver for a television interview with George Woodcock about his Spanish Civil War experiences.

There were certain cities, Vancouver and Ottawa prominent among them, in which Garner always felt himself *persona non grata*. He hadn't much liked Vancouver on his previous visit in 1931, when he had spent most of his time bumming around its skid-row section, and on this trip he managed to get into some really serious trouble. Things began well enough when the interview came off successfully, and he celebrated by taking a few new-found friends and drinking companions back to his hotel room for a rowdy after-hours celebration. When he woke up the next morning they were gone and the hotel's management informed him that he would not again be accepted as a guest, which earned them an equally frank expression of his feelings about the establishment's pseudo-Polynesian décor and into which parts of their anatomy they might consider stuffing it. These pleasantries concluded, he hopped a cab to the airport for his flight to Toronto.

The taxi arrived, he took out his wallet, and now discovered that last night's bosom buddies had departed with all of his cash. But they had left him his credit cards, and so he attempted to explain to the driver that he could use these to get a cash advance at the airline counter. Unfortunately, the driver assumed that this obviously hungover and probably not sartorially elegant passenger was trying to con him out of his fare, and they were soon trading punches while an airport employee yelled for the police. The RCMP arrived and took him off to their Richmond jail, where he was treated as the drunken deadbeat he certainly appeared to be: he had to remove his belt, shoelaces and necktie and surrender his cigarettes, and since it was a Saturday morning and he had no money for bail, he faced the prospect of a weekend in jail before his case would come before a magistrate the following Monday.

Remembering what had happened during his first bout of alcohol-induced illness at the Kingston Road apartment, he screamed for the guard and told him that he was vomiting, which was true, and that there was a lot of blood, which was not. The doctor who was called gave him a mild tranquilizer and told him he'd be fine, which Hugh doubted as he spent the rest of the day alternating periods of sickness with an increasingly desperate need for a cigarette. That night his luck changed for the better when another prisoner on a drunk charge offered to pay his bail after discovering that they were both navy veterans, and he was looked after by his new friend until his case was disposed of and he finally boarded a plane for Toronto.

Safe at home, he prepared to deal with what he assumed would be yet another of the poorly paid, ridiculously overworked and minimally competent editors who seemed to be the norm at Canadian publishing houses. Macmillan's Peggy Blackstock had impressed him with the perspicacity of her comments about *Cabbagetown* thirteen years ago, but ever since then Garner had been dealing with people who as far as he could tell knew little about writing and even less about helping him to improve his own work. He was therefore pleasantly surprised when Jack Rackcliffe proved to be a careful and sympathetic reader of *Silence on the Shore*, who "queried many things that most book editors are too stupid to query." This welcome attention spurred him into one more rewrite of the manuscript. As he told Rackcliffe in a letter:

> Living the multi-schizophrenic life I do, both in my work and other things, I tend to separate its separate parts, and never allow one to impinge on another. For instance, when I write short stories or TV plays I forget about my journalistic bread-and-butter, and when I am scribbling crap about teen-age delinquents or "The Way Television Used to Be" I put out of my mind not only creative writing, but the style of it as well. When I return to work on the book I will become emotionally involved in it and will forget all other interests while I am working on it. This usually consists of several days in a row with time out for meals and a ten to fourteen-hour day at my desk or typewriter, weekends included.

Among the activities in this "multi-schizophrenic life" was a serious effort to get himself sent to Cuba. In February of 1962 the Canadian branch of the Fair Play For Cuba Committee had asked him to be one of its sponsors, and he had replied that he could hardly do this without knowing what was really going on in that country. They then asked him if he would like to go on a tour leaving March 26, and he responded with a deposit of three hundred dollars and an effort to get the *Star Weekly* to subsidize the trip. Although the magazine declined — which meant that he had to scramble to get his deposit refunded — Garner's letter to editor John Clare is of interest for its description of his current political views:

> I am an unreconstructed social radical. Politically I would call myself a left-wing capitalist, although 25 years ago I was a socialist, and a Communist fellow traveller. I believe in the right of individual countries to shape their own destiny, and the right of all people to elect, or otherwise place in power a political group that enjoys the backing of the majority.

Hugh's literary opinions were solicited by his friend Robert Weaver, who asked him what he thought of a forthcoming anthology of short stories originally broadcast on CBC Radio's Wednesday Night programme. People didn't often ask Garner to exercise his literary judgement — the books he was asked to review were usually non-fiction treatments of the Spanish Civil War or the Second World War — and his reply offers a rare opportunity to sample his evaluations of some of his contemporaries. Alice Munro, W.O. Mitchell and Ethel Wilson earned his unqualified admiration, and Morley Callaghan's contribution was praised with the reservation that he should try fashioning a "story line evolved from action and dialogue, and not from what the author told me." Brian Moore was twitted for writing too obscurely, and Mordecai Richler criticized for not seeming to know that "a short story needs a plot, theme and climax." A lighter note was struck by his remarks about his own "Hunky:"

> Garner started out as an excellent fiction writer ..., but unfortunately he didn't live up to his earlier promise. In this story his protagonist (a drunken ex-newspaperman, wouldn't you know) carries out the burning down of a poor farmer's barn and tobacco crop; this is typical Garner, who to my mind is still a Communist, and has no respect for property. But what else can you expect of a hack ...?

Hugh was here satirizing, as he and Weaver were quite well aware, what many observers of the Canadian literary scene had in fact decided was his rightful position in the scheme of things. Although self-parody is not a notable feature of Garner's serious writing, his journalistic, radio and TV appearances often feature similarly wry acknowledgements of the partial truth of these accusations of superficiality and hyper-aggressiveness.

Another literary connection was established with the receipt of a letter from Alden Nowlan in February 1962. Nowlan enthused over the section of the *Star Weekly* series on Spain that had originally been written as "How I Became an Englishman," whose earlier origins he could not have been aware of — it was not published as a short story until 1963 — and thus demonstrated a keen eye for the tale within the tale. Garner responded with a chatty letter that had nice things to say about a Nowlan story, and offered some very practical advice about the writing and marketing of the literary form about which he considered himself to be as knowledgeable as anyone else.

While engaged in his final rewrite of *Silence on the Shore*, Hugh made the mistake of mentioning the Doubleday submission to Jack McClelland during a telephone conversation. McClelland was very upset about it, for which Garner could hardly blame him; and even though they went ahead and worked out a contract for the book in January of 1962, the seeds of mutual suspicion had been sown in the minds of two of the strongest-willed characters ever to liven up the world of Canadian publishing.

Given these circumstances, a kinder fate would have arranged for *Silence on the Shore* to be published without further mishap.

Unfortunately, its production was sabotaged by a series of unforseeable problems: a printer's strike delayed the arrival of bound copies, a bureaucratic snafu left them lying around Montreal for more than a week, and the publicity schedule was completely thrown off by the failure of the books to appear. The upshot was that *Silence on the Shore* wasn't in the stores until late in December 1962, thus missing out on the Christmas gift-book buying that makes or breaks most titles.

Hugh, of course, took all this personally, and although he knew that Jack McClelland wouldn't deliberately do anything to decrease the book's sales, he had good reason to be angry about McClelland and Stewart's performance as a commercial enterprise. The contract he had signed contained a standard clause concerning M & S' right of first refusal on his next work, and he made sure that he would have no further relationship with the firm by offering it a collection that included several of his slightest short stories, among them some that had never found a home in magazine, radio or TV. When this collection was declined, he was free to go elsewhere, and did.

Despite its rocky road to publication, *Silence on the Shore* turned out to be an excellent novel that did much to restore Garner's literary reputation. In the decade since *The Yellow Sweater and Other Stories* Hugh had become known as a journalist who occasionally wrote some pretty good short fiction. In an omnibus volume that evaluated *The Culture of Contemporary Canada* (1957), Roy Daniells described the latter as "a reminder that article writing and factual reporting can go hand-in-hand with story writing and give a robust and objective cast to the creative side." Daniells did not, however, discuss any of Garner's novels — *Storm Below* was not even mentioned in the section of the essay devoted to war fiction — and, as previously described, the 1961 edition of Desmond Pacey's *Creative Writing in Canada* paid them equally short shrift.

Silence on the Shore re-established Hugh as a serious novelist by demonstrating that he could still create a broad, realistic social canvas peopled by convincingly differentiated human types. The rooming-house setting, for example, is presided over by

"Grace Hill," whom he initially imagined as a rather gross and humorous composite of all the strange landladies he had known over the years. As he became more deeply involved with the book, however, Grace Hill began to become an understandable and consequently much more sympathetically observed figure, and in a sense she steals the book from its other dramatis personae.

Garner had originally intended that "Walter Fowler," a middle-aged journalist whose wife and children have left him, would function as a protagonist who expressed the author's thoughts and feelings, but as it turned out, "all the male characters were partial reflections of me at various ages." These included a young man just out of the army, a slightly older French-Canadian labourer, a retired bachelor with a drinking problem and an old-age pensioner, all of whom exemplify some aspect of their creator's knowledge and experience. The female characters were an equally diverse lot: in addition to Grace Hill, they encompass a young evangelical Christian, a French-Canadian housewife and a middle-aged hospital worker, and they are all cogently developed into living representations of credible human beings.

Silence on the Shore follows these lives through a six-month period from May to November of 1959, beginning with Walter Fowler's arrival and ending with the death of Grace Hill. What happens to its characters in between is indicated by a note Hugh wrote to himself during one of his earlier revisions of the manuscript:

> I created these people at the beginning, and they have nearly all changed since. I am sure they will change even more before the book is completely written. I want to show that they are all victims of their own personalities, their neuroticisms, their psychological makeup, but I don't want them to end up as "types" or inflexible blacks or whites. They should all come out tattletale gray, like the next-door neighbor's washing, for that is how people are.

It is this kind of commonsensical, almost domestic realism that was so unassertively but effectively captured in *Silence on the*

Shore, and demonstrated beyond a shadow of a doubt — given that the unexpurgated edition of *Cabbagetown* would not appear until 1968 — that Garner was capable of writing first-class novels as well as excellent short stories.

An amusing footnote to the creation of *Silence on the Shore* concerns the name of one of its characters, the retired undertaker and heavy drinker "Gordon Lightfoot." After the career of the Canadian folk-singer Gordon Lightfoot took off in the early 1960s, Hugh was puzzled by the number of younger readers who wanted to know if there was a sense in which he had been writing about a real person; a 1968 paperback edition reproduced it unchanged until "Gordon" was finally altered to "George" in its next reprinting in 1971.

Garner's usual approach to selecting names for his characters was as down-to-earth as the man himself:

> I take all my names from the Toronto telephone book, ... using a name that is in the public domain, like John Smith, Mary Jones, Walter Jennings and so on. In the case of names I hope are offbeat ... I generally pick a name from the phone book, change one or two letters of the last name, then add a different Christian name. For the names of ethnic characters I find a name that sounds indigenous to his or her nationality, change a letter, and add a fictitious first name.

In a way, his selection of names occurred through a process analogous to that of his technique of fleshing out his fictional characters. Many of the latter, from Ken Tilling to Mrs. Taylor to Walter Fowler, are only slightly disguised portraits of the author and those he knew most intimately; quite a few others, such as Grace Hill and the crew of the corvette "*HMCS River-ford,*" are composite figures drawn from a number of living persons.

Such simple, homely procedures are one of the main reasons why some literary critics have been unable to accept Garner as a "creative" author, although it does not take a great deal of reflection to conclude that writers claiming to have completely imagined their characters are either lying or so remote from social life that their conception of it is unlikely to be of much interest. Here, as elsewhere, Hugh's unwillingness to translate his ideas into acceptable jargon — to describe his characters as Jamesian determinants of incident, say, or as conjunctions of Frye's notions of myth and mimesis — definitely worked against any chance he had of being accepted into the canon of critically anointed authors.

His well-publicized views about universities couldn't have helped much, either. A 1958 *Maclean's* article titled "Why I'm Not Pushing My Children Into College" caused quite a furor. During a 1962 television interview he had some fighting words for those who thought a university degree was a necessity for a writer:

> Anyone who wants to be a writer and goes to university for four years instead of working at twenty different jobs is wasting their time. Take three Nobel Prize winners: Ernest Hemingway, William Faulkner and John Steinbeck. Of the three, Faulkner spent a couple of months at the University of Mississippi and the other two never attended college. Writers need a basic education, but otherwise it's all reading and living.

As Garner put it, "I'm not anti-intellectual, but I am anti-*phoney* intellectual," with the latter term denoting those who thought they were special because they had a diploma from a university.

That he was not anti-intellectual is abundantly demonstrated by the 1959 inventory of his personal library he made for his insurance agent. The great number of short-story collections indicates that his love of the form was matched by his reading in it: as well as fifteen anthologies of various kinds, he had more than seventy volumes of Poe, de Maupassant, James, Chekhov, Joyce, Kafka, Maugham and most of its other notable practitioners. Modern English and American novels were well represented with more than 160 titles, among them the major works of Joyce, Lawrence, Orwell, Hemingway, Faulkner, Steinbeck, Wolfe, Dos Passos and Fitzgerald, and a small selection of their European counterparts included Proust's *Remembrance of Things Past* and Koestler's *Darkness at Noon*. Canadian literature was not much in evidence — three titles by Ethel Wilson and two by Callaghan stand out among the twenty-odd books in this category — and there were a surprising number of classics: most of Voltaire and Ibsen and several volumes each from Scott, Carlyle, Thackeray and Wilde. Speaking now as a former second-hand bookseller who has examined the libraries of several writers with more exalted literary reputations, I can assure readers that Garner's book collection was of higher intrinsic quality than those of many of his peers.

But if Hugh was certainly well-read, he was usually not well-spoken, at least in terms of the norms of polite intellectual discourse. He couldn't, and didn't try to, talk in the euphemistic language of critics and reviewers, where "promising" is a code word for "immature," and "experimental" for "sloppily done." If he didn't like something, he used words such as "lousy," "junk" and "crap" to leave no doubt as to where he stood, and his favourite term for indicating excessive experimentation was "goofy." He was usually the odd man out in any gathering of writers, critics and/or publishing people, and after a while he avoided any occasions he thought might expose him to the babbling of "phoney intellectuals."

The inventory of the Garner's other household possessions illuminates his character from another angle. In the navy Hugh had been required to do regular stock-taking of supplies on hand, and in 1959, when he took out insurance on his family's effects, he got what turned out to be a most enjoyable opportunity to tote up his life's possessions. For several days, as both his wife and daughter vividly recall, their apartment was turned upside-down by his assiduous cataloguing of everything that seemed to have any value, as well as lots of things that didn't. The twenty-five-page, single-spaced list that resulted from this enumeration offered more than anyone, including the insurance company, wanted to know about such items — their cost neatly tabulated in the right-hand column — as:

Vegetable graters, tin, set of three
.75

Rolling pin, wood, 16"
1.00

Corn-on-cob set, plastic (4)
1.00

Tap strainer, non-splash
.98

Trilight Bulb
.85

200 Paper Clips (Commercial)
.58

2 Klenzo, pencil-type Typewriter Erasers
.60

Miscellaneous Erasers
.25

His daughter Barbara claims that he actually counted the paper clips, although this seems unlikely in view of his rather cavalier treatment of the "Miscellaneous Erasers." The point, in any case, is that those who saw Garner careening about in his role as public drunk could not have been aware of — and would probably not have believed if they had been told — how meticulous and painstaking he was in private; and when he was engaged in a serious piece of writing, he applied the same intense concentration to his literary work.

Another interesting aspect of his household inventory was its revelation that his musical tastes had undergone something of a change in the last decade. *Cabbagetown*'s homosexual do-gooder, Clarence Gurney, is contemptuously described as someone who "loved to lounge around in a dressing gown listening to Brahms on his electric phonograph;" one isn't sure whether to take the dressing-gown or the Brahms as the most damning bit of evidence, but it's clear that both are intended to function as indications of decadence and pretension. And in a reflective passage that comes just before this encounter, Ken Tilling lists "oil paintings, symphony records, books of his own, social status or a membership in a club" as examples of the kind of "cultural appurtenances" he can easily live without.

By 1959, however, Garner had acquired quite a few records as well as many books of his own, including Beethoven's nine symphonies, piano music by Mozart, Liszt and Schumann, and three recordings of various works by Brahms. In some "Biographical Notes" written in 1960, he even went so far as to identify his favourite music as "Chopin's waltzes and etudes;" thus it comes as no surprise when a "travelling dressing-gown" and a "kimono" are listed as part of Hugh's wardrobe in the inventory's "Men's Clothing" section.

In February of 1962, with a contract signed for *Silence on the Shore* and their children beginning to make separate lives for themselves — Barbara was now married and Hugh, Jr. had a job and a place of his own — the Garners moved into an apartment house at 51 Parkwoods Village Drive in the northeastern suburb of Don Mills. After a few months in a two-storey maisonette, which they found unnecessarily large, they switched to a one-bedroom apartment in the same building. On the face of it, this was a bizarre thing for them to do: they knew no one in the area, and Hugh would now have to drive every time he went downtown unless he chose to spend several hours travelling by bus and subway.

But on Kingston Road he was constantly reminded of the parts of Toronto where he had spent his childhood — the streetcar line downtown passed through both Riverdale and Cabbagetown — and as he grew older he became increasingly reluctant to return to either of these areas: he refused all invitations to take part in reunions of his public-school classes and seldom exhibited much interest in returning to the haunts of his youth. Although Don Mills proved to be a little too far away from downtown Toronto, the Garners' next move would take them to the northern rather than the eastern part of the city; they would never again reside in the east end.

The year 1962 was ushered out by a series of hassles with the CBC's television drama department. His original teleplay "The Lost Cause" had been purchased in August, under a contract that specified the following schedule of payments: $350 for an outline, $350 for a first draft and $800 for the completed script. Garner completed the first two stages with no more than his usual amount of complaining about the dumb revisions he was being asked to make, but storm clouds developed when the acceptance of his completed script was delayed by the difficulties two CBC editors had in communicating with each other: their respective suggestions for revisions were often contradictory, and at one point they mislaid the script for more than a month. Hugh, using his by now detailed knowledge of the CBC-ACTRA agreement, threatened to invoke its grievance procedures and was once again successful in galvanizing the drama department into action. An abject apology — and, more importantly, an $800 cheque — were immediately forthcoming, as he once again demonstrated that it is the literary squeaky wheels that get the economic grease.

As 1962 drew to a close, the continuing decline of Canadian consumer magazines and the increasingly difficult time he was having getting his TV scripts through the CBC bureaucracy didn't bode well for Garner's prospects. The accumulated frustrations surrounding *Silence on the Shore*, which came to a head when the book's sales were badly hurt by the delays in its publication, deeply upset him; and he could also see that Don Mills wasn't where he should be living, since it tended to cut him off from those editors and publishers with whom he was still on good terms. But he had now survived for almost thirteen years on his writing and his wits, and with both money and experience in the bank he resolved that it would be books, rather than journalism or TV scripts, with which he would make his bid for greater public attention.

Chapter Eight

Awards and Alarums
(1962-1968)

Garner began 1963 with another trip to the West Coast, where he planned to begin a cross-country tour that would produce a series of magazine articles on the plight of Canada's native peoples. In mid-January he flew to Vancouver, where he interviewed members of its Indian community, and made short trips to Nanaimo and Seattle. His stopover in Calgary was enlivened by an evening of carousing at the Palliser Hotel with *Calgary Herald* writers Bill Stavdal and Jamie Portman, and he then visited his old friend W.O. Mitchell at the latter's High River home. A side-trip to Gleichen to profile a Blackfoot Indian reservation brought back memories of his days on the bum thirty years previously, when during a stop at the small Alberta town he had been kicked off a passenger train for riding its "blinds" — the spaces between cars where hobos could hop on as the train left the station.

From Calgary he travelled to Winnipeg, where he spent much of his time interviewing — and of course drinking with — those Indians who frequented the city's skid-row taverns. Then it was on to Churchill, more heavy drinking interspersed with sightseeing and interviewing, and the purchase of a bottle of bootleg liquor that he consumed after returning to Winnpeg's Fort Garry Hotel. But even a stomach as cast-iron as Garner's couldn't take whatever had gone into this home-made concoction and on the plane back to he began drifting in and out of consciousness. When he arrived home he tried to convince Alice that this was just another hangover, but she called an ambulance and had him taken to Toronto General Hospital.

Here he was diagnosed as suffering from kidney stoppage and pneumonia and was put on an artificial kidney machine and given massive doses of penicillin. Alice was told that he would be lucky to survive, and he continued to lapse into comas that were replaced by terrible thirsts when he regained consciousness. But gradually he did begin to improve, and eventually was able to go home in a much weakened condition that made any continuation of the *Star Weekly* series on native peoples impossible. One of the side-effects of this illness was that his stomach problems became less troublesome — possibly because by this time there could not have been a great deal of his stomach left. Hugh had always blamed his stomach ailments on the pressures of producing prodigious quantities of journalism, and now he made yet another resolution to cut down on his magazine writing. This time, he would carry it through: whereas in the 1952-1962 period he had averaged more than thirty full-length articles per year, from 1963 onwards he would seldom produce more than three.

But if he couldn't manage the sort of legwork required by magazine articles, there were lots of other things for a cagey old writer to do. Since the late 1950s Hugh and Alice had been taking to the road for much of the summer as he discovered that motoring about the continent was just as much fun as hopping freights and hitch-hiking. As a way of making sure that they didn't fall into a routine of following the same itinerary on each outing, he inked over each route after they had travelled it; from this it was but a short step to deciding that they would try to drive on all the major roads indicated on his Canadian Automobile Association maps, starting with the Ontario provincial highways, following that with Quebec's, and then moving on to the U.S. interstate system.

This proved to be a highly satisfying hobby, since it combined his love of travel with his penchant for keeping meticulous records. He drove carefully and right at the speed limit, and except for the occasional swear word directed at an errant fellow motorist seemed to be quite calm and relaxed at the wheel. They didn't stop a great deal on these expeditions — the point was to *travel*, not to go anywhere in particular — but at major tourist attractions the Garners would dutifully park and see whatever there was to be seen, and then get back in the car and drive a few hundred more miles before sunset: "on one trip we visited Cape Cod one day, Atlantic City the next, and Williamsburg, Virginia on the third day." His final driving feat was to visit every state in the continental U.S., which he accomplished by the early 1970s. These travel experiences sometimes provided amusing contrasts with those of previous visits during the Depression years: when he told a Lordsburg, New Mexico motel proprietor about his 1933 sojourn in Billy the Kid's old jail cell, for instance, he noticed that his credit cards were subjected to an unusually painstaking examination.

The collection of Garner's stories McClelland and Stewart had declined to take as a sequel to *Silence on the Shore* was also out on the road, and after several more rejections from publishers he decided to submit it to the Ryerson Press. Ryerson wasn't all that excited about this particular batch of stories but did come up with an interesting proposal: if Hugh would permit the inclusion of some of his best contributions to *The Yellow Sweater and Other Stories*, Ryerson would be willing to take a chance on a book that combined old and new material.

Given the generally dismal commercial performance of short-story collections — despite good reviews, Collins had declined to issue *The Yellow Sweater and Other Stories* as a paperback and had let the book go out of print — this was as good an offer as anyone could expect, and Garner quickly accepted it. The rights to his previously published tales had reverted to him, so there was no problem on that score; but there was some difficulty in deciding on a title, with *Hugh Garner's Best Stories* finally selected as a way of indicating that some of its contents had already appeared in print.

The book was published in the fall of 1963, sold moderately well and received almost uniformly positive reviews. It was the older stories such as "The Conversion of Willie Heaps," "One-

Two-Three Little Indians" and "Some Are So Lucky" that evoked the most favourable response; all of these had been written before Hugh got into the have-typewriter-will-write-anything habits of a busy journalist. Among the newer material the poignant domestic realism of "The Father" and the unbridled sentimentality of "Tea With Miss Mayberry" demonstrated how good he had become at writing for "the slicks," as their contributors then referred to the glossier magazines, but none of the more recent stories had anything like the elemental impact of his earlier efforts.

This certainly didn't bother the judges for the Governor General's Award for Fiction, who in the following spring chose *Hugh Garner's Best Stories* as the 1963 winner. Given that 1962's selectors had preferred Kildare Dobbs's *Running to Paradise* to *Silence on the Shore*, this was poetic, if not literary, justice and not at all bad for a former hobo, consorter with communists and graduate of a military detention barracks. Hugh's disreputable past also did not seem to trouble the management of the *Toronto Telegram*, who in the fall of 1963 invited Hugh to become a regular contributor to "Dissent," a column that appeared daily on the newspaper's op-ed page.

Being asked to write for the *Telegram* signified how apolitical an image Garner now had. The newspaper had traditionally addressed itself to a conservative, Tory, Anglophilic readership that represented much of what he had devoted his life to rebelling against; and although in the late 1940s it had attempted to challenge the *Star*'s dominance with a livelier look and tone, the *Telegram* was still basically oriented toward those for whom respectability was next to godliness. In the sixty-three "Dissent" pieces Hugh wrote between October 1963 and October 1965 he did his best to introduce the *Telegram*'s readers to his brand of thinking, and in the process revealed how much he had changed from the committed radical who went off to fight in the Spanish Civil War.

His very first "Dissent" offering, "I'm Against the United Appeal," took an old Garner gripe and expressed it with the idiosyncratic orneriness that had become his journalistic stock-in-trade:

The Metro United Appeal is not a divinely inspired way of taking care of our indigents, cripples and other unfortunates, but is merely the grouping of 82 charities into one giant collection agency. ...

Having been a recipient of Salvation Army charity — plus their religious fundamentalism — as a child, and knowing that last year they appointed a commissioner to look after their very large real estate and investment income, I am pretty cool towards their appeal for funds ...

The Boy Scouts and Girl Guides have no right whatever to ask for alms, and I would just as soon contribute to a pension fund for Baptist choirmasters. ...

... let's kick out those mooching organizations that are run for private profit, and whose main charity is the support of high-priced executives ...

A society that leaves ... the care of its crippled and retarded children to the charity of the public is sick.

Although it is easy enough to read the column as simply an attack on society's do-gooders — and many outraged *Telegram* readers did exactly that — there is also a vaguely socialist ethos present here which champions public rather than private control of important institutions. Elsewhere in his début "Dissent" he argued for a comprehensive medicare system instead of the era's hodgepodge of assorted charitable organizations (five years later the federal Medical Care Act would help to make this a reality). Although by this time it would have been very difficult to classify Garner in conventional political terms, he usually did have a pretty good sense of what issues were really important to those constituents he thought of himself as representing, the average Joe and the little guy.

Another case in point is an August 30, 1963, CBC television debate with a Protestant minister about the vexed question of "Open Sundays." Ever since the 1890s, when the churches had failed in their bid to keep the streetcars from operating on what they insisted was "the Lord's day," there had been a gradual loosening of restrictions on the sabbath behaviour of Toronto's citizenry. Commercial enterprises, however, were for the most part still required to remain closed. As Hugh listened to the Rev-

erend Dr. Leslie Mutchmor defend this on the grounds that it pro-
tected "the working man," he lost his temper. "I think his care
for the working man is a bunch of hooey! His concern is really
about what *he* thinks is sin!" he interjected. A little later in the
conversation, he offered his own down-to-earth view of the
issue: "If some people wish to go without the pleasures of life in
order to get them in the hereafter, good luck to them. Personally,
I'll have the pleasures while I'm here on earth because there may
not *be* a hereafter." During the program Hugh also made a clever
verbal response that demonstrated how much more at ease he
now was in the public spotlight: when Mutchmor unctuously
asked him if he didn't think it was more important to spend Sunday visiting the sick than visiting beer parlours, Hugh was quick
to reply, "What's wrong with going to visit sick people in beer
parlors?"

In the fall of 1963 Garner put together a selection of his best
humorous journalistic pieces and took them to Ryerson Press,
which published them as *Author, Author!* in 1964. Although the
book included entertaining and acutely observed articles such as
"Bohemia on the Bay," "Chatelaines and Charlatans" and
"Cocktails and Canapes" — all of which were used once again
in *One Damn Thing After Another!* — it was a commercial flop.
Three Garners in three years probably was a bit too much for the
reading public. However, since *Author, Author!* is the only collection in book form of his non-fiction magazine articles, it does
provide a sense of the essentially slight but often extremely
amusing work that he referred to as his "bread and butter."

Garner's inability to resume the kind of work schedule that
had produced such a steady flow of saleable articles resulted in
a serious drop in his income, and by the spring of 1964 he was
forced to start dipping into the savings that had been so
laboriously accumulated during the preceding decade. He would
later call the Don Mills period "the most unproductive of my
life," although as a writer who hated to waste anything, he did
later make use of his suburban experiences in the novel *Death
in Don Mills*. But basically his venture into the hinterlands was
a mistake in judgement that happened to coincide with a serious

health problem, and it took a totally unexpected bit of luck to snap him out of the resulting depression.

In March 1964 he was informed that *Hugh Garner's Best Stories* had won the 1963 Governor General's Award for Fiction, which carried with it a one thousand dollar prize. He drove to Ottawa for the presentation, during which he managed to commit the sort of conversational gaffe that deserves to live on in collections of literary anecdotes. When he came forward to accept the award, Governor General Georges Vanier commented, "I've read the stories; they're very good." Perhaps disconcerted by having been addressed with something other than a conventional banality, Garner maladroitly — but undoubtedly with honest curiosity — asked "Do you mean to say you've read them all, sir?" Now it was Vanier's turn to be nonplussed: "Well ... I've read some of them," he replied, while Madame Vanier looked on with an undisguised hostility that carried over into the ensuing reception.

With a spring in his ego and money in his pocket, Hugh felt that it was a propitious time to bid goodbye to Don Mills. He was at this time — there would later be a falling out — on very good terms with his landlords, the Perkell brothers, who told him he would be welcome in their new Erskine Avenue project as soon as it was completed. But since he had made up his mind to move, the Garners decided to spend the intervening period in an apartment at 66 Broadway Avenue in the Yonge Street and Eglinton Avenue area, just one block away from the building they eventually planned to move into. Unfortunately, their new address was inhabited by a rather conservative group of tenants, quite a few of whom objected to Hugh's penchant for public intoxication; during the next two years he would be involved in many hassles with residents who complained about the noise he made when he was on one of his binges.

Hugh had not tried to break into the U.S. market since the early 1950s. Now he made another effort at finding an agent who could help him communicate with what he always thought of as part of his natural audience. As an avid reader of American periodicals — *Newsweek, Esquire* and *Time* were among the many to which he subscribed — he was certainly familiar with the kind of magazine journalism that was commercially viable there, and if he had made the move to New York, he might have been able to place non-fiction articles in the major markets. But writing from a distance meant that he was in practice limited to submitting his short stories, and in terms of both content and style his work was at a disadvantage in capturing the attention of U.S. editors: realistic accounts of sub-middle-class Canadian life must have been extremely low on anyone's list of desirable fictional commodities.

In August 1964, in any event, he signed up with New York's Curtis-Brown Agency in the hope that they would be able to find the right solution to the American puzzle. In a letter to Anne Curtis-Brown, he described his feelings about the United States:

> I ... travelled pretty well all over the U.S. I liked the country very much, and there have been many times when I wished I had moved there. However, in 1937 I served in the Spanish Civil War in the Abraham Lincoln Battalion of the Loyalist army, and so when the time came to try to emigrate to the States, around 1950 perhaps, my way was blocked by the McCarran Act and Senator McCarthy. Not that I was refused admittance by the U.S. Immigration Dept. I just didn't bother trying to get in.

The agency did its best to find markets for his short stories and even tried *Silence on the Shore* on the paperback reprint houses, but there simply wasn't any interest in his work.

It had occurred to Garner that *Silence on the Shore* might make a successful play of some sort, and he now embarked upon a series of moves that would maximize the amount of money to be earned from this process. First he interested the CBC in a radio adaptation, which was eventually broadcast in 1966. Then he convinced them that a TV version would be a good idea, and after a series of battles with editors and executives that he claimed "would have given ulcers to the most phlegmatic dramatist in the world," was paid for a script that was never produced. Finally, he applied to the Canada Council for a grant to turn his TV drama into a stage play, and in November 1964 was awarded three thousand dollars to undertake this project. If *Silence on the Shore* had been a disappointment in terms of royalties from its book publication — it had sold only 1,500 copies as of June 1964 — Hugh subsequently made enough out of it to demonstrate that "One Damn Medium After Another!" would have been an equally accurate title for his autobiography.

A more somber note was struck by Annie Garner's rapidly declining health, which necessitated her placement in first a nursing home and then the Ontario Hospital. Although it was Hugh who as the oldest child had to sign the legal papers and deal with the public trustee, it was his brother Ron who had looked after her at their Winnifred Avenue home, where Hugh had been an infrequent and not necessarily welcome visitor. He and Annnie often argued vehemently at family gatherings ("I should have drowned him at birth!" she once exclaimed, apparently in earnest, during one of their more violent exchanges) and his relationship with his brother wasn't much better. Ron Garner resented the fact that Hugh was almost always drunk when he visited Winnifred Avenue and didn't think that he pulled his weight in helping to take care of Annie. Never close, the two brothers had by now become so hostile to one another that they avoided meeting except on ceremonial family occasions.

Crusty and argumentative though the world often found him, Garner was still capable of acts of gratuitous generosity. Students who had read his work and wrote to ask him about it usually received a polite response, which sometimes stretched out into an extended commentary on his methods of writing. A grade eleven student from Prince Edward Island who asked him for suggestions about how to become a writer must have been delighted with Hugh's thoughtful and extended (three single-spaced pages) reply:

> You learn to write by reading, seeing, experiencing, doing, noticing and living. It is up to you to train yourself to put these things into words on a page, and to do it better than almost anyone else can do.
>
> Don't waste your time or money on "writing courses," even those "creative writing courses" that exist in some universities.

> Nobody can teach you to write creatively, you either have the talent or you don't. You can, however, be taught to write better, and you can also be taught how to write journalism, which is a craft not an art form ... As a matter of fact journalism is a good craft for a writer to learn; I have made my living out of it for years while doing my creative writing on the side, so to speak.
> ... Listen and learn how people really talk in conversation. Learn to describe a person in a few words, so that the reader can form a picture of him in his mind, and never forget him.

When he received his grant from the Canada Council to turn *Silence on the Shore* into a stage play, he began to pay serious attention to the theatrical medium. In his application to the Council he had stated that he looked forward to working in, and planned to devote some effort to studying, a form with which he was not all that familiar, and he was as good as his word. By this time he had patched up his differences with CBC producer Esse Ljungh, who was able to offer some helpful advice about technical aspects of stagecraft, and he also made use of his actress friend Anna Cameron's professional expertise. He also joined the Canadian Theatre Centre in April 1965, which for a confirmed non-joiner was an indication of how interested he was in exploring the possibilities of this new medium.

In *One Damn Thing After Another!* Garner states that he received his Canada Council grant for adapting three TV scripts ("Some Are So Lucky," "A Trip For Mrs. Taylor" and "The Magnet") into a dramatic trilogy, but in fact the award was for the adaptation of *Silence on the Shore*. What the autobiographical version does accurately reflect is the way that he actually used the grant, which resulted in the production of the trilogy *Three Women* but not in a usable stage version of the novel. He did at one point in his correspondence with the Canada Council advise them that he was having a lot of trouble turning *Silence on the Shore* into a play, but otherwise we know only that this project was never completed.

Three Women proved to be less than a roaring success as it accumulated rejections from every major Canadian theatre company. During Garner's lifetime only one of its three parts — "A

Trip For Mrs. Taylor" — was given a public performance (by the Brockville Theatre Guild on November 4, 1966 and by two other small theatre groups in the late 1970s). Garner took this as proof that he wasn't cut out to be a playwright and hereafter confined his dramatic ambitions to writing for radio. His well-developed ear for the way people actually speak was easily translated into theatrical terms; but when it came to getting his characters in and out of rooms on stage or television, he just didn't have the ability to visualize what had to be done to make this appear credible to an audience.

Hugh Garner's Best Stories had by no means used up his backlog of short fiction, and so in the fall of 1965 he offered Ryerson a collection of fourteen tales, most of them quite recent. As an index of how tough things now were for even well-established writers of short stories, it is worth noting that several of these had never been published in a magazine, although most had been broadcast over the CBC. Once again the title was a problem — at one point Hugh exasperatedly suggested that it be called "Hugh Garner's Second-Best Stories" — and finally his own less than scintillating *Men and Women* was accepted.

The book was dedicated to Robert Weaver, an act of homage that acknowledged how important the CBC's literary godfather had been to his writing career. Since their initial encounter in 1950, when Garner had subjected Weaver to some gratuitous and intoxicated abuse, they had become close friends who met regularly for coffee and conversation. As one of the relatively few members of the literary establishment with whom Hugh was always on good terms, Weaver was an important source of advice about such things as Canada Council applications and which universities might be interested in purchasing his papers. They spent hours together in the coffee shop of the Four Seasons Hotel on Jarvis Street, chatting affably and not too seriously about who was writing what for whom and who was doing what to whom; and it was Weaver's loyal — but by no means uncritical — support of his short stories that figured heavily in Garner's decision to continue writing them during a period (1952-1962) when he could have spent almost all of his time on magazine non- fiction.

The hardcover edition of *Men and Women*, which was published in the fall of 1966, showed that Hugh had achieved a compromise between the tough naturalism of his earliest work and the mass-market character of his writing for "the slicks." The new collection contained the odd maudlin sentiment or contrived coincidence, but for the most part dealt with convincingly real people caught up in everyday quibbles and conflicts: "Black and White and Red All Over"'s artful buildup to a shocking conclusion and "Not That I Care"'s affecting evocation of an old love affair were among the highlights of an excellent selection of stories. Unfortunately, the public didn't seem to agree; despite mostly positive reviews, *Men and Women* sold only 1,100 copies in two-and-a-half years, and its 1973 paperback edition added six better-known, older stories in an attempt to attract more readers.

In October of 1965 the *Telegram* asked Hugh if he would like to do a regular weekday column in place of the occasional "Dissent" pieces, and with an old free-lancer's inability to turn down a job, any job, he agreed. He had averaged a "Dissent" every two weeks, which for a person with more than his share of unconventional opinions meant that he had no difficulty choosing topics to write about; but the pressure of a five-days-a-week schedule soon told on him, and he found that he was beginning to brood about his next column as soon as he finished the one he was working on.

Since his new column ran on the editorial page instead of opposite it, his work was now being judged by an ever-changing retinue of editorialists who seemed to be much more concerned about what readers might think than their op-ed page counterparts had been. During the next year nine of his columns were killed for one reason or another: one for sheer bawdiness when he tried to recycle the story of how as a randy young seaman he had been taken to a nunnery in Belfast, another because it probably would have offended the ethnic politicians who were its subject, and a third for its nasty remarks about evangelical religion. After a year of this anxiety and irritation, Garner went on a month-long binge that helped the *Telegram*'s management decide to replace him, but they parted friends and he would later do some more free-lancing for the newspaper.

The year 1966 was ushered in by two projects that for entirely different reasons strongly appealed to Garner. The first was a travel book on Ontario, for which he requested funding from the Centennial Commission when it began to consider ideas for activities that would contribute to the celebration of Canada's one-hundredth birthday. This would probably have been the only travel book ever written that concentrated on highways and beer parlours, and it's a pity that his was not one of the applications allotted a grant.

His second idea was one that had been nagging at his consciousness for some time. As early as 1948 he had written that "I am seething with ideas about a novel dealing with the decline and apprehension of a sexual psychopath," and now he finally began to work in earnest on the manuscript that would become *The Sin Sniper*. The fact that the book was a paperback original, had superficial similarities to the police-procedural genre and was followed by two rather badly written sequels (*Death in Don Mills* and *Murder Has Your Number*) featuring its protagonist, "Inspector McDumont," have all worked against its being taken seriously; but in terms of its autobiographical and sociological revelations, *The Sin Sniper* is as important as *Cabbagetown* and *Silence on the Shore* for an understanding of Garner's persona, and it is nearly their equal in literary quality. Although it did not find a publisher until 1970, it will be discussed here on the grounds that it was conceived almost twenty years earlier and deserves to be separated from the two later Inspector McDumont titles.

At first sight, *The Sin Sniper* appears to be just another cops-and-criminals opus. Someone is shooting prostitutes in Toronto's tenderloin district, and after a long investigation during which the city's sociology is colourfully explored, a series of coincidences leads to the police gunning down an innocent suspect. The real killer, a newspaper reporter with severe sexual problems, dies shortly thereafter of natural causes, at which point McDumont belatedly realizes the true state of affairs.

Inspector McDumont is obviously modelled on Garner: he is an abrasive, curious and generally perceptive detective who is also a bit of a bully as well as something of a sentimentalist. The similarities extend to their tastes in food and detestation of rock music and, as Hugh would later tell an interviewer, "Sure, McDumont is me." But it is his relation to *The Sin Sniper*'s other main character, the journalist and psychopath "George Pethwick," that has — understandably enough — gone unnoticed by those unfamiliar with Garner's background.

Pethwick, like *Silence on the Shore*'s Walter Fowler, Ben Lawlor in the 1970 novel *A Nice Place to Visit*, and the protagonists of several of his short stories, is yet another of those down-at-the-heels journalists who frequently appear in his work. Although these characters differ from McDumont in that they are much less self-assured, they are otherwise equally recognizable self-portraits that reflect Garner's awareness of to some extent being a "hack," in that he produced a lot of hackwork and was thus often dismissed as one by unsympathetic critics; they also seem to represent his idea of what he might have become without his wife and family, since his journalist protagonists are usually divorced and friendless loners. Their drinking and health problems also resemble their creator's, with George Pethwick's painful ulcer a reminder of the stomach ailments that troubled Garner for the last twenty-five years of his life.

Except for the concluding one, each chapter of *The Sin Sniper* ends with a stream-of-consciousness passage narrated by the killer, who is revealed to be Pethwick only at the end of the book. Hugh was a great admirer of William Faulkner's use of stream-of-consciousness technique in the opening pages of *The Sound and the Fury*, although his own ideas about fictional realism meant that he usually avoided such relatively experimental procedures. In *The Sin Sniper*, however, he made extremely effective use of it; and just as he had always rummaged about in his past for memories that would lend credence to his fiction, so does he appear to have relived his youth in sketching Pethwick's troubled upbringing.

This is, of course, fiction, and there is no way of ascertaining how exactly it corresponds to the realities of his early life. Given what we do know about his ambivalent feelings toward Annie Garner and his hatred of at least one of the men with whom she was involved, however, it seems reasonable to take the following as an emotionally true account of what he as well as his protagonist, whose nickname is "Twitch," experienced:

> When he was ten years old ... his mother ... frequently entertained a married-but-separated boyfriend ... called Gordon Yearby. During the night he had been jarred from sleep twice by the cadenced banging of the head of his mother's bed against the wall that separated his kitchen cot from the room in which she and Yearby were "doing it" again. At that time he had only a vague idea what "doing it" entailed, but he knew it was physical, and that the man lay on top of the woman, who sometimes moaned, laughed or swore.
>
> ... When he heard them getting up in the morning, he turned his face to the wall and pretended to be asleep.
>
> "Young Twitch is still sleeping", Yearby said, crossing the kitchen to wash up in the sink.
>
> "That's what I told you," Etty said. "Nothing could wake that kid once he hits the pillow. I have one hell of a time getting him up before I leave for work.
>
> "Well, don't get him up before I get out of here," Yearby said. "He hates me, even though I done nothing to him."
>
> "Kids don't like their mothers to have any fun of their own," she said, lighting the wood-burning stove with newspaper and bark and chips. "They like to keep their mother's attention only on them."

If this is a substantially accurate representation of what he observed during his childhood, it is now clear why he later used the phrase "lamentable and injurious" to describe his mother's conduct toward him.

From such beginnings Pethwick gradually turns into a sexual psychopath whose experiences are analogous to some of those detailed in Krafft-Ebbing's *Psychopathia Sexualis*, that catalogue of socially tabooed practices that Hugh had first discovered in Los Angeles and had a copy of in his library. Although Pethwick develops into a tormented creature clearly based on fantasy rather than fact, snippets of Garner-like autobiography periodically suggest that there is a connection between them: both work "bagging shavings in a wooden ruler company," both educate themselves by reading in libraries, and the name and serial number of Pethwick's weapon is exactly the same as the "Lee-Enfield Jungle Carbine" Garner listed in his 1959 inventory of household effects.

These correspondences did nothing to convince editors to publish the book, of course, and Ryerson's Robin Farr was quick to exercise his right of first refusal when he handed back the manuscript "as if it were burning his fingers." It was then turned down by all the major and most of the minor publishers in Canada; only in 1970 would it find a home at Simon & Schuster of Canada, an American-owned firm that recognized its possibilities as a paperback original.

In the spring of 1966 Hugh was invited to be an instructor at that summer's creative-writing workshop at the Quetico Centre, a continuing-education facility in the north-western Ontario town of Atikokan. He accepted with alacrity, and from July 24 to 30 taught a class in the basics of short-story writing. Although he had earlier (and would again) dismissed creative-writing courses as wastes of time, he found this one quite a pleasant experience: his students were an interestingly varied lot, including two schoolteachers, a nurse and a guide for the Ontario Department of Forestry, and they seemed to enjoy his no-nonsense approach to the writing business.

Much of the fall of 1966 was spent finishing up his stint at the *Telegram*, making promotional appearances for *Men and Women* and moving into a new apartment. The residents of 66 Broadway Avenue had drawn up a petition demanding that he be asked to leave the building; fortunately the Perkell Brothers had a place for him in their 33 Erskine Avenue property. By December he and Alice were comfortably settled in a one-bedroom apartment where he would reside for the remainder of his life.

All this activity had made 1966 a relatively quiet year in terms of his abuse of alcohol — although the tenants at 66 Broadway Avenue would obviously have disagreed — but as 1967 dawned with no regular column to write and *The Sin Sniper* finished and embarking upon its long round of rejections, the binges came with disturbing frequency. As was often the case, it was the Christmas season that seemed to trigger his need to drink himself into unconsciousness. Shortly after the beginning of the new year he went on the first of what would be a series of drinking bouts, four of which required hospitalization at the Homewood Sanitarium in Guelph.

From now on "Homewood" would become part of the everyday vocabulary of the Garner household. Hugh came to view his increasingly frequent sojourns there not as a treatment for his alcoholism, which by this time was probably beyond any humane form of therapy, but as a kind of vacation from the cares of the outside world. Here he became a favourite of the doctors and nurses and made vast quantities of rather hideous ashtrays, which he delighted in pressing on even his slightest acquaintances. He also met a number of socially prominent fellow guests and told a 1971 CBC TV interviewer that the atmosphere was in many ways "just like a gentlemen's club."

Garner spent a total of fifty-six days as a patient at Homewood on four separate occasions between January 30, 1967 and January 26, 1968. Each admission was preceded by a period of approximately two weeks during which he drank so heavily and continuously that it became painfully obvious he was not going to stop. In between stays at Homewood he tried to continue leading the life of a successful author, but his drinking was beginning to catch up with him. Early in May he started on another binge, and when a CBC producer phoned to confirm a radio appearance Hugh agreed verbally while retaining no memory of their conversation. Although he had experienced occasional blackouts during previous drinking sessions, they now became much more frequent: he was liable to visit the bank or go for a walk without any conscious recollection of what he had been doing.

After spending May 12-23 at Homewood, he thought that a change of scene might perk him up. In the middle of June he and Alice left for a long motor trip through the Canadian and American West, during which they visited the Grand Canyon as well as some of the places Hugh had last seen as a 1930s hobo. When they returned in mid-July, however, he immediately started another round of heavy drinking, and from August 2 to 16 he was back in Homewood. Since travel at least suspended his imbibing even if it didn't seem to cure it, he and Alice then headed off to Montreal, where Expo '67 was in full swing.

During his final days at the *Telegram* Garner had written two columns in which he mocked Expo '67's ambitions to be a world-class event, and it was mainly at Alice's instigation that he finally did agree to visit the exposition. Once there, he was delighted with its amenities, and in a letter to R.F. Shaw, the Deputy Commissioner General of Expo '67, confessed that he deserved to eat "a large helping of crow" for his previous sceptical remarks. Buoyed up by this experience as well as the news that next year Ryerson was going to bring out *Silence on the Shore* and *Hugh Garner's Best Stories* as quality paperbacks, he decided to apply to the Canada Council for a grant to undertake a project that had long been in the back of his mind.

After finishing *Silence on the Shore*, Garner had conceived of writing a sequel that, with it and *Cabbagetown*, would make up a "Toronto Trilogy." When *Cabbagetown* had originally been published in 1950, Collins had asked him to consider writing some additional chapters that would bring Ken Tilling's life up to the present day. Although he rejected the idea at the time, Hugh and his protagonist were so closely interlinked that in a sense the Tilling story would continue as long as his real-life counterpart survived. Garner now proposed to take Tilling and several characters from *Silence on the Shore* and weave them into a novel tentatively entitled "Dance to a Different Drum," which would bring their lives to a dramatic conclusion. While occupied with drafting his application to the Council and making some preliminary notes, he kept his consumption of alcohol to a minimum through most of December. But on Christmas Day, 1967, with the forms in the mail and nothing that needed to be immediately written, he began to drink with grim intensity, and from January 8 to 26, 1968 he was again a resident of Homewood.

By the time he was released there were, fortunately, a number of things that did require his attention. The drinking tapered off as he got back into the routine of being a professional writer, his nerves somewhat calmed by a prescription for tranquilizers. After years of asking every publisher he met to issue the unexpurgated version of *Cabbagetown*, Ryerson had agreed to bring it out in the fall of 1968, and so he had to get busy restoring and revising his original text. There was quite a bit of free-lance work as well: he adapted a story for CBC Radio, selected two others for inclusion in Robert Weaver's anthology of *Canadian Short Stories* and queried *Star Weekly* about an article on neurotic housewives that would make use of the psychological expertise of the staff at Homewood. He also had his eyes tested for new reading glasses, went to the dentist and caught up on the many everyday sorts of things that had been interrupted by the previous year's bout with the bottle.

In February 1968, he engaged in what he considered one of his finest hours, a victorious battle with his son's former landlord. The latter was refusing to return Hugh, Jr.'s security deposit despite the fact that the lease had expired and he had legally moved out, and Hugh leapt into the fray with righteous enthusiasm. He had himself sworn in as a bailiff and personally presented the landlord with a summons for the amount of money involved, which was paid with no further delays. It was "one of the highlights of my life," he wrote one of the doctors at Homewood, once again demonstrating that enjoyment of litigation which *Mayfair* editor Jeann Beattie had found so disconcerting.

Some other things that he found himself enjoying, much to his and everyone else's astonishment, were the arts-and-crafts activities Homewood offered its patients as a means of relaxation. In addition to the ashtrays he turned out in prodigious quantities while resident there, he created a "Picassoesque multi-tiled plate [that] now occupies a place of honor on our dinette sideboard" and a somewhat less successful pair of mocassins. Back at the Erskine Avenue apartment he continued his tile work:

I have done a couple of plates to join the gigantic one I did at Homewood. Right now I have two brass bowls to do, and am currently finishing a half dozen coasters whose insides became shabby from spilt beer and stuff; I am lining them with tile. I don't know how long it will take me to get sick of this particular caper, but I will be concentrating on tiling a large tray probably next winter or fall, as a release from the work I'll be doing on my novel.

His fifty-fifth birthday on February 22 was made a happier occasion by the news that the Canada Council had awarded him a Senior Arts Fellowship worth seven thousand dollars to write "Dance to a Different Drum." Before getting down to work on this, he and Alice decided to celebrate by taking a long automobile trip to Mexico, for which Hugh prepared by reading a pocket Spanish dictionary and trying to remember some of the more polite phrases from his soldiering and sailoring days. They left at the beginning of April, travelled leisurely along the eastern and southern coasts of the United States, crossed the border at Brownsville, Texas and continued down Mexico's Gulf Coast to Mexico City. After sightseeing by taxi — Garner found the traffic a terrifying example of anarchy in action — they returned home via the inland Mexican highway to Nuevo Laredo, where they re-entered the U.S. and took a western and midwestern route back to Toronto.

This holiday gave him the material for an excellent story, "Violation of the Virgins," which was based on their attendance at a festival in a small village north of Mexico City. As a further indication of how closely his fiction sometimes followed his life, Hugh later chortled when a friend commented that he had created a powerful symbol of civilization's destruction of nature in another story inspired by the trip, "Step-'n-a-Half." Here he presented the image of a jaguar's carcass, sprawled at the side of the road after having either been shot or hit by a car, as what his friend took to be a foretaste of the narrative's subsequent depiction of human depravity. For Garner, however, this was simply something that he had seen and remembered when describing a particular stretch of highway; a wilier person would have taken credit for this imagined coup, but with his usual blunt forthrightness he made it clear that his fiction was — as always — based on realities rather than symbols.

Back in Toronto by the end of May, Hugh tried to buckle down to writing "Dance to a Different Drum." But after making some notes about his principal characters and drawing up a floor plan of the apartment building in which Ken Tilling resided, he was unable to go any further. Since he had experienced similar difficulties with *Silence on the Shore*, this wasn't yet serious cause for concern, and there were other matters competing for his attention. He had agreed to teach creative writing at an August workshop held at the Ryerson Polytechnical Institute in Toronto, but a more serious concern was Annie Garner's failing health.

Since she had entered a nursing home, Hugh's attitude toward his mother had undergone something of a change. Once vociferous in his condemnation of her relations with men, he gradually became somewhat more sympathetic and sentimental about how she had coped with making a new life in a strange country. When she passed away on July 7 he was surprised by the emotions her death evoked in him: relief, guilt, sorrow and shame were mixed together in overwhelming combination. Annie Garner had been a part of his life to an extent that he had not fully realized; and in his autobiography he concludes his portrait of her with the confession that "I didn't cry for her when she was buried, for crying wouldn't have been enough."

Chapter Nine

One Damn Thing After Another (1968-1973)

In the fall of 1968 Hugh tried to resume work on "Dance to a Different Drum," but he simply couldn't get anywhere with it. He fiddled around making lists of major and minor characters, crossing out a name here and adding one there, and even tried to cannibalize parts of his long out-of-print novel *Present Reckoning* as a way of getting the book off the ground. Ironically, these difficulties were occurring at the same time that the original version of *Cabbagetown* was finally seeing the light of day, attractively presented in a hardcover edition that sparked a number of serious and generally favourable reappraisals of his work.

Viewed whole, *Cabbagetown* could at last be granted its due recognition as an ambitious and largely successful combination of psychological character study and the sociological examination of a community. Its protagonist's political development was effectively integrated with the maturation of his adult persona, and several figures who had played minor roles in the book's first incarnation were now brought forward as important pieces of its structural mosaic. The 1968 edition convincingly established that when Garner lavished time and care on his work, as he had also done with *Silence on the Shore*, many of his short stories and to a lesser degree *The Sin Sniper*, he had few peers as a writer of psychologically charged and vividly realistic fiction.

On the other hand, he could also dash off some pretty slight stuff that satisfied only the more uncritical among his readers, and he also seemed to take a perverse kind of professional pride in how quickly he could churn out minimally acceptable copy. Having seen that *The Sin Sniper* was a bit too raw for Ryerson Press, with which he had now been publishing for five years, he decided to write a novel that would combine the investigation of a murder with the journalistic portrayal of a community. *A Nice Place to Visit* actually took quite a long time to finish — it was written between the summer of 1968 and the fall of 1969 — but this was primarily because he had difficulties with its structure: it began as a short story, ballooned into a manuscript almost as long as the original *Cabbagetown*, and had to be pared down into the still rather prolix form in which it was published in 1970.

A Nice Place to Visit is set in Graylands, a small town west of Toronto that probably reflects Garner's growing familiarity with the area around Guelph, where Homewood Sanitarium is located. Although the book contains some acute if rather jaundiced observations about small-town life, both its plot and its people take far too long to develop; and you have to go back to the unrelenting awfulness of *Waste No Tears* to find a Garner title in which the dialogue is so leaden and characterless. The protagonist, Ben Lawlor, is one of those grizzled old journalists who often feature in Garner's fiction, and he provides a certain amount of comic relief with his abrasive style of researching his story. But on the whole, *A Nice Place to Visit* is about as stimulating as the overworked catch-phrase to which its title refers, and it did not bode well for the books to come. There is a notable difference in quality between much of his pre-1968 fiction and the novels and stories written afterwards, and it may be that 1968's monumental drinking spree marks the beginning of what would by the mid-1970s be clear indications of serious brain damage.

In the spring of 1969, while working *A Nice Place to Visit* into publishable shape, Hugh asked Robert Weaver about the possibility of selling his papers to a university archive. Weaver contacted Queen's University professor Douglas Spettigue, who was indeed interested in acquiring them; and after some brief and amicable negotiations during which a figure of seven thousand dollars was agreed on, Garner's literary files became the property of one of those "snob institutions" against which he liked to fulminate.

Hugh took great delight in this connection with one of Canada's major universities. During most of the remaining years of his life he made an annual expedition to Queen's to drop off another accumulation of material, speak to English classes there and to inmates of the Kingston and Joyceville penal institutions. On one occasion, a student at a Queen's graduate English seminar asked him about the symbolism of a *Cabbagetown* character who was scalded to death in a vat of boiling chocolate. Once again, Garner had to disappoint an eager academic interpreter: "I was flabbergasted. I had to tell him that I did know a boy who died that way when I was young, after he had an epileptic fit while he was working in a chocolate factory."

Throughout all these varied activities, Hugh was painfully aware that he was using up both the money and the time earmarked for "Dance to a Different Drum." As someone who prided himself on being as good as his word, he was well aware that he had been using his grant for "Dance to a Different Drum" to revise *Cabbagetown* and to write *A Nice Place to Visit* and several short stories. But he was still anxious to complete the "Toronto trilogy," and he finally decided that he would own up to what he had been doing while at the same time asking the Canada Council for further funds.

Accordingly, he drafted a long and somewhat less than convincing letter that attempted to simultaneously explain, apologize and solicit additional support in one rambling missive. After a garrulous preamble in which he congratulated himself for having written about Toronto for so many years, he went on to rant about how the "the fear and nice-Nellyness of my publisher, The Ryerson Press, and of other foreign-book-jobbing so-called Canadian 'publishing houses'" had kept *The Sin Sniper* from being published. He then argued that since he had written *A Nice Place to Visit* and nine short stories during the past year, he had really earned his first grant and was entitled to another one for "Dance to a Different Drum." The whole thing read like an unbalanced tirade from someone with so much reason to be defensive that he had decided to be offensive; not surprisingly, the Canada Council decided that for the next year, at least, it would take a break from subsidizing Garner's adventures in novel writing.

At the same time, he was applying to the Ontario Council for the Arts (now The Ontario Arts Council) for a grant to write "Dance to a Different Drum." When making such applications, it is customary to provide some sort of outline or idea, however vague, of what the book is about; but with his usual contempt for those conventions with which he happened to disagree, Hugh told the Council's Awards Committee that he wasn't going to bother with such irrelevant details:

> I have no intention of giving you a synopsis of the book, DANCE TO A DIFFERENT DRUM, at this time, as it is against my policy ... to *talk* [about] a book's theme, plot, or denouement before *writing* it. You'll just have to take my word, and the evidence of my history and success as a writer, that the grant will be used to support me while the book is being written, and that it will be published as Book No. 2 of my Toronto Trilogy.

It took the Ontario Council for the Arts until the fall of 1969 to act on Garner's somewhat unusual request for funds, and its response will be discussed a bit further on in this chapter. For the moment, it is enough to note that in these two applications the arrogance and combativeness Garner so often displayed in personal confrontations and communications have been carried over into what should have been an entirely impersonal business correspondence.

The frustrations with publishers that were such an inappropriate part of his letter to the Canada Council came to another head when he learned that almost a thousand copies of his short-story collection *Men and Women* were languishing in Ryerson's warehouse. He kept bugging the company to do something with the books and finally offered to buy the whole lot if they were priced as remainders. As a result, the basement storage cubicle allotted to the Garners at 33 Erskine Avenue was soon crammed with 970 copies of *Men and Women*, and Hugh made his entry into the wholesale end of the book business.

For a more ivory-tower sort of author, this impulsive purchase could have been a disaster; but for someone who had sold men's clothing, groceries and soap flakes — the last door-to-door to Depression-era housewives — selling books was a piece of cake. Carting the books around town in the trunk of his car, he made major sales to the Toronto library system, the Readers' Club of Canada and a local high school, and during his summer stint at the Ryerson Polytechnical Institute's creative-writing workshop he sold his students autographed copies for one dollar each. The approximately two hundred copies left over went to the Coles bookstore chain for slightly more than what he had paid for them, and by the time he was finished he had made a substantial profit, enjoyed himself immensely, and reinforced his conviction that he knew more about selling books than did any of his publishers.

The money was needed, because in the summer of 1969 both his children required loans for pressing family matters, and the cheque from Queen's had been invested in a pension fund that, since he would have no other nest egg if he had to retire from writing, Garner was becoming increasingly anxious about augmenting. With *The Sin Sniper* still making the rounds of publishing houses and *A Nice Place to Visit* not yet ready for submission, he as he had so often done before turned to his friend Robert Weaver at the CBC. After Annie Garner's death he had made a new will that named Weaver as his literary executor, and in a July 26, 1969 letter told him "without you I don't know where the hell I'd be." Weaver once again came through by buying *The Sin Sniper* and the story "Artsy- Craftsy" for radio adaptation, and purchasing "The Sound of Hollyhocks" — a short fictional portrait of a stay at Homewood Sanitarium — for his quarterly *The Tamarack Review*.

From August 11 to 22 Hugh was back at Ryerson's creative-writing workshop for the second year in a row. He liked to pretend that he did these workshops strictly for the money, but he also enjoyed the chance to talk about his own approach to authorship and help younger writers avoid some of the difficulties he had experienced. Among the several students who wrote to express how much they had enjoyed his classes, at least one — short-story writer Robert Knight — did go on to have some of his work published, and in a letter to Knight Hugh offered some of the eminently practical advice that he had himself followed:

> a university education is not too important to a writer, for whom there are far more important things. Among these things ... I would list as varied a life as possible, in jobs, contacts with the opposite sex, travel, and learning from the writings of others. You may not be able to fight in a war, and you certainly can't have a baby ... but you must be able to write about them, from the inside. You must *know* a million things, and be able to write about them as if they have happened to you. To sum up this bit of literary philosophy, *a writer is a person who has a shallow knowledge of a great many things, but is not necessarily an expert in any.*

In September the Ontario Council for the Arts finally responded to his application for a grant to write "Dance to a Different Drum" when a secretary called to ask about the amount and duration of his previous Canada Council awards. Smelling a rat, Garner fired off a broadside to the Council's chairman, Professor Anthony Adamson, in which he said he was "immediately suspicious" that someone was trying to "portray me as a literary mendicant, existing from grant to grant as a beggar exists between alms or handouts." After providing more information than he had offered to date about the novel he wanted to write, he launched into a scathing attack on Ron Evans, the Council's film and literary officer:

> After attending a meeting of Mr. Evans' "inner-city" quasi-arts/welfare group, and visiting a couple of east-central Toronto groups, one of which has been supplied with movie equipment and a part-time instructor ... I am certain that Evans is not using the money allotted to him for films and literature as it should be used. For instance the $18,089.30 spent on the "Dick & Jane" artsy-

craftsy Annual Report could have kept quite a few writers writing, and might have brought forth an excellent young novelist out of those who can't afford to write a book. Let Evans forget his goddam lunches at Le Pavillon, his embossed letterheads, his no-talent escape into fantastic and impossible dreams of making artists out of slum kids (I'm a slum kid and I know more about the slums than any petit bourgeois dilettante will ever know) and spend the money he is allotted on what it has been allotted for, namely helping and instructing writers and unpublished writers of promise in this province.

Garner closed this letter by describing himself as "a person who has always burnt his bridges, not after crossing them but before even reaching them," thus concluding his splenetic tirade with an appropriately mixed metaphor.

With this off his chest, Hugh a week later favoured the Council with a long letter listing various suggestions as to how it could do a better job of distributing its largesse. Some of these reflected personal quirks — taking control of the Governor's Medals for non-fiction, which he bitterly resented never winning, out of the hands of the University of Western Ontario was the prime example — but most were sensible enough. Prizes for high-school age writers, support for the smaller presses and the encouragement of regional writers' workshops were advocated in what may have been an attempt to convince the Council that he was not the deranged misanthrope who had written the previous letter. But whatever his intentions, the result was a carefully phrased — he was told that "Council members were particularly admiring of your work, sir, and intrigued by the possibility of assisting in its creation" — but nonetheless negative reply that in effect meant that "Dance to a Different Drum" would never be written.

Aside from the fact that he was by this time probably incapable of the concentrated effort that had gone into *Cabbagetown* and *Silence on the Shore*, Hugh had painted himself into a psychological corner with his refusal to write a serious novel unless he could count on being paid for it. Since he was having trouble with "Dance to a Different Drum" anyway, the rejections from the two arts councils gave him — as he saw it — legitimate reason to abandon the book; and because he was unable to provide even a simple outline of what the novel was about, it was perfectly understandable that awards committees preferred to subsidize projects that looked as though they had some chance of actually being completed. The aspiring author who had persevered with *Cabbagetown* in the face of poverty and lack of encouragement was no more; in his place was a professional writer whose notions of merit were now bound up with monetary considerations.

As 1969 drew to a close, with *The Sin Sniper* and *A Nice Place to Visit* still looking for publishers and two unsuccessful tussles with arts councils fresh in his memory, Garner began looking around for a job that would pay him a regular salary. He applied to the *Toronto Star* for the position of book editor and in his letter included many detailed suggestions for improving its book pages. He indicated his general state of mind in a letter to Robert Weaver: "I've definitely made up my mind not to write another book. That's definite. More than twenty years in this business has been enough." But nothing came of these efforts, and not too long thereafter both his novels suddenly found a home.

When Ryerson had turned down *The Sin Sniper*, as he had known quite well it would, Hugh was then, under the terms of his contract, free to take his books elsewhere. But since no one else seemed to want either *The Sin Sniper* or *A Nice Place to Visit*, his enjoyment of his new freedom was rather short-lived. At the beginning of 1970 he swallowed his pride and submitted the latter book to Ryerson. It happened to be the first manuscript that the press' new general manager, Gavin Clark, picked up to read, and he liked it so much that the negotiations were concluded without difficulty and a contract signed on February 19.

Much heartened by this demonstration that he wasn't yet on the publishing scrap-heap, Garner took *The Sin Sniper* to the Canadian branch of Simon & Schuster, who were aggressively seeking titles for an original mass-market paperback line. He hit it off well with the firm's general manager, James Smallwood, who also had a journalistic background, and on March 13 they agreed to terms on a book that would easily sell out its first paperback printing of fifty thousand copies. *The Sin Sniper* had been turned down by every major and many of the minor Canadian-owned presses, a revealing display of the lack of commercial acumen that contributed to the series of crises which struck the Canadian publishing industry in the 1970s.

With two advance royalty cheques topping up the family's bank account and two books set for fall 1970 publication, Hugh and Alice decided they would celebrate with a trip to Europe. Alice had never been there, and Hugh wanted to make a return visit and wasn't getting any younger. Early in May they flew to England for the start of an ambitious journey through the Britsh Isles, France and Italy. Unfortunately, Hugh was not on his best behaviour for much of the trip and provoked several near-riots with his impatience and obnoxiousness on the crowded continental trains, where he often got into shouting and shoving matches with his fellow passengers.

During a short stop in Nice, returning to their hotel after a long and liquid dinner, Hugh experienced an overwhelming need to empty his bladder. He chose a narrow alley-way alongside a tavern that, judging from the number of motorcycles parked outside, was a biker's hangout. While attempting to negotiate his way in the pitch dark, his foot slipped and he lurched against one of the motorcycles. All hell now broke loose: one after another, the gleaming chrome machines fell like a row of dominoes, and their irate owners boiled out of the tavern, doubtless expecting to confront an attack by a rival gang. What they found was an obnoxiously unrepentant tourist and his terrified wife; as Alice begged for their forgiveness, Hugh shouted epithets that fortunately defied translation and they were fortunate to escape from the bewildered bikers.

The Garners spent the last two weeks of their holiday in Paris, where they stayed in a pleasant, small hotel in the St.-Germain-des-Pres quarter and dined at famous cafés such as the Brasserie Lipp and Les Deux Magots. Alice had thought it would be easier to manage Hugh without the strain of getting him on and off trains and buses, but he now came up with a new method of getting on everyone's nerves. When he saw someone doing something that piqued his interest, he would pester Alice to ask them about it in her fluent French; when she told Hugh the person's answer, he would come up with more queries that would eventually provoke a response of the "Leave me alone!" variety. Hugh would get his back up, and Alice would have to apologize to everyone concerned; by the end of their vacation, she felt more like her husband's keeper than his wife.

Back in Toronto, Garner threw himself into the sort of pre-publication publicity whirl that he hadn't experienced since the 1966 appearance of *Men and Women*. In July he taped several shows for CBC Radio, was interviewed by newspaper reporters and an Ontario Institute for Studies in Education researcher, and made sure that review copies of his new books went to the right people. This was easy enough in the case of Simon & Schuster, which was adept at the marketing of solid commercial properties when it saw one, but at Ryerson there was total confusion: the United Church of Canada had decided to unload the long-unprofitable company, and the only bidder with cash in hand was the American firm of McGraw-Hill.

As Canadian nationalists tried to pressure either the federal or provincial governments into blocking Ryerson's sale to McGraw-Hill, Garner once again demonstrated that the former left-winger who in the '50s had become a "left-wing capitalist" was now simply a capitalist. He refused to take a public stance against the takeover and made an ostentatious point of crossing a picket line thrown up by its opponents. When he wrote his autobiography a few years later he was still fuming about what he saw as the phoney sentimentality of the anti-McGraw-Hill forces. As usual, he didn't mince his words:

> I didn't care if the firm had been taken over by a Zulu publishing company, and anyhow it had been running in the red long enough, supported by the dimes from the Sunday school collections of the United Church. ...
> ... The Ryerson Press hadn't even come close to doing a job for Canadian literature for years, as can be proved by their almost non-existent stable of novelists by the time the United Church sold them off.

Garner made himself some new enemies and reinforced the distaste of his old ones with his stand on this issue, and he further
irritated those in the nationalist camp when he opted to keep the
company now known as McGraw-Hill Ryerson as his publisher.

This decision, which reflected both Hugh's characteristic
stubbornness and his dislike for those who espoused the cause
of Canadian nationalism, would have far-reaching consequences
for his literary reputation. In the 1970s there would be a discern-
ible downgrading of his work by younger academic critics such
as Frank Davey, whose influential *From There to Here* (1974)
announced that even Garner's short stories — which unlike his
novels had up to this point received almost uniformly respectful
attention — were now out of favor. Davey described them as

> lacking in subtlety and in depth of characterization. Most of them
> present personality types rather than firmly drawn idiosyncratic
> characters. The situations in which the characters find themselves
> are usually more interesting than the characters themselves. Al-
> though the world-view of these stories is simplistic and often banal,
> most of them can provide an enjoyable and provocative reading
> experience at the secondary school level.

By the 1980s, there would be no Garner presence in anthologies such as George Bowering's *Fiction in Contemporary
Canada* (1980) and John Metcalf's *Making It New: Contemporary Canadian Stories* (1982), and his short fiction would
indeed be relegated to collections aimed at secondary-school students.

There are certainly literary grounds for this attitude, the number of Garner's stories that show their slick-magazine origins
prominent among them, but it also reflects the fact that his often-
expressed pride in being a "loner" had by this time distanced him
from most younger Canadian writers. He definitely wasn't part
of what was going on as he had been in the 1950s and the early
1960s, and he simply did not comprehend the reasons for the
post-1967 explosion of literary nationalism; and just to make

sure that no one missed his alienation from its adherents, his 1973 autobiography took dead aim at

> The semi-literate natives now become Canadian nationalists, as dumb as their forebears but far more gross and rude. Where a business suit and necktie used to be *de rigeur* among authors, now the uniform has changed to a pseudo proletarian-cum-revolutionary denim jacket and dungarees. What hands me a laugh is that their wearers are neither proles nor revolutionaries but middle class dropouts playing the latest literary charade.

An additional factor that tended to push him to the fringes of 1970s literary society was the generally dreadful quality of the fiction he produced during the decade; and for reasons that will be spelled out in detail when the editorial contribution to *One Damn Thing After Another!* is discussed, this to some extent reflected the fact that he was one of McGraw-Hill Ryerson's few remaining Canadian authors of any stature.

The literary fruits of his relationship with McGraw-Hill Ryerson began promisingly enough when he offered them his latest gathering of short fiction, *Violation of the Virgins*, which featured the novella-length title story resulting from his trip to Mexico. The variable quality of the other inclusions is suggested by their original appearances in everything from *The Tamarack Review* and *Queen's Quarterly* to *Chatelaine* and *The Star Weekly*; but on balance, it was a worthwhile collection that earned the applause of those reviewers sophisticated enough to appreciate why Hugh wrote — as George Woodcock had put it — "up and down the scale of fiction."

In the fall of 1970 Garner had been approached by Jim Foley, an English teacher at Port Colborne High School, for help in organizing a "Canada Day" celebration in the Niagara Peninsula community. Perhaps because Foley was himself an old Cabbagetowner, the two hit it off by mail long before they ever met each other on the first Canada Day, February 18, 1971. On this occasion the school's library was rechristened the "Hugh Garner Resource Centre," and as Foley wrote shortly thereafter, Hugh made a strong impression:

this day would not have had half the punch it did if you had not been here ... you may deny it, but how do you account for you being singled out by the papers ... how do you account for the kids that flocked about you ... how do you account for the number of people that kept asking (the organizers) to introduce you to them. How do you account for the fact that a lady waited all the while you spoke to a group of young people outside the cafeteria just to say "hello." How do you account for a resolution put through the student council and filed with the Principal today, that in a little while the students raise money and pay you for your time and have you alone down for the day.

... You spoke to these kids straight from the shoulder and they liked it. You were their authority on Canadian literature. Today in class, one of my students related the incident wherein some students told you about the teacher [who] had them reading between the lines.

You answered to the effect that the teacher didn't know what he was doing ... etc ... they thought that was great.

For anyone sceptical about Garner's ability to relate to high-school age students, there is a tape of a CBC Radio School Broadcasts programme that displays him doing a wonderful job of it. He seems to particularly enjoy the directness of questions such as "Where do you get the ideas for your characters?" and "What are your working habits?," and answers them in his usual candid manner. When one of the students wants to know if he has a favourite contemporary novel, it turns out that they are all fans of Ken Kesey's *One Flew Over the Cuckoo's Nest*; Garner exhibits an easy familiarity with the novel and even comments — perhaps remembering his two weeks at the Point Edward Detention Barracks — that the book's protagonist brought about his own destruction when he went too far in challenging the sway of authority.

As this programme suggested, Hugh was far more aware of what was going on in the world than anyone would have guessed from his frequent public appearances in the role of cantankerous old curmudgeon. In May of 1971 *Maclean's* asked him to contribute to a survey on how some well-known Canadians kept up with current events, and he responded at length. A daily reading of the *Star* supplemented by the weekend editions of *The Globe and Mail* and *Telegram* represented his newspaper intake, and subscriptions to *Time, Maclean's, Newsweek* and *Life* kept him abreast of newsmagazine coverage. He also subscribed to *Saturday Night, Esquire, The Tamarack Review* and *Canadian Literature*, was a more occasional reader of *The New Yorker, Harper's* and *The Atlantic Monthly*, and quipped that he picked up the *New York Sunday Times* when his health permitted him to do so. His television viewing included variety shows, newsmagazine programmes and dramas; radio was primarily a source of morning newscasts on the CBC.

For all of his public and often well-publicized battles with the bottle, a more typical evening for Hugh would consist of reading or TV viewing at home. Once or twice a week he and Alice might go to the movies, but otherwise they were content with each other's company. Alice was more of a night person, and often stayed up to watch The Johnny Carson Show; Hugh usually retired early, often by ten o'clock, and got up with the dawn. If he was tired of reading and there was nothing interesting on TV, he would take a portable radio into the bedroom and sit at his desk, "bathed in nostalgia hearing once again the jazz and swing music of my youth."

In March 1971 Garner made his annual visit to Kingston, where he spoke to classes at Queen's University and at Joyceville Institution. Although he got on well with both groups, it was meeting the prison's inmates that he enjoyed "far more than I did talking with the kids down at Queen's;" he felt an instant kinship with men whose counterparts he had met in his own brushes with the law. In addition to his visits, he ensured that a steady supply of books kept coming, canvassing his publishers for contributions and himself donating most of his review copies of new titles after he had finished writing about them.

One of the odder episodes in a life not exactly deficient in them began that May, when York University's Winters College asked him if he would be willing to become an "Associate Fellow." This came about through the aegis of the poet Miriam Waddington, who taught at Winters and had become a friend of Hugh's at the 1955 Canadian Writers' Conference at Queen's. Since Garner was far more impressed by such honours than he liked to admit — it was the same side of his personality that loved a good old- fashioned parade — he accepted and duly appeared at a dinner for the College's fellows. Here he felt like "Mark Twain's Yankee in King Arthur's Court ... having more affinity with Toronto's Don River than with college dons," and never again attended a Winters' function.

In the summer he began writing the book that was eventually published in 1975 as *Death in Don Mills*, which he began with the idea that it would make another best-selling paperback original for Simon & Schuster. He carried over Inspector McDumont from *The Sin Sniper*, but otherwise left the latter book's funky downtown settings behind for the wide-open spaces of suburbia. As had been the case with his previous novel, *A Nice Place to Visit*, he found that a plot that wasn't drawn from his own experiences was much harder to manage, and he was soon bogged down in what was supposed to have been a "quickie" murder mystery. At one point he even picked up "Dance to a Different Drum" again and had another go at concluding his "Toronto trilogy;" but since this didn't work either, he was soon staring at two problematic writing projects.

The result was an increase in the frequency of his binges, one of which forced McGraw-Hill Ryerson to cancel the November promotional tour it had arranged to coincide with the publication of *Violation of the Virgins*. Since this would have been an all-work-and-no-play grind from Halifax to Vancouver, it's more than likely Hugh took the easy way out by simply stepping up his consumption of alcohol. By the early part of 1972 he was back in circulation, attending a CBC conference of writers and producers at the King Edward Hotel early in January; and he was once again the star of the Port Colborne Canada Day festivities on March 7- 8. But after fulfilling speaking engagements at Hamilton Teacher's College and Brock University on the same south-western Ontario swing, he began drinking heavily again and was in Homewood Sanitarium for a two-week stay at the end of March.

When he got out he took up his Inspector McDumont novel again and got a bit further into it, working in some material about hippies and the drug culture that he had researched with the aid of his much younger friend Doug Fetherling. Fetherling had met Garner in the spring of 1968, and despite their differences in politics, lifestyle and age, they enjoyed each other's company; Garner would sometimes telephone for no other reason than that he "just wanted to yack." Fetherling now conceived the idea of doing a short book on Garner for the "Canadian Writers & Their Works" series that Forum House was putting out, and Hugh obliged by writing him a long autobiographical letter as an aid to his research. Never one to waste anything that could profitably be recycled, Garner used this and several other journalistic pieces in putting together *One Damn Thing After Another!*, with which he would shortly test McGraw-Hill Ryerson's commitment to retaining its most famous Canadian author. And to make things even sweeter, the Canada Council granted him an Arts Award to complete the book, which he now went ahead and did without getting into the sort of muddle that had sabotaged his 1969 application for subsidy.

When he accepted the University of Ottawa's invitation to deliver a lecture there in April, the stage was set for what Garner buffs usually refer to as "the battle of the revolving doors." Although Hugh was usually very good about doing whatever he was supposed to do before he began his serious drinking, his Ottawa hosts got him off to a regrettably early start. When it was time for his talk he wasn't capable of anything more than an informal question-and-answer session, after which he blacked out almost completely for the next two days. As he weaved his way into the lobby of the Chateau Laurier after an evening's boozing, a doorman did get his attention by telling him to "Go sleep it off, buddy." Garner promptly knocked him through the glass panels in the revolving door, and after paying the bill for damages he found that he had come out a net loser on his Ottawa excursion.

He had to be driven home from Ottawa by his sister June, who found him comatose in his hotel room with very little notion of who she or anyone else was. But once back in familiar climes he made one of the characteristically rapid recoveries that often amazed his family and friends. His interest in putting together an autobiography helped to keep him out of serious mischief, and there were also quite a few special events on the horizon. On May 17 he was presented with the City of Toronto's Civic Award of Merit, which prompted him to remark to his friend Jim Foley that the last time the city had given him anything it was Judge Mott's sentence of "a $10 fine or 60 days in the Working Boys' Home" for his 1928 ship-vandalizing escapade. On June 7 he gave a talk about writing as part of a series at the Royal Ontario Museum. This was originally supposed to have been a reading from his work, but Garner "cased" — as he so idiomatically put it — the performances of two of his peers, Hugh Hood and Douglas LePan, and after hearing them read decided that authors should leave the public presentation of their books to the acting profession.

From July 31 to August 11 he taught at a writers' workshop held on the campus of York University's Glendon College and finished up some publishing odds and ends. The firm of Simon & Pierre wanted to issue his stage adaptations of a trilogy of short stories as *Three Women*, and they quickly agreed upon terms for its 1973 publication; and he sold the paperback rights to the collection *Men and Women* to Simon & Schuster, which wisely insisted on beefing it up by adding four older and two very recent stories to the 172 pages of the original volume. And he continued to work on his autobiography, even though McGraw-Hill Ryerson had as yet shown only minimal interest in publishing it.

This lack of interest may possibly have reflected the company's chagrin at Hugh's discovery that it had been remaindering copies of *A Nice Place to Visit* without having first offered him the opportunity to purchase them. Regardless of contractual small print, this is the sort of elementary courtesy that almost all publishers extend to their authors, and Garner had good reason to be angry. He immediately drove out to the company's warehouse and bought all of the 464 copies that were left, as well as 84 copies of the hardcover edition of *Cabbagetown* that he suspected they might remainder without telling him. Disposing of the books was no problem: the Reader's Club of Canada took them all, and once again he had demonstrated that, as he had long ago told Jack Kent Cooke, he could sell as well as write.

Another major sale was the optioning of The Sin Sniper's film rights to the firm of Jim McCammon & Associates, Film Production Co-ordinators. This set in motion a process which would, after many changes of producers, directors and script-writers, result in the artistically and commercially disastrous movie version released as *Stone Cold Dead* in 1979; but by then Garner would have lost all interest in a project that he had little to do with after 1973. The sale did, however, open his eyes to the relatively large sums film companies seemed willing to pay for options, and during the years that remained to him he made several unsuccessful efforts to interest them in the rights to his other books.

Garner completed his first draft of *One Damn Thing After Another!* in December 1972, and after sending it off to McGraw-Hill Ryerson he went on an extended binge. Christmas was, as so often the case, the occasion that seemed to trigger a serious episode of alcohol abuse, although he seemed to enjoy the exchanging of presents and visits from his children and their growing families; he now had four grandchildren, for whom he and Alice often babysat when he wasn't engaged in a drinking bout. Early on Christmas Day, while packages were being opened and wrappings strewn about the apartment, he roamed around with a garbage bag at the ready for each new bit of litter. But later in the day he would begin the serious imbibing, which would then continue until it became evident that institutionalization was necessary.

This year was no exception, and by early January he was at Homewood Sanitarium for another drying-out period. This was one of his more serious benders: he missed the 1973 Canada Day weekend at Port Colborne, and was taken to the Addiction Research Foundation Clinical Institute in Toronto for tests when he did not recover as quickly as he usually did. When he was well enough to go home, he had to deal with McGraw-Hill Ryerson's suggested revisions of his autobiography, which he did in a manner that also sheds an all too revealing light upon the reasons for the poor quality of his next three published novels.

The McGraw-Hill Ryerson editor assigned to *One Damn Thing After Another!*, Toivo Kiil, was an unfortunate choice for a task that would have been extremely difficult for even the most experienced editor. Kiil's initial "Editor's Critique" accurately identified many of the weaknesses of the sprawling and badly organized manuscript Garner had submitted, but it did so in English that called into question the user's familiarity with the language:

> The author's encounters (run-ins) with other persons need not be of a vengeful report. This is not to muzzle the truth or even the substantiated impression. That would take all the author's characters and life out of the book and the people. I think kindness is the essential requisite for a biography that contains episodes of such frustration, but restraint, "being above pettiness" can add real punctuation to the work. When a real spade shows up, it's worth noting and editorializing. But obscuring without anonymizing the target of the attack is a far more effective means of exposing incompetence than a specific, if not libelous, diatribe.

With these general remarks unlikely to bolster anyone's confidence in Kiil's idiomatic appreciation of English prose, it isn't surprising that Garner fought tooth and nail against the more specific changes that were suggested. Hugh's copy of this part of his "Editor's Critique" is inked over with negative, profane and contemptuously dismissive comments, and he apparently returned a photostat of it directly to Kiil.

This document is much too long to quote in full, but the following examples will convey something of the author-editor relationship that it so graphically depicts. When Kiil suggests that excerpts from the fiction might be used to flesh out some of the sparser passages, Garner writes "No! Don't talk shit!" An admonition to "Try to avoid unnecessary references to names and details" earns the response "You are full of shit!" The proposed deletion of two proper names provokes "Fuck off!" The comment that some of Hugh's prose is "plodding" is answered by "You're a very smart-assed unpedantic pedant, Kiil!" And a criticism of Garner's discussion of psychopathology prompts "So now you're a psychiatrist? In this case you're just plain full of shit!" Hugh did accept some of Kiil's ideas concerning minor revisions of the manuscript, but his general attitude is summed up by his reply "How in hell can I remember dates?" to Kiil's perfectly valid observation that the chronology of many of the events in *One Damn Thing After Another!* is unclear. Thus what should have been a monument to Garner's literary achievements instead became a disjointed assemblage of old journalism, rambling reminiscences and new axes to grind. Robert Fulford's *Toronto Star* review demonstrated that both Hugh's bullying of his publisher and the resultant quality of the book had not gone unnoticed:

> Most of it meanders pointlessly from anecdote to anecdote to anecdote, with no sense of structure or purpose. Old magazine articles are flung in here and there, usually for no good reason. ...
>
> The editing is atrocious: apparently the people at McGraw-Hill Ryerson were helpless in the face of Garner's mangled syntax, were incapable of checking the spelling of proper names, and have not yet decided when you use "who" and when you use "whom."

During the last week of June 1973, while *One Damn Thing After Another!* was being printed in just about the form Garner had submitted it, he was among a select band of Canadian literary folk — Irving Layton, Al Purdy, and *Globe and Mail* book columnist William French among them — flown to Los Angeles for that year's American Booksellers Association Convention under the auspices of the federal Department of Trade and Commerce. Here he engaged in some of the inebriated shenanigans that were by now an expected part of his behaviour on such occasions. As Al Purdy put it in a November 1974 letter that recalled their stay at the Marina Del Rey Hotel outside Los Angeles:

Do you remember the sandwich I made for you, which you knocked off the third floor balcony? And then knocked off the coffee, too, and I had to chase down for my wife's plastic cup? I've seldom seen a guy so plastered as you were then, or perhaps a little later when you wanted to take on all the taxi drivers in Hollywood.

Garner replied that he didn't remember anything about those events but did have flashes of vivid memory regarding his adventures after the convention was over. Feeling nostalgic about his last visit to Los Angeles, he had checked into a downtown hostelry — he thought this was probably the Ambassador Hotel, but he couldn't be absolutely certain — and continued with his programme of serious drinking. He described this to his friend Glen Sorestad as

what the French call *nostalgie de la boue*, or "a return to the mud." I had a sport jacket stolen from my room which had my glasses in a pocket, but luckily I was flaked out in my clothes on the bed and had my wallet in a trouser pocket. Such contretemps is about par for any trips I take out of town. One of the house dicks gave me an old jacket to fly home in, which I did at the end of the week.

When he got back he had to finish off an original TV play called "The Outsiders," which had been commissioned by the CBC, and he was also involved in the negotiations for another movie option on *The Sin Sniper*. In August, with his work up to date and Alice away on a visit to her relatives, it was back to drinking and another stay at Homewood, from which he was released just in time for the late-September publication of *One Damn Thing After Another!* From October 9 to 20 he made a string of public appearances to promote the book, and in the following month he was involved in the sort of unmitigated disaster that suggested the book's title was something of an understatement.

The producer of the CBC TV show Take Thirty thought that it might be fun to portray Garner returning to his roots at an old-style beer parlour in Toronto's east end, where he would be filmed chatting with host Paul Soles and two younger writers about the perils and perks of authorship. Doug Fetherling and Nancy Naglin were booked to appear on the programme with him, and around noon on the appointed day they all arrived at a Gerrard Street East tavern. Garner, unfortunately, had gotten an early start on the day's drinking: he was less than steady on his feet and began engaging in the aggressive camaraderie with strangers that represented the midway point in his typical — and inexorable — transition from gracious social drinker to obnoxious lush.

By the time everything had been set up to the satisfaction of the technical crew, Garner was in no condition to be filmed. Doug Fetherling recounts what happened next:

> At the next table a couple of old fellows with Legion pins began to make off-camera remarks about Garner's apparent flirtation with show business, and he excused himself several times to go threaten violence against them. At another point he slammed his lapel-mike down on the hard table, causing the soundman some grief. Paul Soles bore up with professionalism and grace, but after about ten minutes the director called a halt and the crew began to pack up. All the while, Garner, a chain-smoker, had been gesticulating wildly with a lighted cigarette. Once Nancy and I were outside, she told me that he had unwittingly brought it to rest against her trouser leg. There was a hole about the size of a quarter in her corduroys with a corresponding burn beneath. "I didn't want to call his attention to it lest the smell of burning flesh excite him further," she said.

With his day beginning in this fashion, it's no surprise that Hugh went on to make a complete shambles out of it. In a letter to another younger literary friend, Ray Fraser, he related the various damn things after another that had happened next:

> I tried to punch out a taxi-driver, first outside a liquor store where he'd gone to buy me three jugs of Walker's Special Old, next as we were driving up Toronto's main street, and the third time inside my neighborhood police station. Unknown to me — not that I was in any shape to give a damn — a police squad car was following right behind us when I tried to climb over the front seat to get at the driver.

Anyhow, the outcome was a shit-kicking from the fuzz, a summons on a charge of common assault, another one as a common drunk, several hours in a police cell until the welts on my head went down and they sprung me, and then down to the criminal courts. The cab-driver was a hell of a nice young guy, twice my size, who could have taken me like Grant took Richmond. ... When we stepped before the judge the cab-driver withdrew the charge, and the case was dismissed. I gave him ten bucks for the trouble I'd caused him. The cops still have my three jugs of liquor, and I hope to hell they choke on them. I'm too old for those capers any more.

Garner might not have been very good at dealing with the police during his binges, but he had by this time made several friends among the upper echelons of Toronto's finest. He was on very good terms with Syd Brown, the head of the Metropolitan Police Association, and as part of his research for his next Inspector McDumont novel he had become chummy with some of the detectives at 33 Division in Don Mills. With all his major projects completed and remorse at his latest alcoholic escapade temporarily ascendant, he once more started working on the book that was now tentatively entitled *Death in Don Mills*.

Chapter Ten

An Inspector Calls (1973-1979)

In *Death in Don Mills* Garner attempted to write about what
in the early 1970s was known as "the youth culture," and if
the results were on the whole pretty awful, it wasn't because he
was completely isolated from the youth of the day. Since he had
met and immediately hit it off with Doug Fetherling in 1968,
Hugh had also struck up friendships with angry young writers
such as Juan Butler, Jim Christy and Ray Fraser, all anti-estab-
lishment mavericks who appealed to his own residual rebellious-
ness. He was particularly taken with Butler, whose *Cabbagetown
Diary* (1970) was in a sense a modern version of *Cabbagetown*,
and was happy to recommend him for a Canada Council grant;
he did the same for Fraser, and was instrumental in having the
latter's *The Struggle Outside* published by McGraw-Hill Ryerson in 1975. But the communication was by no means all one
way: Christy used Garner as a character in his short story "How
I Became Champ," and Fetherling wrote an excellent profile of
him for a May 1973 issue of *Saturday Night*.

Making use of the hippie slang and sociological insights
offered by his younger friends, Hugh worked away at his manuscript and completed it in May 1974. He knew, as he wrote to
Ray Fraser, that it was "just a pot-boiler," but then, he had never
pretended that it was anything else: he had begun it with the idea
that it would be a paperback-original sequel to *The Sin Sniper*,
and if it had been released in that form, the damage to his reputation would have been minimized. But with his successful
browbeating of McGraw-Hill Ryerson about publishing *One
Damn Thing After Another!* "as is" still fresh in his mind, he

thought that he might as well offer the company *Death in Don Mills* on the chance of the more prestigious — and of course more profitable — publication of the book in a hardcover edition.

McGraw-Hill Ryerson accepted it immediately, scheduled it for its 1975 spring list, and suggested only a few minor editorial changes. This has led some observers to conclude that Garner had the company so much under his thumb that it would print anything he submitted, and given the abysmal quality of the three novels he published with them between 1975 and 1978, there are certainly literary grounds for this view.

Focusing on the intrinsic worth of these books, however, ignores the fact that at least two of them — *Death in Don Mills* and *Murder Has Your Number* — were commercially very successful, and it would probably be more accurate to say that McGraw-Hill Ryerson was simply following the logic of the profit motive in publishing them pretty much as they had been submitted. Having had the experience of trying and largely failing to improve a title that nonetheless sold very well, from the company's point of view it would be a waste of editorial time and tempers to go through the same unpleasant process with Garner's subsequent manuscripts. And even though Hugh's abrasive tirades were by now part of the folklore of Canadian publishing, it is still difficult to believe that he would have been able to intimidate a firm owned by a major American corporate empire.

Whatever McGraw-Hill Ryerson's internal dynamics, its evident willingness to accept almost anything he submitted soon had Garner working hard on another project. In 1973 he had written an original TV play, "The Outsiders," for the CBC, but its production had been plagued with difficulties. The filmed version, shot in early 1974, did not turn out well, and despite various attempts to rewrite, restructure and reshoot it, the play was never shown on television. With his usual disinclination to waste any writing that might possibly be recycled, Garner began to work the play into the form of a novel, at first referring to it as "The

Invaders" but soon settling on the title under which it would be published, *The Intruders*.

On March 8, 1974 he attended the Port Colborne Canada Day celebrations, where for the first time he was something less than an overwhelming success. He became terribly drunk at a dinner held the evening before the major events on the programme, was sick all over himself and a couple of people who tried to help him and got through the next day only by keeping his remarks to a minimum and avoiding informal conversations afterwards. On the same trip, he did make a positive impression on the students he addressed at Lord Elgin High School in Burlington, and then he was off to Ottawa for a TV interview.

Hugh was now beginning to turn down many requests for public appearances, as the increasing frequency of his binges and his growing dislike of travel combined to keep him closer to home. In May 1974 he declined a lucrative offer to address Montreal's prestigious St. James Literary Society, and he rejected McGraw-Hill Ryerson's suggestion that the sales of his books would be boosted if he attended that year's Canadian Booksellers Association convention in Halifax. With the odd exception, the once hard-travelling hopper of freights and intrepid automobile explorer would spend the rest of his life in the immediate vicinity of his native Toronto.

He spent a quiet summer working on the book that would become *The Intruders* and negotiating improved terms with Simon & Schuster for the early 1975 release of the paperback edition of *One Damn Thing After Another!* He also sold two stories — "Moving Day" and "Jacks or Better, Jokers Wild" — to Robert Weaver and made plans for a Western Canadian tour in September of 1974, which would have taken him to Regina and Moose Jaw and points west. On August 22 he had a new experience when a theatrical producer asked him to read for the part of a crusty old Colonel in the TV play Enter the Flower. Although he wasn't chosen, he did enjoy this glimpse of life from the actor's perspective. But just before he was due to leave on his trip to the West, he became seriously ill in Ottawa while visiting his sister June and had to cancel his travelling plans at the last minute.

This episode began when, after an evening of heavy drinking, he seemed to have an unusually persistent hangover. What he really had was pneumonia, and back in Toronto he had to spend two days in a hospital intensive-care unit, lying under an oxygen tent and being fed intravenously while he recovered. This pattern of a binge or illness just before leaving on a trip is a recurring feature of Garner's later years; and it's difficult not to conclude that, on at least some of these occasions, he induced his own sickness as a way of avoiding obligations that he no longer felt capable of meeting.

When he had fully recovered from his pneumonia, Hugh went back to work on *The Intruders*, continuing to translate it from TV play to novel. He made things as easy for himself as possible by carrying over the names and dialogue of most of the characters without making a great many changes, but he still had a lot of trouble writing the descriptive passages. The book was set in the new, "under renovation" Cabbagetown of the early 1970s, where middle-class "white-painters" and the traditional working-class population co-existed in a sometimes uneasy truce, and Garner found that the Cabbagetown locales he had known forty years earlier had been very much altered by the passage of time. All the houses Annie Garner and her family had lived in had long since been torn down, and as Hugh walked along the area's once familiar streets he felt little sense of connection with what remained.

At the end of October he felt well enough to participate in a series of lectures and discussions on the theme "Encounter: Canadian Literature" at York University's Vanier College. Garner's attendance at conferences such as this and Canada Day became a regular feature of his life in the 1970s, and helped to fill the void left by his inability to work on magazine journalism. In the ten years between 1969 and 1979 he wrote a total of only eight magazine and newspaper articles, most of them commissioned and all for better-paying publications, and several of these were actually rehashes of pieces he had written earlier. At Can-Lit conferences he was paid a modest fee to attend and got to hob-nob with old friends whom he might otherwise not see much of any more; and perhaps most importantly, he could count on being received well by the students, with whom he always seemed to have a natural empathy.

Christmas was, as usual, the occasion for an extended drinking spree and a trip to Homewood, and then it was time for the promotional activities connected with the March 1975 publication of *Death in Don Mills*. Since Inspector McDumont's début in *The Sin Sniper* had by now sold more than 100,000 copies in paperback, McGraw-Hill Ryerson did its best to make his return appearance a major event. Hugh made visits to Montreal and Ottawa to plug the book, and he fulfilled a busy schedule of interviews with Toronto's electronic and print media.

With the appearance of *Death in Don Mills*, it became painfully obvious that Garner was just going through the motions as a writer of fiction. If the short stories he wrote for "slick" magazines in the 1950s weren't masterpieces, they were good examples of their kind; but the three novels he wrote in the 1970s didn't even have this distinction, as they demonstrated that the old pro was by now quite willing to be regarded as an old hack. The plotting is laborious, the characters are either stereotypes or nonentities and it's only the crusty crankiness of Inspector McDumont that gives the two mystery novels an occasional breath of life.

In scenes such as the following interrogation of a woman suspected of the murder of "Zelda Greenless," the reader can watch some of Garner's typical pet peeves get a good airing:

> He stared hard into the woman's face. "I know that you, Dolly Bullay, are a schoolteacher down at Berkeley Street Public School. At three-thirty, like the rest of your tribe, you beetle back to Don Mills, and you probably speak to women's groups about the unfortunate slum kids you have to teach, your speech liberally punctuated by your amateur sociological jargon like 'inner city,' 'programmed,' 'playback,' 'one-parent families,' and all the rest of that middle-class baloney. Right now though I want to know what you thought of Zelda Greenless?"
>
> Dolly Bullay, whose face had become livid, answered, "I knew nothing about that woman! To me she was lower class scum like

some of the parents I meet at Berkeley Street. And she wasn't a missus, she was an unmarried miss!"

"That's where you're wrong," the Inspector said. ... "I have Mrs. Greenless's marriage licence in my office right now. I am certain *she* had one, but have you?"

The Inspector turned on his heel and ... left the Bullays' doorway. The Bullays' door slammed. ... He said, "I'm going to get a search warrant for the Bullays' apartment. That broad trying to put on the class! I had to stand her brand of bullshit when I was a kid, but I don't now."

After the autobiographical connections have been duly noted, it has to be said that as Garner portrays him, McDumont makes an extraordinarily unbelievable police inspector. When he isn't making extended sociological analyses of everything in sight, he spends most of his time alternately terrifying and charming the people with whom he comes in contact; then, if he hasn't got a meal to eat or an errand to run, he occasionally takes a stab at actually solving his case. For all of Hugh's attempts to get the correct police procedures down accurately, the central unreality of McDumont makes it impossible to take *Death in Don Mills* seriously as a mystery or any other sort of novel.

Although its reception by the press was generally favourable, Garner couldn't help but notice that this was "my first book to receive quite a few adverse reviews." Established writers turning out obvious pot-boilers are usually given the benefit of the doubt in situations such as this, and his contemporaries were far kinder to the book than posterity would be; but an author as sensitive to criticism as Garner was could be expected to lash back at his tormentors, as he did in an October 1975 talk at the public library in Kitchener, Ontario. Among the types he identified as typical book reviewers were the "failed writer," the "friend or mistress of an editor who only reads the book jacket copy" and the "copy boy or secretary on a newspaper," whose bad reviews "can't really hurt a writer with clout." This was sheer whistling in the dark as far as Hugh was concerned — he was among the most thin-skinned of authors — but it did indicate just how upset he was by negative notices.

Regardless of what the reviewers thought, *Death in Don Mills* sold extremely well. It stayed on Canadian best-seller lists for almost four months, was chosen as an alternate selection of the Literary Guild book club and became the object of a spirited battle for paperback rights, with Bantam finally outbidding Simon & Schuster. McGraw-Hill Ryerson, it turned out, was an excellent judge of what the market-place wanted; and now the company forcefully demonstrated that it was by no means prepared to publish everything Garner wrote.

Toward the end of March 1975, with *Death in Don Mills* selling well and McGraw-Hill Ryerson presumably at its most receptive, Hugh brought in a collection of short stories for the firm's consideration. Of these fourteen stories, three ("The Man With the Musical Tooth," "The Old Man's Laughter" and "The Predetermined Death of Samuel Glover" — with "Predetermined" changed to "Predestined" in the later version) were from the 1952 *The Yellow Sweater and Other Stories*, and two ("Losers, Weepers," "A Walk on Y Street") had appeared in the 1973 paperback edition of *Men and Women*. Garner didn't bother to mention this to McGraw-Hill Ryerson, and Toivo Kiil and David Nelson, the two editors who read the manuscript of what would eventually be published as *Legs of the Lame*, don't seem to have been aware of it. But regardless of the history of its contents, they were not impressed by the stories' intrinsic merits: both found it an uneven and, on balance, a rather poor collection. After Garner read their critiques he dashed off an angry note to McGraw-Hill Ryerson president Ronald Besse that began with a vicious attack on Nelson:

> This psychotic, pill-popping bastard would be flogging panty hose if his old man hadn't been George Nelson, onetime president of Doubleday Canada.
>
> The fallback cliche of all amateur short story critics is the line "this is an uneven collection," as if a fucking short story writer was building a goddam picket fence.
>
> Nelson, who is a perfect companion to Toivo Kiil, has no critical judgement at all. Of the 14 stories making up THE LEGS OF THE LAME, 12 have been broadcast over the CBC's most pres-

tigious literary radio show, "Anthology," and 11 of them have been published in 9 Canadian magazines, all of them without a rejection. Do you think I don't pay more attention to the CBC and magazine editors — all of whom have read more short stories than Nelson will read in his life — than I do to that congenital misfit!

Since it was his short stories that he particularly prided himself on and which he also thought would earn him a degree of literary immortality, this rejection might better have been phrased in terms of how difficult it is to market collections of short fiction. The point, in any case, is that McGraw-Hill Ryerson certainly wasn't about to publish anything just because Garner wanted it to, and its commercial judgement of *Legs of the Lame* was vindicated when the 1976 Borealis Press edition sold very poorly.

About a month later, Hugh got a few more things off his chest in a long letter to Besse. His basic gripe was that he wasn't being treated properly by McGraw-Hill Ryerson's editors, although he also complained about the company's unwillingness to remainder *Violation of the Virgins*, all but accusing it of sharp practice in its interpretation of his contract. In discussing the issue of publisher's advances, he revealed that Simon & Schuster had given him advances of first one thousand and then fifteen hundred dollars on the paperback reprints of his books, which by this time in his career was extremely important to him: he was convinced that publishers as a matter of course cheated authors out of the royalties their books had earned, which meant that a cheque in the hand was much better than a high-percentage sales royalty in the bush.

A good deal of Garner's indignation was sheer bluster, since at the same time that he was treating the company's employees as a bunch of mental defectives and con artists he was finishing *The Intruders* and planning on giving the firm first chance at its publication. He didn't have to do this, since McGraw-Hill Ryerson's rejection of *Legs of the Lame* meant that he could take his next book wherever he liked; by 1975, however, Hugh had burnt quite a few publishing bridges behind him, and no matter what he thought about some of the firm's policies, he was well aware that it had done an excellent job of promoting and marketing *Death in Don Mills*.

Most of the spring and summer were devoted to work on *The Intruders*, which he submitted to McGraw-Hill Ryerson in September. Writing another novel set in downtown Toronto had revived his love-hate relationship with the city, and when the *Star* asked him for an article on the city as it had been, he was happy to oblige. "They Called it Hogtown — with reason" was based on several earlier pieces of the same sort, although some of its offhand remarks were of more recent vintage: "half its university dodos are semi-illiterates" and "the mama's boy dingbats down at city hall" were typical of the slangy aspersions that often crop up in his later casual writings.

In October he attended a literary luncheon in Kitchener where, as we have already seen, he spent much of the time allotted for his address in lambasting a local newspaper reviewer for a negative notice of *Death in Don Mills*. A November appearance at London's Fanshawe College showcased Garner speaking on the topic "How to Make a Living Without Working," during which he reminisced about his days with Jack Kent Cooke and used the story of an unfortunate Savarin Hotel drinking crony as an example of why vocations should be based on avocations. Hugh drew a vivid word picture of how his friend, born into a socially prominent family and possessing all the advantages of wealth and education, ended up in the gutter when he tried to force himself to succeed at a lucrative but unsatisfying career. Although this may not be a true story — Garner always had a weakness for those "semi-fictional vignettes" Pierre Berton had once complained about — it succinctly expressed the value system of a writer who probably could have made much more money doing things he would have hated.

Hugh spent much of December going over the revisions McGraw-Hill Ryerson editor Robin Brass suggested in the manuscript of *The Intruders*. This time, the tone of Garner's response to his editor was quite different from that of his blasts at Toivo Kiil, even though he peppered his remarks with "goddam"'s and argued vociferously on almost every point, and this can be directly attributed to the cogency of Brass's comments. In this more relaxed and expansive atmosphere, several of Garner's replies veered off into discussions of his basic literary principles.

When Brass questions his habit of providing detailed physical descriptions of characters as soon as they have been introduced, Hugh argues that this is a crucial factor in determining the reader's image of them; here it might be noted that Garner's often literal brand of realism — in which the most important fictional characters are almost always drawn from real-life models — in a sense requires that readers see things his way. Elsewhere, he demonstrated the sharp eye for social behaviour that explains why his work was often selected for inclusion in anthologies of social-scientific, as well as literary, readings. Responding to Brass's querying of how some of the novel's characters react to a violent incident, he suggested that the editor might

> listen sometime to the onlookers and uninjured participants walking away from the scene of an accident. The tendency of human beings is to rid themselves of traumas and stress by concentrating on subjects not even wildly connected with what they have recently viewed or undergone. ... I am a realistic or naturalistic writer, and I think a similar group of people in real life would have acted precisely as they did.

With the revisions to *The Intruders* finished and nothing else on the immediate horizon, Garner followed his habitual pattern of heavy drinking over the Christmas holidays. Although it wasn't necessary for him to go to Homewood this time, there were a number of indications that his mental functioning was being adversely affected by his periods of heavy drinking. Doug Fetherling noticed that he seemed to have experienced a degree of memory loss: he forgot common words and was increasingly unable to remember the names of past acquaintances. When he failed to keep a coffee date with Robert Weaver, which he had never done before, Weaver was concerned that he might have been in an accident; but Hugh had simply forgotten, and was mortified when he learned that he had committed what he described as "an unforgiveable breach of etiquette" toward his most important literary friend and supporter.

He was certainly not getting any younger. In responding to a February 1976 request from *Saturday Night* for information about his literary preferences, he went off on a political tangent: "I think all young people should be radicals of one tinge or another; they will discover later, as I did, that today's teenage radical is tomorrow's conservative, a theory I used to jeer at." He did, however, show that he had been doing his best to keep up with literary developments, indicating that he had read William Burroughs, Jean Genet, James Baldwin and William Golding, and reiterated the view that Ken Kesey's *One Flew Over the Cuckoo's Nest* was the finest novel of recent times. A vintage venting of Garner spleen occurred when he was asked if F. Scott Fitzgerald's *The Great Gatsby* captured the sensibilities of the interwar generation:

Today [Scott and Zelda Fitzgerald] would be looked upon as phony upward strivers, doing stupid things such as diving fully clothed into the Hotel Plaza fountain, throwing parties they could not afford, not paying their debts, dunning Fitzgerald's publisher for money, and finally ending their roles as leading idiots of the grounded jet set with Scott, a terminal alcoholic, living in a Hollywood hotel bungalow, called appropriately enough "The Garden of Allah," and Zelda a committed psychotic.

What seemed to offend him most was that the Fitzgeralds were "strivers," a key word in the Garner vocabulary of disparagement. He had earlier used it in *One Damn Thing After Another!* to describe a couple who tried to impress him with the news that they had dined with a member of a prominent Toronto family, and we will soon see him making fictional use of it in *The Intruders*.

March was largely taken up with publicity appearances and the onerous task of correcting the galleys and page proofs of *The Intruders*, the sort of work which had been a labour of love when he was a younger writer but was now merely labour. One thing that did cheer him up was Robert Weaver's purchase of "The Conversion of Willie Heaps" for CBC Radio, which was an indication of how much more elastic public attitudes about religion had become in the twenty-five years since he had first submitted it to Weaver.

He was also happy to receive a translator's request for permission to do a German-language version of *Death in Don Mills*, which incidentally points out how relatively little foreign interest there was in his work. "One-Two-Three Little Indians" did appear in several German anthologies and was also translated into Romanian, and there were occasional out-of-the-blue requests, as one for a Swedish translation of "Some Are So Lucky" and another for an Afrikaans version of "One Mile of Ice." But otherwise his foreign-rights earnings were minimal, which is on the one hand not surprising — given the style and subject matter of his novels — but is on the other hand indicative of how badly he needed a professional literary agent. When he had started out as a writer, there simply weren't any competent Canadian agents, and so he had gotten into the habit of working out most things by trial and — all too often — error.

Hugh prided himself on being a good manager of his literary properties, and to some extent he was right to do so. He had worked out, entirely on his own, a system of selling his short stories that maximized their earning potential: he first sold the radio rights to the CBC, then sold the first serial rights to a magazine and finally sold them in collected form to publishers. At each stage in this process, he was careful to retain all subsidiary rights, which meant that he might eventually receive income from adaptations in other media — as radio, TV or stage plays, and as films — as well as any and all appearances in anthologies. "One-Two-Three Little Indians," for example, was first sold to CBC Radio for one hundred dollars, and then to *Liberty* for fifty dollars. When collected in *The Yellow Sweater and Other Stories*, its share of the advance was twenty-one dollars, and there were no royalties; after two years it had earned a total of $171, and it becomes obvious why Garner had to turn out seventeen stories in 1951 if he was going to pay his bills with his writing. In the period between 1952 and 1979, however, "One-Two-Three Little Indians" earned more than $5,600 in fees of various kinds, and in combination with the revenues from his other stories provided Garner with a steady if unspectacular source of income.

His novels were another matter entirely. Of the five major novels that preceded *Death in Don Mills* — *Storm Below, Cabbagetown, Silence on the Shore, The Sin Sniper* and *A Nice Place to Visit* — none earned as much as "One-Two-Three Little Indians" in the course of its existence, although if his Canada Council grant for *Silence on the Shore* is figured in, he could in a sense be credited with writing at least one novel that was more lucrative than his most popular short story. This is partially the fault of peculiar circumstances, such as *Cabbagetown* beginning life as a paperback and then being allowed to go out of print, but the primary culprit was Garner's inability to settle down with any one publisher. It wasn't until McGraw-Hill Ryerson took him on that he had something resembling a stable relationship with a publishing house, and by that time he was probably incapable of writing as well as he had in the 1950s and early 1960s.

The Intruders was certainly not going to add anything to his reputation. Where *Death in Don Mills* had been treated as a slight effort in the mystery genre, *The Intruders* was judged as a serious novel, and reviewers couldn't help but make unflattering comparisons with *Cabbagetown*. For the first time in his career he had to face a generally negative reaction to one of his books, as even old fans like *The Globe and Mail*'s William French found it difficult to be enthusiastic about his latest volume.

The Intruders depicts the conflict between the long-time residents of Cabbagetown and the middle-class renovators who by the early 1970s were moving into the area in droves. Garner has no difficulty in portraying this from the point of view of the working-class population; but when he attempts to describe how things seem to the new arrivals, it becomes painfully obvious that he really doesn't know very much about them. The following description of a renovator's bedroom exemplifies the combination of spleen and unlikely factual information to which he resorts:

The bed, a brass artifact of the kind thrown away in 1930 and revived as chic in 1965, had been bought ... just after they had moved
into the house, along with a cityscape in oils of the "Paris as seen
from Sacre Coeur" type that was hanging on the opposite wall. The
dresser and highboy were good modern "Spanish" pieces which
belonged with their matching bed, now relegated to the back guest
bedroom. The ancient brass bed offered a laughable contrast not
only to the room's furnishings but to the lack of taste and even san-
ity of the room's occupants.

The detail about the painting is particularly amusing in view of
the fact that reproductions of "2 Parisian Scenes, Utrillo," were
listed on Garner's 1959 household inventory, although one
doubts that they would have turned up on the corresponding list
of the Bay-Street lawyer whose bedroom this is supposed to be.

Garner's outrage at these "strivers" is reflected in the name he
chose for the book's smarmy arts-council representative,
"Donald Strivener." Strivener is continuously castigated as the
sort of spineless bureaucrat who toadies to those above him and
is nasty to those below him. He is the object of several long
tirades by "Syd Tedland," an old Cabbagetowner who articulates
the Garner viewpoint on things. The collection of crude stereotypes in *The Intruders* also includes a thinly disguised caricature
of a Toronto alderman, a gay dance instructor and a gang of juvenile delinquents who speak a language that seems to have been
lifted from 1930's films:

"If we have ta knock over the joint, we gotta have one of us inside
before the scoop's put in the cracker er hid someplace." ...
"One a yous has got to get into that closet before, hide in er till
ya hear the last a the clerks an butchers change inta their street
clothes an leave, then come out and herd the manager an his gofer
inta the back cold room. Gettin the gofer's keys first, unnerstand?"

Here the use of "scoop" in the sense of a sum of money, and
"cracker" to refer to a place for its safekeeping, are based on
older usages that don't even appear in dictionaries of slang published after 1950. The wavering between "inta" and "into," the

incongruous precision of "herd" and the general Dead-End Kids tone of these supposed 1970s street toughs all point out that here Garner just doesn't know what he is talking about.

As he wrote to Al Purdy later that summer, *The Intruders* was "a bomb," and for quite different reasons he was also upset about the Borealis Press edition of *The Legs of the Lame and Other Stories.* Not used to dealing with small presses, he raved and ranted at how long it took Borealis to do things, and by May 1976 was demanding "a little fucking courtesy" in his increasingly irate letters. When the book finally did appear shortly thereafter, the paucity of reviews and its poor distribution resulted in very disappointing sales, turning what should have been a banner year — with both a new novel and a new collection of stories coming out — into one that he would attempt to forget.

One of the few rays of sunshine on the horizon was provided by the producers of a TV show called Connection, who chose Hugh as one of their panellists. He was flown to CJOH's studios in Ottawa for rehearsals, "dolled up" in a dinner-jacket and trotted out before a live audience for the pilot episode, which seemed to go quite well. The director liked his "raspy whisky tenor" so much that he had Garner do some demonstration tapes of commercial messages; although nothing further came of this, it was a welcome change from staying home and brooding over negative reviews of *The Intruders.*

In the middle of June he began one of his binges and spent all of the month of July at Homewood. By this time Alice was well aware that there was nothing she could do to stop him drinking once he got started, and she left to visit her relatives in the Gaspé. Early in August Hugh drove down there to pick her up, making what would be the last long automobile trip of his life. When they returned to Toronto he made a tentative start on another Inspector McDumont novel but wasn't able to get the book under way to his satisfaction. At the end of September he was back in Homewood for almost three weeks, but this time when he was discharged there was enough accumulated business awaiting him to put a temporary hold on the drinking.

Four more episodes of Connection were being shot at the beginning of November, and he had to be measured for his rented dinner-jacket — which he really enjoyed wearing — before leaving for Ottawa. There were negotiations about the paperback rights to *The Intruders* and yet another movie option on *The Sin Sniper* to be attended to; and, perhaps inspired by the compliments he had recently received about his voice, he unsuccessfully tried to interest CBC Radio in a series of fifteen-minute readings from *Death in Don Mills*. He was also able to make some headway on the Inspector McDumont novel that would eventually be published as *Murder Has Your Number*, and during the next year worked on it slowly but steadily until it was done.

Garner's perenially short fuse, which during his final years became if anything even shorter, was now touched off by an inexperienced young filmmaker's request for the rights to the story "Step-'n-a-Half." In a handwritten letter that both got the name of the story wrong and implied that its author's permission wasn't absolutely necessary, Garner was offered "a token payment of several hundred dollars." His response was ferocious:

> For chrissakes how much faith do you think I'd put in an amateur would-be movie-maker who can't even get the title of my story right? ... you're just an ignoramus about writing and/or movie-making, and I have had nearly thirty years in the business.
>
> Sentences like "I don't want to make this film without your permission ... " just bolster my belief that you are completely out of touch with the realities of movie-making or anything else connected with the media. If you ever tried making a film, TV play, or anything else remotely resembling STEP-'N-A-HALF or any other of my more than 90 short stories I'd sue you for enough to keep you broke for the rest of your life. HAVE YOU NEVER HEARD OF THE LAWS OF PLAGIARISM?

Unlike most of Garner's temperamental explosions, this one had a happy ending. The young man wrote again, apologizing for the ineptitude of his approach, and in the course of describing his background mentioned that he had laboured as a road paver and factory worker in order to raise what money he did have. Hugh, his memories of what it was like to be young, broke and ambitious perhaps reawakened by this story, apologized in turn for the "snotty reply" he had made and offered some practical advice as to how funds for the film could be raised.

Another letter of a quite different kind received a warmer response. To a British Columbia man who wrote that Garner had become "an old acquaintance" through the medium of his books and articles, Hugh responded with the courtesy he typically afforded writers of fan letters. During the course of his career he received many such communications, which were often sparked by some place or event mentioned in his writings that he and his correspondents had in common. When he didn't feel he was being pointlessly bothered by people — and toward the end of his life he did become much more suspicious about the motives of others — he would often go to great efforts to answer their requests. In the case of a student asking for information about his work, for example, he typically replied at some length while offering personal asides about all sorts of peripheral matters.

In December 1976 he was a judge for that year's *Miss Chatelaine* short-story contest. In the garrulous style now typical of his correspondence, he rambled on, making plot summaries and offering free advice about how the writers could have improved their work. In discussing the awkwardness with which several of the entrants used a first-person narrative viewpoint, he advised them to tell their tales "in the third person, preferably from the point of view of an anonymous onlooker." Here Garner was accurately describing his own practice, although his onlookers often did play some peripheral part in the story.

With more episodes of Connection scheduled to be shot in January 1977, Hugh managed to get through the Christmas holidays without starting on a binge. After his work on the TV show was finished, however, he began drinking with a vengeance, and early in February was admitted to Homewood. The day after he arrived, his heart began beating irregularly, and he had to be rushed to the coronary-care unit at Guelph General Hospital. There he spent a week under observation, during which it was determined that there was nothing organically wrong with

his heart, and then spent four days at Homewood before returning home. Garner did some more work on *Murder Has Your
Number* before returning to the sanitarium in April for an eight-
day stay. When he got out, he finished his mystery novel and sent
it off to McGraw-Hill Ryerson, which accepted it immediately.

During the summer of 1977 his left leg developed a long, ul-
cerous sore that was quite painful and did not respond quickly
to treatment, and he had to keep the leg elevated while he was
sitting down. With his body beginning to betray him, the periods of heavy drinking, which since about 1966 had changed from
sporadic to frequent, now became chronic. He was often up all
night, careening around the apartment singing and yelling while
Alice attempted to calm him down, and his neighbours at 33 Erskine Avenue made a number of complaints to the building's
management. Those who knew what Alice was going through
asked her why she didn't leave him, but she refused to seriously
consider it: "The thought would cross my mind, but I would immediately reject it. If I left him, no one else would take care of
him, and he would have to be put in an institution. That would
have killed him immediately."

On one occasion, when Alice needed to make an emergency
trip to the Gaspé because of her parents' health, she left Hugh in
what she thought would be stable condition for at least a few
days. But he immediately began drinking heavily and made so
much noise that his neighbours' complaints brought a visit from
an employee of the building's owners. This person found Garner
almost helpless, lying on the floor in a pool of urine; only Alice's
timely return kept Hugh from yet another hospital admission.

During his intervals of lucidity, Hugh began to tidy up his affairs in a way that suggested he was consciously preparing for
the end. In October 1977 McGraw-Hill Ryerson accepted his
proposal for *A Hugh Garner Omnibus*, which would collect his
best work into a fitting literary memorial, and he devoted much
of his time to thinking about what should go into it.

Later that same month his drinking passed the point at which
Alice felt able to deal with it, and he was admitted to the Addiction Research Foundation in Toronto for a drying-out period. Be-

cause of the serious health problems that were now beginning to manifest themselves, it was felt that he needed to be closer to the kind of care available in Toronto; when he had to be rushed to Toronto Western Hospital after his liver started to malfunction, the wisdom of this became apparent.

After being discharged, he made what was in a sense a symbolic resignation from the kind of existence that he had until recently led. In November he declined to renew his American Express Card on the grounds that he was suffering from ill health, thus tacitly recognizing that his travelling days were over. Garner had been inordinately pleased when his application for the company's card was originally accepted — it was one of those small snobberies that reflected how proud he secretly was of having clawed his way out of the working-class — and he only gave it up when it became obvious that he would have little further use for it.

In the same spirit of tidying up loose ends, he resigned his Associate Fellowship at York University's Winters College. This, again, was something that he had been very proud of, even though he had attended only one meeting of the College's Fellows, and it was the kind of thing that he would let drop whenever he thought anyone was "high-hatting" him. The turning inward that these resignations represent was also expressed in Hugh's treatment of his published writings, to which he now began to devote the kind of methodical attention to detail that he had given to his earlier inventory of household effects.

As part of the inventory of his literary effects, Garner decided to figure out which of his short stories had been the most popular. This was exactly the sort of complicated, time-consuming task he had always enjoyed. With the help of the "LOGBOOK" in which he kept careful records of the history of his work, he devoted much thought and effort to it:

> I first approached the compilation of this collection by choosing the thirty short stories which have earned me the most money. Next I went over the logs of my 90 short stories and made a list of those having the best sales record [by which he means number of sales

rather than gross income], and discovered not surprisingly that both lists were different one from the other, though some stories held their places at the top of both. I then made allowances for the length of time each story had been on the market, the one-time opposition of the public to eroticism or pornography in relation to today's acceptance, the fact that an original story had been written for sale to, say, a woman's periodical or to network radio, and for the tenfold increase in fees since the days when I was referred to as "a promising *young* writer." Finally, ignoring the criteria of monetary and publishing records, I allowed myself to be the sole judge, through personal preference, of one or two stories that I substituted for some with better sales.

Thus "The Conversion of Willie Heaps," which had earned much less than most of his stories, went to the top of the list; and "One-Two-Three Little Indians," despite its high earnings, barely squeaked in as number thirty. Although the quality of his short fiction is too variable to make a complete edition advisable, a book consisting of "Hugh Garner's Thirty Best Stories" would make a sensible tribute to his accomplishments in this demanding form.

Hugh was very concerned that the forthcoming omnibus volume show his work at his best. Between frequent letters to McGraw-Hill Ryerson about the omnibus and the April 1978 publication of *Murder Has Your Number* — for which he insisted on a jacket photograph showing him in the new, non-moustached state he had decided was more appropriate for a man of his age — his drinking temporarily abated. When *Murder Has Your Number* appeared it was much more kindly treated than *The Intruders* had been: it was obviously an entertainment rather than a serious work of fiction, and even the less than enthusiastic reviews seemed to be tempered by sympathy for a writer whose health was widely known to be failing.

But Inspector McDumont was still in characteristically abrasive form. Whether he's chewing out an incompetent psychiatrist—

How the hell would you know? You graduated from the U of T medical school in 1967 with a standing of 114 out of a class total

of 123, not a very impressive record. You went into private practice on Harbord Street, but found you couldn't hack general prac-
titioning. Through your father, who is the owner of a large clothing
company, you returned to university and switched to psychiatry.

or an ex-army officer who tries to pull rank on him —

I see you still have the poor working-class manners of a Junction
kid whose old man worked for Massey-Harris. You can put on all
the high-tone crap you want, Cosgroom, but there are working-
class mannerisms and manners you'll never be able to shake —
and don't 'So?' me, you son of a bitch. I didn't like you when you
tried to put me down at the Snelgrove house last night for having
been only a corporal while you'd reached the dizzying heights of
captain. I found out from Ottawa today that you were only a brigade headquarters wallah in Korea, and not a field officer at all. To
me an army headquarters clerk is lower than shark shit.

McDumont was a wonderful vehicle for expressing his fierce
opinions on matters of social class, and despite health ailments
that meant he now had to print rather than type his manuscripts,
in the summer of 1978 Garner began another novel about him,
which remained unfinished at the time of his death.

During the last year of his life Hugh drank pretty well continuously. By the time *A Hugh Garner Omnibus* was finally published in 1979, he was beyond the point at which its appearance
might have stimulated even a momentary decrease in his consumption of alcohol. Along with the increase in drinking went
an increase in medical problems: his left leg had to be encased
in a knee-to-toe cast, he experienced loss of feeling in both legs
and there were periodic episodes of kidney failure. His general
health was now too poor for him to be safely treated at drying-
out centres such as the Addiction Research Foundation's facili-
ties in Toronto, and his last three admissions for alcohol overdose
were to Sunnybrook Hospital.

Each of these admissions required emergency transportation
by ambulance, and the second was necessitated by severe
haemorrhaging that his doctors thought would probably be fatal.
But there was one more recovery left in a constitution that had

often defied medical opinion, and he returned home for a final brief stay. On June 5, 1979 he was readmitted to Sunnybrook with serious respiratory problems, where he remained in critical condition until his death. Encased in an oxygen tent, he continued to have great difficulty breathing, and by the evening of June 30 was drifting in and out of consciousness. As his wife and daughter kept vigil by his bedside, Alice took his hand to let him know that he was not alone. He came to for a moment and, obviously not knowing where he was, made one last request: "Alice, get me a drink — get me a big one." Then he quietly passed away, almost sixty years to the day after a young English lad had with mounting excitement stared at the silent Canadian shore that contained the secret of his future.

Hugh Garner's funeral could not help but be something of a literary occasion. Joining his family in their mourning were old friends and associates such as Robert Weaver, William French, Robert Fulford, Doug Fetherling and Jack McClelland, whose names were prominent among those mentioned in the media coverage of the ceremony. But for many of those present at the funeral, the most remarkable aspect of the day was the large number of anonymous individuals who turned up to pay their respects.

Nondescriptly and in many cases even shabbily dressed, they seemed to know neither family nor literary acquaintances nor each other, and stood apart from the other mourners during the course of the service. Following its conclusion they left as inconspicuously as they had arrived, without speaking to anyone present or coming forward to sign the guest book. If no one else knew who they were, it was clear that they had known Hugh Garner: he had spoken to them, he had spoken about them, and in giving voice to the thoughts and feelings of people who lived with loneliness every day of their lives, he had always spoken for them.

Epilogue

Although almost a decade has passed since Hugh Garner's death, it is still too soon to tell if posterity will admit him to the pantheon of Great Canadian Authors. His work's wild variations in quality, its avoidance of sophisticated literary techniques, his contempt for the arbiters of intellectual taste — all of these are serious obstacles to his occupying a significant place in future histories of Canadian literature. But there is one factor very much in his favour: say what you like about his deficiencies as a writer — and much has necessarily been said in the course of this narrative — his books continue to sell, continue to remain in print and continue to attract new generations of readers.

As I researched this biography, I met people from all walks and conditions of life who had one thing in common: they enjoyed reading the work of Hugh Garner. This thoroughly unscientific but perhaps significant survey suggests that he may achieve in his own country's literature something like the status hels by H.G. Wells and Sinclair Lewis in English and American literature: continually dismissed and left for dead by the critical establishment, and just as continually resurrected by readers who know good, solid literary workmanship when they see it.

What it comes down to, I suspect, is that Hugh Garner aimed at comparatively simple goals and more often than not achieved them. Where much of twentieth-century literature has proceeded from the assumption that observable reality is fraudulent, and profoundly inadequate when not deliberately and perversely misleading, Garner worked along much more straightforward lines. His writing rests upon a bedrock of firmly held axioms — the reality of reality, the conditioning of individuals by society, the existence of moral standards — that are contemptuously dismissed by many of our intellectual luminaries but nonetheless form the common coin of much of our mundane conversation. Easy to snigger at and surprisingly difficult to avoid, these simple strictures may well be part of the required response to the chaos that we seem to have made out of the modern world.

But as the subject of this discussion would probably have said about such speculations, "That's all a lot of hooey." As a teller of interesting tales who sought to entertain his readers with the fruits of his varied experiences, Hugh Garner found ample satisfaction in the artful communication of what he knew to those who were eager to know it. Novels such as *Cabbagetown* and *Silence on the Shore*, and short stories such as "The Conversion of Willie Heaps," will be read and appreciated as long as there is an audience for honest and impassioned literature.

While writing *The Storms Below*, I often wondered what Hugh Garner would have had to say about the book. When things were going well, I imagined him remarking, "Pretty good for a college guy, Stuewe;" when they weren't progressing so smoothly, it wasn't difficult to picture him dismissing the whole enterprise with a "Who are you trying to kid, kid?" In trying to provide the maximum of factual evidence and the minimum of tenuous speculation, I have certainly been conscious of his presence in a way that perhaps integrates this book with his subject. Both Hugh Garner and his biographer approach life with a sometimes awkward combination of realism and sentimentality, and in our own different but comparable ways we have done our best to speak directly to our contemporaries and descendants.

Source Notes

The most important sources of information regarding Hugh Garner are his autobiography, *One Damn Thing After Another!* (Toronto, 1973), three major journalistic articles ("Depression Memories," three parts, *Liberty*, October and November, 1960, and January, 1961; "The Spanish Civil War," three parts, *Liberty*, April and May, 1961; and "My First Hundred Years as a Writer," *The Star Weekly*, December 29, 1962), and the various articles, letters and other material in the Queen's University Archives. The latter contains copies of most — but not all — of the numerous autobiographical pieces Garner published over the years, although his personal "LOGBOOK" does list all magazine articles and much of his writing for newspapers. Many of these are identified by the titles Garner suggested rather than the titles under which the pieces were actually published, but they can be correlated by comparing dates of appearance.

In the notes that follow, all letters to and from Garner are contained in the Queen's University Archives unless otherwise indicated; where the source of a quotation has been identified in the text, it has not been repeated here. Direct quotations from individuals other than Garner are taken from interviews conducted by the author, or from their letters where indicated.

Chapter One: Early Years in England and Toronto (1913-1929)

The description of West Yorkshire housing is from Paul Thompson's *The Edwardians* (London, 1975). Matthew Garner's military records are in the Personnel Records Centre of the National Archives of Canada in Ottawa, and Annie Garner's attempt to take legal action against him is documented in the Police Court records at the archives in Toronto City Hall. The description of Toronto's housing crisis is based on James Lemon's *Toronto*

Since 1918 (Toronto, 1985) and G.P. de T. Glazebrook's *The Story of Toronto* (Toronto, 1971). The addresses and dates of school attendance are taken from records still on file at each of the schools indicated, supplemented by city directories; Annie Garner's family does not appear on the Assessment Rolls for this period. Hugh described being hit by an automobile on the CBC Radio programme Metro Intercom on December 24, 1968 and remembered his past Christmases in "Some Ghosts of Christmas Past" (*Saturday Night*, December 26, 1953) and in "The Way It Was" (*Toronto Telegram*, December 10, 1966). The anecdotes regarding playing in a band and singing "The Mermaid" are from "Schooldays, 1919 to 1926" (*Saturday Night*, September 19, 1953) and "What I Didn't Learn at School" (*Canadian Home Journal*, March 1951), respectively. His memories of bullies and teachers are from the "Schooldays" article. The description of 1925 Toronto is from "Whatever Happened to Those Wonderful Summer Holidays in the City?" (*The Star Weekly*, July 2, 1960). Garner recounted his multiple-picnic prowess in "Ivan McGeery and the Rhode Island Red" (*Saturday Night*, June 6, 1953) and in an interview on the CBC's "Judy" programme on March 2, 1976. He reminisced about the CNE in "The 'Ex' Is My Home-town Fair" (*Toronto Star*, August 24, 1963). Copies of the *Tech Tatler* can be consulted at the archives of the Toronto Board of Education, and Garner's high-school grades are on file at Danforth Technical School. His youthful poetry is contained in "'Longer Torture' and Other Poems" (*Saturday Night*, April 18, 1953). The details about his vandalism of the lake boat are taken from "Confessions of a Frustrated Psychopath" (*Saturday Night*, February 27, 1954); unfortunately, the juvenile court records for this period have been destroyed.

Chapter Two: On His Own, and Down and Out (1929-1936)

Garner's service in the militia is documented in his military records at the Personnel Records Centre at the National Archives of Canada. The Queen's Own Rifles parade is mentioned in

"Toronto — Dialectic on the Don" (*Saturday Night*, January 31, 1953). The description of his early sexual experience is from "The Women in My Life" (*The Star Weekly*, February 13, 1965) and in "Toronto the Terrible" (*Toronto Telegram*, July 12, 1969); the lonely-hearts club episode and the pleasures of Depression-era entertainment are recounted in "The Gang," the transcript of a 1961 CBC "Project '61" broadcast. In addition to the primary sources previously identified, "On the Road Through the Thirties" (*Weekend Magazine*, February 27, 1971) and "Where Has the Hobo Gone?" (*Maclean's*, July 29, 1961) help to flesh out the on-the-road years. His stay at the Fresno YMCA is related in the previously mentioned "Some Ghosts of Christmas Past", and "Fame, Fortune and Famine" (*Saturday Night*, May 9, 1953) is a detailed account of his stay in New York.

Chapter Three: Spain and Radical Politics (1936-1939)

Hugh Thomas's *The Spanish Civil War* (London, 1961) and Stanley Weintraub's *The Last Great Cause* (New York, 1967) offer an excellent background account of this period. Victor Hoar's *The MacKenzie-Papineau Battalion* (Toronto, 1969) quotes extensively from Garner's letters from Spain. The advertisement in the *Toronto Star* appeared on November 28, 1936, in the Personal Column. The quotation regarding the field-telephone course comes from "The Tired Radical" (*Saturday Night*, October 24, 1953), which is primarily about Garner's friend Reid. The visit by Hemingway and Dos Passos to XVth Brigade headquarters is described in Townsend Ludington's *John Dos Passos* (New York, 1980). The autobiographical character of the pieces originally published as fiction is asserted in an undated piece called "Biographical Short Stories" in the Queen's University archives. The dates of Garner's stay at the Gota de Leche hospital are provided in documents now in the possession of his family, which will eventually be deposited in the Queen's University Archives. The quotation describing the treatment of International Brigades passports is from Thomas's *The Spanish Civil War*. Copies of *New Advance* are available at the Central Reference Library in Toronto.

Chapter Four: At War in the Atlantic (1939-1945)

Garner's service in both the artillery and the navy is outlined in documents at the Personnel Records Centre in the National Archives. The account of the 30th Battery of the Royal Canadian Artillery is from Bruce West's *Toronto* (Toronto, 1967). The circumstances surrounding the writing of "The Conversion of Willie Heaps" are described in a CBC press release written by Garner and dated June, 1967. Joseph Schull's *Far Distant Ships* (Ottawa, 1950) and James Lamb's *The Corvette Navy* (Toronto, 1977) are helpful sources for the naval background. The account of *Battleford*'s Christmas party is in "Some Ghosts of Christmas Past". The articles "Let's Splice the Brain Mace" (*Saturday Night*, June 27, 1953) and "Home Port" (*The Legion Magazine*, May 1978) offer additional information on rum-rationing and shore leave, respectively.

Chapter Five: Reckoning With Toronto (1945-1952)

As of January 1947, Garner began to keep copies of both incoming and outgoing correspondence, and thus the balance of *The Storms Below* is based on documents now at the Queen's University Archives. *Waste No Tears* is not listed among the holdings of any Canadian library; I was able to read it only because Stephen Temple Books in Toronto loaned me a copy. George Woodcock's review of *The Yellow Sweater and Other Stories* appears in *Northern Review*, 6, No. 1 (April-May 1953).

Chapter Six: Selling Everything You Write (1952-1957)

The title of Garner's original article on Reid is "The Tired Radical" (*Saturday Night*, October 24, 1953). Except for the CJBC interview, all CBC Radio and Television appearances referred to here and in subsequent chapters are in the CBC archives. Hugh described his work habits in some "Biographical Notes," dated 1960, in the Queen's archives. For the O'Leary Commission's excellent account of the plight of Canadian magazines, see *Report, Royal Commission on Publications* (Ottawa, 1961).

Chapter Seven: The Play's the Thing (1957-1962)

The genesis and progress of *Silence on the Shore* is related in "Writing a Novel," an undated, twenty-four-page essay in the Queen's archives. The remarks about writers, university degrees and intellectuals were made on CBC TV's Seven-O-One programme on November 26, 1962. Garner used "junk" and "goofy" in reviewing Donald Barthelme's *Unspeakable Practices, Unnatural Acts* on CBC Radio's Speaking of Books, September 8, 1968. Copies of his "Book Inventory" and "Household Inventory" are in the Queen's archives.

Chapter Eight: Awards and Alarums (1962-1968)

Garner talked about his driving habits on CBC Radio's This Country in the Morning, May 14, 1974. His first "Dissent" column appeared on October 18, 1963. He made his remark about the unproductivity of the Don Mills years on CBC Radio's This Country in the Morning on March 10, 1975. Homewood is described in detail in "How I Got Over My Last Drunk" (*The Star Weekly*, June 3, 1967).

Chapter Nine: One Damn Thing After Another
(1968- 1973)

The anecdote about the *Cabbagetown* character who fell into boiling chocolate comes from a CBC Radio School Broadcast Series programme taped on March 10, 1972. A copy of his four-page response to the *Maclean's* survey, in which he also describes a typical evening at home, is in the Queen's archives. Doug Fetherling's book is *Hugh Garner* (Toronto, 1972). Robert Fulford's review of *One Damn Thing After Another!* appeared in the September 26, 1973, *Toronto Star*. Garner discusses talking to the 33rd Division detectives on CBC Radio's This Country in the Morning, March 10, 1975.

Chapter Ten: An Inspector Calls (1973-1979)

The text of his October 1975 talk in Kitchener, "Book Reviews," is in the Queen's archives, as is that of "How to Make a Living Without Working." "They Called It Hogtown — with reason" appeared in the *Toronto Star* on August 2, 1975.

Printed in Canada